FIXING PARENTAL LEAVE

Fixing Parental Leave

The Six Month Solution

Gayle Kaufman

NEW YORK UNIVERSITY PRESS

New York

NEW YORK UNIVERSITY PRESS
New York
www.nyupress.org
© 2020 by New York University
References to Internet websites (URLs) were accurate at the time of writing. Neither the author nor New York University Press is responsible for URLs that may have expired or changed since the manuscript was prepared.

Part of Chapter 1 was originally published in P. Moss, A. Duvander, & A. Koslowski (Eds.), *Parental leave and beyond: Recent developments, current issues, future directions* (pp. 147–163). Re-published with permission of Policy Press (an imprint of Bristol University Press, UK).

Library of Congress Cataloging-in-Publication Data
Names: Kaufman, Gayle, author.
Title: Fixing parental leave : the six month solution / Gayle Kaufman.
Description: New York : New York University Press, [2019] |
Includes bibliographical references and index.
Identifiers: LCCN 2019012034| ISBN 9781479810369 (cl : alk. paper) |
ISBN 9781479885039 (pb : alk. paper)
Subjects: LCSH: Parental leave.
Classification: LCC HD6065 .K38 2019 | DDC 331.25/763—dc23
LC record available at https://lccn.loc.gov/2019012034

New York University Press books are printed on acid-free paper, and their binding materials are chosen for strength and durability. We strive to use environmentally responsible suppliers and materials to the greatest extent possible in publishing our books.

Manufactured in the United States of America

10 9 8 7 6 5 4 3 2 1

Also available as an ebook

To my parents

CONTENTS

LIST OF FIGURES

LIST OF TABLES

Introduction

What do the United States and Suriname have in common?

These are the only two countries in the Western Hemisphere that do not have any government-funded paid parental leave. What about the rest of the world? Well, we could add Papua New Guinea to the list. You might not be surprised that Canada offers up to fifty-two weeks of paid maternity and parental leave, but did you know that our neighbor to the south, Mexico, offers up to twelve weeks of maternity leave at full pay? How about countries like Bangladesh, Somalia, and Saudi Arabia? Yes, yes, and yes. Surely not North Korea. But yes, even North Korea. The point is, we are on a short list—and I mean very short—of countries that do not offer paid parental leave (Figures I.1 and I.2 illustrate this stark reality). The lack of paid leave might make sense for a country that is largely based on subsistence agriculture and mining, but does it really make sense for the world's largest economy? Basically, every other country has some form of paid maternity leave and an increasing number of countries have paid paternity leave. Why is the US such an outlier?

The only federal parental leave policy we have is the Family and Medical Leave Act (FMLA), a bill that was introduced in Congress each year between 1984 and 1990, passed but vetoed by President George H. W. Bush in 1991 and 1992, and finally signed into law by President Bill Clinton in 1993. The FMLA provides up to twelve weeks of *unpaid* leave. Barely 60 percent of American employees are eligible for this leave once you take into account the requirements for minimum time in employment, work hours, and company size.

You might have better luck if you live in California, New Jersey, Rhode Island, or New York (or Washington starting in 2020 or Massachusetts starting in 2021), states with paid parental leave, or if you work for a company such as Netflix, Etsy, Facebook, or Google. But then consider that, as of 2018, only 15 percent of American workers in the private sector have access to paid family leave.[1]

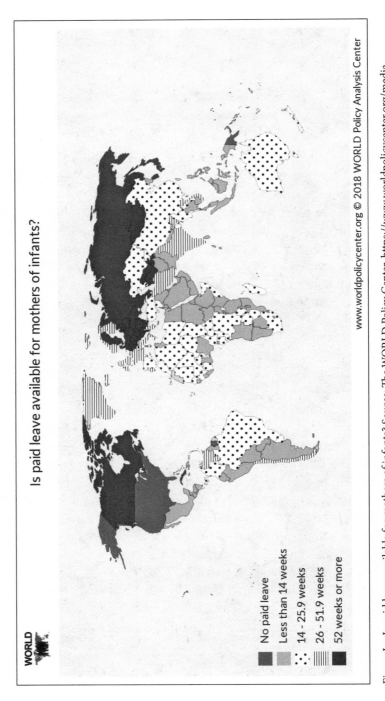

Figure I.1. Is paid leave available for mothers of infants? Source: The WORLD Policy Center, https://www.worldpolicycenter.org/media /no-cdn-images/maps/91.png

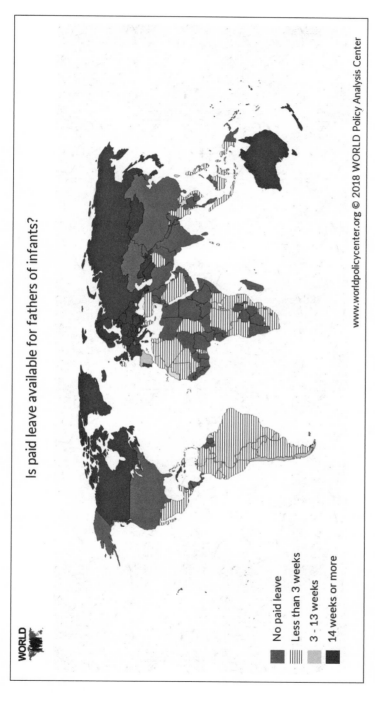

Is paid leave available for fathers of infants?

WORLD

- No paid leave
- Less than 3 weeks
- 3 - 13 weeks
- 14 weeks or more

www.worldpolicycenter.org © 2018 WORLD Policy Analysis Center

Figure I.2. Is paid leave available for fathers of infants? Source: The WORLD Policy Center, https://www.worldpolicycenter.org/media/no-cdn-images/maps/93.png

These are the kinds of statistics that drove me to study parental leave, first in the US and then in Sweden and the UK. In my research on American fathers, published in my book *Superdads: How Fathers Balance Work and Family in the 21ˢᵗ Century*, I found that most fathers were scraping together vacation days to take time around the birth of their child, while hourly employees simply had to take a day or two without pay if they wanted time off. This contrasts sharply with Sweden, a country that provides sixteen months of paid parental leave, with three months earmarked for each parent. It's not quite perfect, but those pictures of Swedish fathers pushing strollers around town in the middle of the day are real.

How late are we to this party? Some might say one hundred years. After all, it was in 1919, at the first International Labour Conference, that the International Labour Organisation (ILO) adopted its first maternity protections. In 1952, the ILO added a maternity leave provision of at least twelve weeks to the nine branches of social security at that convention. In 1981, the United Nations issued a convention aimed at eliminating gender discrimination, which included paid maternity leave. A stunning number of countries have signed this convention—185—and yet the US is not among that list.[2] In 2000, the ILO specified that all countries should provide fourteen weeks of paid maternity leave and now recommends at least eighteen weeks of leave. Since first adopted in 1919, sixty-six countries have ratified at least one of the conventions' maternity protections.[3] Needless to say, the US is not one of these countries.

There is plenty of evidence showing that parents, children, and even businesses benefit from parental leave. Clearly, parental leave policies, perhaps more than any other type of policy, are important for work-family balance.[4] Several polls have shown that a majority of Americans support paid parental leave. Could it ever happen in the US? It has been over twenty-five years since FMLA was passed. As long ago as 2013, Senator Kirsten Gillibrand of New York and Representative Rosa DeLauro of Connecticut introduced the Family and Medical Insurance Leave (FAMILY) Act, which offers paid leave to all workers. What are we waiting for?

There is more to parental leave policies than whether a country provides time off or not around the birth or adoption of a child. While virtually all maternity and parental leave policies are designed to help women return to employment, they do not all provide similar support. Further, women's employment is only half of the gender equality puzzle. The second half of the gender revolution requires men to become equal partners at home.[5] One of the best ways of encouraging this change is to offer equal parental leave for men and women and to encourage both parents to take equal time—the first step on the way to promoting gender equality at home. This is no small issue, given that much of the lingering inequality in the workplace is due to women's greater burden at home.

Fixing Parental Leave focuses on parental leave policies and gender equality in three countries—the US, the UK, and Sweden. These case studies will highlight how differences in policy encourage (or discourage) gender equality. This type of in-depth case study and international comparison is crucial for understanding policy variations and determining what works.[6] I ask how policies from other countries can be applied to the US. I'm not naïve. I know we will not adopt the Swedish model. We are above all a capitalist country in which the majority of people have a positive view of small business, entrepreneurs, and capitalism (though in 2018 Democrats and young adults under the age of thirty were more likely to have a positive view of socialism than capitalism—so, never say never).[7] I do think we can learn from Sweden, about what works, and also from the UK, a country similar to the US in its capitalist tendencies, but with a generous maternity leave policy, which, on the surface, appears better than the US situation, but which has ultimately failed to promote gender equality. Through a comparative policy study, I offer six lessons about parental leave and gender equality: 1) The US is way behind the rest of the world when it comes to parental leave; 2) Parental leave is good; 3) Too much parental leave can be bad, especially for mothers; 4) Fathers should be partners, not helpers; 5) The UK is not a good model for parental leave and gender equality; and 6) The Swedish model is great—but not perfect. Based on these lessons, I offer recommendations that will enable the US to develop a strong parental leave policy, one that will promote gender equality at work and at home.

This introduction sets the stage for the connection between parental leave and gender equality by providing an overview of parental leave and measures of gender equality around the world. Spoiler alert: Sweden is ranked highest, the UK in the middle, and the US lowest.

Some Basic Concepts

Since there may be some confusion over the different terms related to parental leave, I will begin by providing some working definitions:

Maternity leave is employment-protected leave available to employed women around the time of childbirth. This generally includes some time before birth in late pregnancy as well as time following childbirth. The aim of this leave is generally to ensure the health and well-being of the mother and her child.[8] This is often, but not always, available to employed women who adopt children.[9] In *all* cases outside of the US, maternity leave comes with some form of payment.

Paternity leave is employment-protected leave that is available to employed men. Paternity leave tends to be much shorter than maternity leave, commonly ranging from two days to two weeks, and focused immediately around the time of birth.[10] This policy is often designed not simply for infant care but also for the father to care for and assist the mother. It may include adoption.

Parental leave is employment-protected leave available to new parents. This leave is often longer than paternity leave, may be longer than maternity leave, and is generally meant to follow maternity leave. This leave is more focused on caring for infants and young children than on birth recovery or partner assistance. While it is available to either parent, mothers generally make greater use of it. This type of leave may be paid, but often it is unpaid or paid at a low flat rate.[11]

The *father's quota* is a type of leave that is reserved specifically for the father or partner of the mother. This policy is designed to promote gender equality and the sharing of leave by incentivizing fathers' use of leave. This kind of leave is also referred to as "use it or lose it" leave because it is non-transferable, meaning that if fathers do not take the specified amount of leave, it will be lost (i.e., mothers cannot take it). The father's quota is often combined with an equal mother's quota or with longer time for maternity or parental leave.

Family leave is employment-protected leave available to employees who meet eligibility requirements. This type of leave covers childbirth and adoption, but also care for oneself or for a sick family member. The combination of parental leave and medical leave in one policy is fairly unique to the US.

It is more common for parental leave to be funded by the government than by employers. In about half of countries, the government fully pays for leave, while in 30 percent of countries, employers pay for it. The remaining one-fifth have a combination of government and employer funding for parental leave.[12]

Parental Leave Policies around the World

The European Union (EU) has had a series of directives on parental leave. The 1992 EU Directive (92/85/EEC) required member states to offer a minimum of fourteen weeks of maternity leave. To address health concerns, this directive also made two weeks of leave, around the time of birth, compulsory for new mothers, with a corresponding monetary allowance. The 2010 EU Directive (2010/18/EU) emphasized parental leave rather than maternity leave. Clause 2 of this directive states:

1. This agreement entitles men and women workers to an individual right to parental leave on the grounds of the birth or adoption of a child to take care of that child until a given age up to eight years to be defined by Member States and/or social partners.
2. The leave shall be granted for at least a period of four months and, to promote equal opportunities and equal treatment between men and women, should, in principle, be provided on a non-transferable basis. To encourage a more equal take-up of leave by both parents, at least one of the four months shall be provided on a non-transferable basis. The modalities of application of the non-transferable period shall be set down at national level through legislation and/or collective agreements taking into account existing leave arrangements in the Member States.

Point 1 of this clause sets out requirements for parental leave and necessitates parental leave to be an individual right for all parents. The purpose of this was to avoid excluding fathers through maternity leave. Point 2 sets the minimum length of time for parental leave at four months, which was somewhat longer than the 1992 directive. It also focuses on "equal treatment between men and women." Given that men often do not take parental leave when it is transferable because it is seen

TABLE I.1: How much paid leave is available for mothers of infants in high-income countries?

52 weeks or more	26–51 weeks	14–25 weeks	Less than 14 weeks	No paid leave
Austria	Belgium	Andorra	Antigua and Barbuda	United States
Canada	Chile	Australia	Bahamas	
Croatia	Finland	Cyprus	Bahrain	
Czech Republic	France	Israel	Barbados	
Denmark	Greece	Liechtenstein	Brunei	
Estonia	Iceland	Malta	Equatorial Guinea	
Germany	Ireland	Monaco	Kuwait	
Japan	Italy	New Zealand	Oman	
Latvia	Luxembourg	Spain	Qatar	
Lithuania	Norway	Switzerland	Saudi Arabia	
Poland	Portugal	The Netherlands	Singapore	
Republic of Korea	United Kingdom	Trinidad and Tobago	St. Kitts and Nevis	
Russian Federation		Uruguay	United Arab Emirates	
San Marino				
Slovakia				
Slovenia				
Sweden				

Source: WORLD Policy Center, https://www.worldpolicycenter.org

as more important for mothers to take leave, this directive sought to encourage countries to offer non-transferable parental leave to parents, which would mean fathers would need to take at least one month of the four months of leave; otherwise that leave would not be available to their family.

It is more appropriate to compare the US to high-income countries, given that the US has the highest gross national product in the world. Table I.1 shows paid parental leave for mothers in fifty-six high-income countries. Of the fifty-six countries classified as having high income, seventeen (or 30 percent) provide new mothers with at least one year of maternity and/or parental leave. This includes Sweden. Another twelve (or 21 percent) of countries provide between six months and one year of paid leave. This includes the UK. Almost one-quarter of countries (thirteen) provide between fourteen and twenty-five weeks of paid leave and another almost one-quarter (thirteen countries) provide some paid leave but less than fourteen weeks. This latter category includes mainly island countries and countries in the Middle East. That leaves one high-income country that does not offer any paid leave to new mothers—the United States.

Table I.2 shows paid parental leave for fathers in fifty-six high-income countries. Half of these countries provide new fathers with at least fourteen weeks of paternity and/or parental leave. This includes Sweden and the UK. Four countries provide between three and thirteen weeks of paid leave and nine countries provide some paid leave to fathers, but less than three weeks. That leaves fifteen countries that do not offer any paid leave. Considerably more countries offer no paid leave to fathers than mothers. The US is thus not alone in this category. However, nine of these countries have populations below 1.5 million; several of them are small islands, and four are in the Middle East. Interestingly, Switzerland is not in the EU and not subject to EU directives. Thus, both Switzerland and the US are unusual as high-income Western countries in this category.

Why Study Sweden, the UK, and the US?

When I set out to examine parental leave policy and gender equality, the comparison between the US and Sweden seemed to provide the obvious extremes. Sweden was the first country to introduce parental leave back in 1974 and the US may be the last country to introduce paid parental leave. It was also clear that the US would not adopt a Nordic-style parental leave policy. There are dreams and then there is reality. The UK, on the other hand, is a liberal market similar to the US. The UK has generally seen family and corresponding strains between work and family as a private concern, just as the US has. If Sweden is the dream, maybe the UK is the attainable reality.

Sweden and the UK both offer leave that covers parents through the first eighteen months of their child's life. But if we focus only on

TABLE I.2: How much paid leave is available for fathers of infants in high-income countries?

14 weeks or more	3–13 weeks	Less than 3 weeks	No paid leave
Australia	Andorra	Bahrain	Antigua and Barbuda
Austria	Chile	Greece	Bahamas
Belgium	Israel	Ireland	Barbados
Canada	Spain	Malta	Brunei
Croatia		Monaco	Cyprus
Czech Republic		Saudi Arabia	Equatorial Guinea
Denmark		Singapore	Kuwait
Estonia		The Netherlands	Liechtenstein
Finland		Uruguay	Oman
France			Qatar
Germany			St. Kitts and Nevis
Iceland			Switzerland
Italy			Trinidad and Tobago
Japan			United Arab Emirates
Latvia			United States
Lithuania			
Luxembourg			
New Zealand			
Norway			
Poland			
Portugal			
Republic of Korea			
Russian Federation			
San Marino			
Slovakia			
Slovenia			
Sweden			
United Kingdom			

Source: WORLD Policy Center, https://www.worldpolicycenter.org

well-paid leave (at least 66 percent of wages), the UK only offers six weeks to mothers, whereas Sweden offers over thirteen months to both parents. Furthermore, since the early childhood education and care services (ECEC) entitlement (i.e., childcare services) begins at twelve months in Sweden, there is no gap between paid parental leave and ECEC. In contrast, ECEC does not begin until three years in the UK, which leaves a gap of eighteen months (any leave) to thirty-five months (well-paid leave) between parental leave and ECEC.[13]

We might best be able to understand these policy differences through the concept of *father-care-sensitive leave*. Sociologist Margaret O'Brien states that "father-care-sensitive leave is adopted to signify that the leave period formally allows fathers to be away from the workplace to undertake child and partner care obligations rather than engage in economic breadwinning functions."[14] Two factors are crucial to her framework: leave duration and level of income replacement. Sweden provides an example of "extended father-care leave with high income replacement," the UK provides an example of "short/minimalist father-care leave with low/no income replacement," and the US provides an example of "no statutory father-care sensitive parental leave" (a fourth category exists for "short father-care leave with high income replacement," but this provides less of a contrast than the other three categories, and there is no category for lengthier leave with low/no income replacement).[15]

Political scientist Diane Sainsbury classifies Sweden as an earner-carer regime, which means that it emphasizes both earning money through a paid job and caring for children and family members at home for both men and women.[16] It supports this through a generous parental leave policy as well as heavily subsidized childcare and other laws to ensure gender equality at work and home. These programs, as with other social safety-net programs, are inspired by Sweden's democratic socialist ethos. It is also clear that the Swedish see gender-equal relationships as ideal.[17]

In contrast to Sweden, Sainsbury classifies the US as a universal breadwinner state, which means that it expects that all individuals will hold jobs and earn money.[18] There is not much of a focus on the family, since it is considered a private institution, with the result that policies to alleviate potential conflicts between work and family are limited. This has likely affected employment rates for new mothers. Before 1987, about 70 percent of mothers took time out of the labor market following childbirth, but after 1993, taking time out became less common and after that year, less than 40 percent of women took time out of the labor market when they had a child.[19] This speaks to the pressures American women face to earn money and the lack of availability of paid parental leave.

According to Helene Dearing's calculations, Sweden and the UK have similar durations of leave. The duration of total leave, both paid and unpaid, is eighteen months in Sweden and twenty-one months in the UK. However, when we look more closely at the duration of specifically well-paid leave (defined as at least 1,000 euros per month, or 2/3 or more of earnings), we see that Sweden provides 13.4 months of well-paid leave, whereas the UK provides only 1.4 months, the second lowest amount in Europe (only Slovakia is lower). Dearing also develops an "Equal Gender Division of Labour" indicator based on how well countries' leave policies conform to an ideal model of leave for gender equality. Sweden scores 0.74, which places it at the top as one of only two countries with high scores (the other is Iceland).[20] Note that this rating was calculated before Sweden introduced a third daddy month, which suggests that it would score even higher now. In contrast, the UK is in the low category, with a score of 0.3, mainly because of how little well-paid leave it provides.

The OECD reports the full-rate equivalent, which is the duration of parental leave in weeks multiplied by the payment rate. This measure allows us to compare countries that offer paid leave but at different rates. Before applying the full-rate equivalent, Sweden offers sixty weeks of paid leave to mothers, the UK offers them thirty-nine weeks of paid leave, and the US offers mothers no paid leave. When we look at the full-rate equivalent for mothers, this is thirty-eight weeks for Sweden, twelve weeks for the UK, and zero for the US. While the above numbers are based on leave *available* to mothers, for fathers we must think in terms of the amount of paid leave *reserved* for them. Sweden reserves twelve weeks of paid leave for fathers compared to two weeks in the UK and none in the US. It is thus not surprising that Sweden spends more than the OECD average and the UK spends less than the OECD average on maternity and parental leave. The question remains whether a skewed parental leave policy benefits gender equality.[21]

These three countries—Sweden, the UK, and the US—provide lessons for potential parental leave policy in the US. Sweden has provided a model for many countries as it was the first to introduce parental leave and has continued to tweak its leave policy to encourage father uptake and ultimately gender equality at work and home. The UK is closer to the US in its welfare state approach (both are considered "liberal" regimes with limited state intervention according to Danish sociologist Gøsta Esping-Andersen's frequently cited classification).[22] Yet their policies have maintained gender divisions and therefore provide lessons on what to avoid. It is clear the US needs to adopt paid parental leave, and this book provides a better understanding of what kind of policy will help parents and children while creating opportunities for greater gender equality.

One Day in the Life of an American Family

An incredible 59 percent of first-time mothers in the US return to work within three months after giving birth.[23] When I had my first child in the spring of 2000, there was almost no parental leave to speak of in the US. The FMLA existed, but no states had paid leave. Few companies offered much paid parental leave. Even at the top-ranking liberal arts college where I worked, there was no leave policy. That is unless you count the one-course reduction the college offered new mothers. That's right, out of a five-course teaching load over an academic year, you could take one course off and teach four courses instead. Fortunately for me, I gave birth toward the end of the spring semester and had already put together my final exams. So I was off the hook for the summer. Well, at least once I graded my exams and entered my final grades. My daughter was four months old when I returned to classes the next fall.

I wasn't so lucky the next time. Almost three and a half years later, in the fall of 2003, nothing much had changed in terms of parental leave policy, including at my top-ranking liberal arts college. Enter child number two, on a beautiful September day just a few weeks into the semester. What to do with a one-course reduction? Keep in mind this was not the 1950s. There was one income in my family, but it came from my job. What else was there to do? After assigning three weeks of independent readings, films, and projects, I returned to my classes. Let me now, on the record, apologize to my fall 2003 classes. As you can imagine, it was not my best work. The thing is, I was yet again fortunate. My husband stepped in. After finishing law school, passing the bar (first try), and landing a job with the D.A.'s office, he pushed back his start date and stayed home with our son until the end of that semester. Yes, I realize that I just said that my husband was a lawyer, but 1) he had just finished school so why start a new job and have me stay home when he could stay home, and 2) he wanted to work in the D.A.'s office (which he did for several years) because he didn't want to be one of those lawyers who works eighty hours a week and never sees their family, which meant an embarrassingly low starting salary (even lower than mine). In any case, Kevin took care of our son, and I ran back and forth to breastfeed and such.

The following spring, several female faculty members realized that it was not great to only have one course off when having a child. After gathering parental leave policies from other comparable colleges, we brought this to our dean of faculty and requested a change in the policy. This resulted in a change from a one-course reduction to a two-course reduction for female faculty, which allowed my female colleagues to go on leave for one semester during or after birth or adoption, with a return to three courses in the next semester of teaching. We followed up by making sure the semester of leave included a break from committee and other service work. Based on my research on parental leave and gender equality, I spearheaded efforts to extend the two-course reduction policy to male faculty by taking gender references out of the policy. This happened in August 2016.

The State's Role in Promoting Gender Equality

We can't talk about parental leave without discussing gender equality. There has been a lot of theorizing about gender equality and the welfare state. I draw heavily on feminist theory and in particular on the ideas about "state feminism" put forth by Helga Hernes, a Norwegian political scientist, diplomat, and Labour Party politician. Hernes coined the term "woman-friendly state," a state in which women are able to fully engage equally in work life, family life, and public life. In her book *Welfare State and Woman Power*, she writes:

> A woman-friendly state would not force harder choices on women than on men, or permit unjust treatment on the basis of sex. In a

woman-friendly state women will continue to have children, yet there will also be other roads to self-realization open to them. In such a state women will not have to choose futures that demand greater sacrifices from them than are expected of men.[24]

For Hernes, the state could play an important role in reducing gender inequality. This process involves feminism from above, in the form of policy. Sociologist Ann Shola Orloff adds:

> Because of the power relations in families, shifting decision-making about the distribution of resources or the provision of services from families to polities is parallel to shifting decision-making from markets to states, for it is a shift from an arena in which resources are disproportionately controlled by men to one in which power may be more equally distributed between men and women . . . The failure to recognize gender relations and power within the family and outside the family blinds the power resources analysts to aspects of social policy regimes that affect gender relations . . . The state is woman-friendly to the extent that policies reduce the sexual division of labor by shifting the burden of domestic work to public services and to men.[25]

Feminist theorist Nancy Fraser considers two conventional models for achieving gender equity and introduces a third model. The two models often debated by feminists are the *universal breadwinner* model and the *caregiver parity* model. The universal breadwinner model seeks to achieve gender equity by supporting women's employment and largely focuses on the idea that men and women are equal and should take on similar roles at work and home. The caregiver parity model seeks to realize gender equity by providing support for caregiving work and focuses on the idea that men and women may have different roles that are valued equally. Fraser suggests that both are problematic because notions of equality generally rely on the male as norm, with women fitting into a system structured for men, whereas notions of difference generally rely on essentialist notions of masculinity and femininity, which reinforce gender stereotypes. Fraser further suggests that gender equity requires five normative principles: an anti-poverty principle, an anti-exploitation principle, an equality principle, an anti-marginalization principle, and an anti-androcentrism principle.[26] For my purposes, I will focus on the latter three. More specifically, the equality principle consists of income equality, leisure-time equality, and equality of respect. Beyond addressing the pay gap, there is a need to avoid having the second shift of household labor fall only or mainly on women. Anti-marginalization seeks to promote the economic and political participation of women in public life. Anti-androcentrism seeks to shift gender normative ideals. Fraser argues:

> Social policy should not require women to become like men, nor to fit into institutions designed for men, to enjoy comparable levels of well-being. Policy should aim instead to restructure androcentric institutions so as to welcome human beings who can give birth and who often care for relatives and friends, treating them not as exceptions, but as ideal-typical participants. The antiandrocentrism principle requires decentering masculinist norms . . . It entails changing men as well as changing women.[27]

While Fraser suggests that both the universal breadwinner model and the caregiver parity model are good at alleviating poverty and exploitation, she argues that the universal breadwinner model does a poor job of promoting leisure-time equality and anti-androcentrism, whereas the caregiver parity model does a poor job of promoting income equality and anti-marginalization. Ultimately, Fraser proposes a third option, the *universal caregiver* model, in which women's work and family patterns become the norm and men become more like women. This is no small task, since it entails deconstructing gender. But a very usable aspect of this model is that "all jobs would assume workers who are caregivers, too."[28] In other words, the workplace needs to adapt to the fact that most people have some caregiving responsibilities and that the state must support this through appropriate family policies.

Danish feminist scholars Anette Borchorst and Birte Siim have applied both Hernes's and Fraser's concepts to Sweden, Norway, and Denmark in an attempt to theorize Scandinavian gender equality. They see Fraser as "too optimistic" and are skeptical of the ability of the universal caregiver model to fully realize gender equality. At the same time, they acknowledge that Sweden has come the closest to realizing the universal caregiver ideal. They also comment on the idea that woman-friendly policies would lead to "reproduction going public," as Hernes has suggested. While Borchorst and Siim take issue with this happening in a directly linear fashion, they point to the importance of blurring the boundary between public and private realms for the achievement of Scandinavian gender equality.[29] These models may also be useful for considering the cases of the UK and the US. I would argue that the UK has been closest to the caregiver parity model without actually achieving parity, while the US has been closest to the universal breadwinner model. This may provide a partial explanation for the greater success of the US, relative to the UK, in promoting women's economic participation and opportunity.

Business professor Jill Rubery builds on Fraser's work by elaborating a multi-dimensional framework and proposing a gender agenda for reform. Rubery suggests examining gender equality through two types of work—reproductive work and wage work—and five components of gender equality—time, opportunities, resources, respect, and security.[30] Well-designed parental leave policies can promote gender equality by addressing these components in both reproductive and wage work. Likewise, policies might support a "dual-earner-dual-carer" society in which men and women both earn and care, with particular time set aside for the intensive caring needed for infants.[31]

Parental leave policies can be grouped into a larger category of policies, namely family policies. Economist Olivier Thévenon identifies six aims of family policies. One aim is to reduce poverty. A second aim is to compensate parents for the cost of raising children. A third aim is to promote employment, particularly women's employment. A fourth aim is gender equity, both in the workplace and at home. A fifth aim is improvements in childhood development, both through supporting parental care and public childcare. A sixth aim is increasing fertility rates. Thévenon suggests that the main objectives of family policies in the Nordic countries, including Sweden, are child well-being and gender equity, which are accomplished through generous parental leave and public childcare. These policies also tend to reduce poverty and increase female employment. Anglo-Saxon countries, on the other hand, including the UK and the US, seem more motivated by poverty reduction. These countries often provide means-tested (need-based) or work-tested transfers in order to encourage employment and choices in childcare.

While these programs alleviate some poverty, these countries tend to have higher poverty rates than the OECD average and they further serve to reproduce a gender-based division of labor as women are the ones expected to take employment breaks to care for children.[32]

While a great deal of focus has been put on the need for parental leave policies to ensure women's employment and ultimately gender equality, such policies also have the potential to promote gender inequality. Policies that provide generous parental leave that is mainly used by mothers actually may serve to encourage a gendered division of labor and gender inequalities at home and work.[33] It is therefore important that such policies do not simply focus on women but also on men. As political scientist Christina Bergqvist and colleagues state: "parental leave in Sweden is rarely referred to as a "women's issue," but as a gender equality issue."[34]

According to the 2018 Global Gender Gap Index, Sweden ranks number three in the world in gender equality with a score of 0.822, and ranks particularly high in economic participation and opportunity and political empowerment. The UK ranks fifteen with a score of 0.774, and the US ranks fifty-one with a score of 0.720.[35] Even though the UK ranks above the US on overall rating, the UK falls behind the US in economic participation and opportunity (fifty-two versus nineteen, respectively). Notably, the UK ranks fifty-one on labor force participation, sixty-four on wage equality, and sixty-eight on professional and technical workers while the US ranks highly on professional and technical workers and wage equality.[36] Sweden has the highest maternal employment rate at 83 percent and the highest rate of dual-earners, including 68 percent of couples having both partners in full-time employment, compared to 45 percent in the US and 31 percent in the UK. Sweden also has a high rate of women's political representation, with women comprising 46 percent of members of Parliament, compared to 32 percent in the UK and 21 percent in the US.[37] It is probably worth noting that the Swedish government has adopted gender mainstreaming, a strategy used to incorporate gender equality into all aspects of government rather than pigeonholing it as a single issue in a single organization. To achieve its goal of gender equality, the government has assigned the Swedish Gender Equality Agency to help integrate gender into all operations within fifty-eight government agencies.[38]

A Note on Methods

Much of this book is based on case studies of the US, the UK, and Sweden, with a policy analysis of parental leave policies in those three countries. I have a close familiarity with these policies and with both government sources containing details about the policies as well as empirical studies of the effectiveness of such policies. I draw from the websites of the three governments as well as reports from government agencies like the US Department of Labor and from groups such as the Swedish Social Insurance Agency and the Trades Union Congress (TUC) in the UK. I also use reports from national and international organizations such as the Organization for Economic Cooperation and Development (OECD), the International Labour Organization (ILO), the World Economic Forum, the WORLD Policy Analysis Center, and the National Partnership for Women and Families.

In addition, I draw on my own primary research over the past several years, including interview data I collected in the US and the UK, supplemented with secondary interview data from Sweden. For this particular project, I spent a semester in the UK, conducting research on recent changes to UK parental leave policies. Prior to this, I had collaborated with researchers at City University in London on a project in which we compared my American data to their British data on fathers' experiences with paternity leave.[39] I have personally conducted over one hundred qualitative interviews with American and British parents about parental leave. Participants include ninety-one Americans residing in California, North Carolina, and Texas and twenty-four British individuals residing mainly in the midlands.[40] I used a semi-structured interview approach, placing particular focus on participants' decision-making processes concerning parental leave, how they divided parental leave with their partners, their experiences during parental leave, and the gendered dynamics in their workplaces and at home. I have also spent a good deal of time in Sweden conducting research on the stability of gender role attitudes in Sweden and the influence of egalitarian attitudes on fertility plans and work adjustments.[41] For this book, I have access to two different sets of Swedish interviews, conducted by Swedish collaborators. One set of interviews was conducted with thirty-two first-time parents living in two Swedish counties, one in the northern part of the country, the county with the highest rate of parental leave taken by fathers, and one in the southern part of the country, the one with the lowest rate of uptake by fathers.[42] The second set of interviews was conducted with twenty Swedish parents of preschool-aged children living in the northern region of Västerbotten.[43] In all cases reported in this book, names have been changed. Personally, some of my favorite places in the world include Djurgården in Stockholm, Stadsliden in Umeå, and Victoria Park in Leicester. I have a deep affection for all three countries.

Outline of Chapters

The rest of the chapters focus on the six lessons outlined above regarding parental leave and gender equality. Chapter 1 focuses on the first lesson—the US is way behind the rest of the world when it comes to parental leave. The US has mainly resisted efforts at introducing paid leave and is currently the only industrialized country without any form of national paid leave. This chapter provides the background of policy development at the federal and state level and considers employer policies. Chapter 2 focuses on the second lesson—parental leave is good—and thus outlines the benefits of parental leave for women, men, children, employers, and society. Women benefit when they take leave, but they also experience employment and health benefits when their partners take leave. Men themselves benefit from leave in bonding and building relationships with their children and developing parenting skills. Children enjoy health, educational, and behavioral benefits when their parents take parental leave. Employers gain in areas of competitiveness, recruitment, retention, and positive company culture. Societal benefits include a stronger economy and higher fertility rates. Chapter 3 focuses on the third lesson—too much leave may not be good either, particularly for women. This chapter explores the question of how much leave is too much by considering evidence of gender dynamics at home and in the workplace. Long leaves have detrimental consequences for women and men's careers as well as for women's health.

Chapter 4 focuses on the fourth lesson—we need to think of fathers as partners, not helpers. This chapter examines gendered leave taking. It looks at parental leave decisions and experiences and highlights how parents rely on gender expectations but also seek to challenge these same expectations. As expected, based on policy differences, British parents experience more gendered dynamics than either Swedish or American parents. Chapter 5 focuses on the fifth lesson—the UK is not a good model for parental leave and gender equality. British policy lagged behind Europe's on parental leave, then introduced and expanded maternity leave until their policy was extremely lopsided with one year for maternity and two weeks for paternity leave. The UK has attempted to increase fathers' uptake of leave by introducing various policies but these have had limited success. Chapter 6 focuses on the sixth lesson— the Swedish model is great but not perfect. This chapter provides historical context for Sweden's parental leave policy and describes its current policy. Sweden was the first country to introduce parental leave in place of maternity leave back in the 1970s. It now offers three months of leave to each parent as well as ten additional months to be divided between parents. Finally, in the conclusion, I offer policy recommendations, based on these six lessons, for the US. The six month solution is the product of these lessons. It is still possible, I conclude, for the US to develop a strong parental leave policy that will promote gender equality at work and at home.

1

The US Is Way behind the Rest of the World

Why is maternity leave so terrible in this country?
New York Magazine, March 8, 2016[1]

US dead last among developed countries when it comes to
paid maternity leave.
Forbes, April 6, 2016[2]

Paid parental leave elusive twenty-five years after Family and
Medical Leave Act—The US ranks last on this important
issue.
CNN, February 5, 2018[3]

The United States stands out as one of the very few countries in the
world (with Papua New Guinea and Suriname) that do not offer any
cash benefits during maternity leave.[4] This despite the fact that, all the
way back in 1952, the United Nations' International Labor Organization
(ILO) recommended that countries implement at least fourteen weeks
of paid maternity leave. According to the Bureau of Labor Statistics, 85
percent of American workers have access to *unpaid* family leave, mainly
through the Family and Medical Leave Act (FMLA).[5] However, the same
report shows that only 12 percent of workers have access to *paid* family
leave, mainly through employer policies. This has increased slightly in
the last few years, but as of 2018, only 15 percent of civilian workers in
the US had access to paid family leave.[6] This is even the case when it
comes to paid maternity leave. According to a recent survey of a national
sample of working mothers, only 41 percent received paid leave, and the
average amount of paid leave was just 3.3 weeks, at 31 percent of wages.[7]

On top of that, a recent study by economist Jay Zagorsky shows that
the number of women taking maternity leave in the US has not changed
significantly in the past two decades.[8] Specifically, in 1994, on average,

278,454 women took maternity leave each month compared to 299,861 in 2015. Since the number of births in 1994 and 2015 were similar (3.95 million versus 3.98 million, respectively), the rate of maternity leave changed little. On the other hand, the number of men taking paternity leave more than tripled over this time period. In 1994, the average number of men taking paternity leave each month was 5,798, compared to 21,703 in 2015, with a corresponding increase in the rate of leave-taking from 14.7 per 10,000 births to 54.6 per 10,000 births. Keep in mind that most of those taking leave did not receive paid parental leave. Certainly, many more American women would take paid maternity leave if it were available to them, and the tremendous increase in American men taking paternity leave suggests that there is a huge, growing, unmet need in the US for paid paternity leave. But American parents, practically alone in the world, have no national policy to rely on. How can this be? Why is there no paid leave at the national level? What has happened at the state and local level? Have employers stepped in to fill the need for paid leave? Will we ever see the US adopt paid parental leave?

This chapter attempts to address these questions by focusing on parental leave policy in the US, namely the absence of a paid statutory parental leave policy at the national level and efforts to fill the gap at the state and local levels. While there is no federal paid parental leave, eight states have passed legislation to implement it at the state level, and others have used short-term disability to offer paid maternity leave. This is a distinct feature of the US, where many policies that are not supported at the federal level are left to be determined by individual states. In addition, private employers are increasingly creating and expanding paid parental leave policies, though these tend to benefit more professional workers.[9] The following sections focus on leave policies at the national, state, city, and employer levels. To contextualize the tensions between broader policy and individual experiences, I draw from company statements and news releases as well as from interviews with American fathers. The final section discusses the policy possibilities moving forward.

Before reviewing the development of parental leave policies in the US, it may be useful to provide an overview of relevant terminology. We must first make a distinction between paid and unpaid leave. There is no paid leave at the federal level, but some states and employers provide a percentage of employees' wages or salary. Those who are eligible for unpaid leave may be able to use paid vacation or sick days, if available from their employer, to cover their pay. Some states and employers make distinctions between maternity and paternity leave, but most policies refer to parental or family leave, the latter being inclusive of leave to provide care for sick family members.

The Absence of Statutory Paid Parental Leave at the National Level

The only US federal policy that addresses parental leave is the Family and Medical Leave Act (FMLA), which was passed in 1993 and signed into law by Democratic President Bill Clinton. There was much resistance to this act as it was introduced in Congress each year between 1984 and 1993. It finally passed in 1991 and 1992, only to be vetoed by Republican President George H. W. Bush. Much of the opposition to FMLA focused on the potential damage to businesses and employers.[10] On the other hand, much of the motivation for introducing family leave centered on women's increasing participation in the labor force. In particular, legislators noted the need to respond to the dramatic rise in employment among mothers of young children and the growing need for two-income households, as well as the surge in single-parent families.[11] Arguments in favor of FMLA raised the potential benefits to businesses, including lower turnover rates and increased productivity. Interestingly, some politicians at the time also noted that the US was out of touch with the rest of the world on this issue. Notably, however, there was very limited discussion of fathers and paternity leave at this time.[12]

The final version signed by President Clinton in January 1993, which has been in effect since August 1993, allows up to twelve weeks of unpaid leave for eligible employees. When first drafted, the bill provided eighteen weeks for parental leave and twenty-six weeks for medical leave.[13] Although Dr. Berry Brazelton, pediatrics professor at Harvard and host of "What Every Baby Knows," testified before Congress that parental leave should be at least four months to allow for healthy bonding between parent and child, in order to gather enough support to pass the bill the length of leave was reduced to twelve weeks.[14] Pressure for paid leave from women's organizations was unsuccessful, as the political environment during the Reagan era emphasized small government, and the sponsors realized that an unpaid leave benefit would have the best chance of passing.[15] It was not ideal, but it was the best we could do at the time.

FMLA, as its name suggests, covers family and medical reasons for leave. Medical leave includes time off to care for oneself or a family member (spouse, child, parent) who is experiencing a serious medical condition. Family leave includes time off for pregnancy, adoption, or foster placement and care of newborn or newly adopted children. FMLA also covers time off for family military leave related to an injured service member or to deal with needs that arise from a family member's deployment. FMLA leave is an individual right of each eligible employee. However, there is an exception to this: when two spouses work for the same employer. While each spouse is able to take the twelve weeks for their own illness or to care for a spouse or child with a serious health condition, there is a combined limitation of twelve weeks for the birth, placement, and bonding of a new child (as well as to care for an ill parent).

To be eligible, an employee has to work for an eligible worksite, which includes only firms that have at least fifty employees. Even if an employee works for an eligible employer, they must have worked for the same employer for at least one year and must have worked at least 1,250 hours during the previous year. There is the possibility for some flexibility in the form of intermittent leave or a reduced schedule for use with bonding leave, but this is left to the individual employer's discretion. Leave is job-protected, which means that the employer must allow the employee to return to their original job or an equivalent job (as determined by pay, benefits, and other conditions) and must continue health insurance coverage for the employee while on leave. Those working for small businesses, particularly those with fewer than ten employees, and those working in service and retail comprise much of those not covered by FMLA.[16]

A few states have extended the number of weeks covered by FMLA, lowered the requirement that employers have at least fifty employees, or broadened temporary disability insurance (TDI) to include pregnancy and childbirth (all of these states but Hawaii have introduced paid family leave and are covered in the next section). For example, Hawaii's TDI program offers up to twenty-six weeks of leave for eligible employees (those who have been employed with their employer for at least fourteen weeks, worked twenty or more hours per week, and earned $400 or more per week) at 58 percent of wages. Most states do not provide these benefits, and therefore there is no paid leave for many new parents, including mothers who are recovering from childbirth. Sometimes their only protection comes from the Pregnancy Discrimination Act of 1978, which mandates that employers with fifteen or more employees cannot discriminate against an employee based on current pregnancy, past pregnancy, potential pregnancy, or medical conditions related to pregnancy or childbirth. It also requires employers to treat pregnant employees the same as they would treat other temporarily disabled employees. This may involve paid leave, but that is not required.

So this is what we have to work with. But how is it working? Is it serving the needs of America's new parents? In order to assess the effectiveness of FMLA, the Department of Labor commissioned surveys in 1995, 2000, and 2012. In the most recent survey, only 17 percent of worksites report that the policy applies to them and another 30 percent are unsure if FMLA applies to their worksite. Meanwhile, Klerman, Daly, and Pozniak, researchers at Abt Associates hired by the Department of Labor, impute that only 10 percent of worksites meet eligibility requirements.[17] In considering employee eligibility for FMLA, only 59 percent of employees meet all of the requirements (worked full-time or at least 1,250 hours at a worksite with fifty or more employees continuously for the past year). Awareness of FMLA increased from 56 percent of workers in 1995 to 66 percent of workers in 2012, with the most common way of learning about FMLA coming from Human Resources or a poster at work. Based on an analysis of the Current Population Survey for 2011–2014, only 38 percent of working adults who are eligible for FMLA can afford unpaid leave. This varies from 28.6 percent in Idaho to 44.7 percent in Virginia.[18] The bottom line is that few workplaces are covered under FMLA, 41 percent of employees are not eligible for FMLA, and even fewer workers feel they can afford to take unpaid leave.

Nevertheless, family and medical leave-taking is fairly common among American workers, with 13 percent of *all employees in the country* taking leave for a new child, their own illness, or to care for a sick family member each year. Extended over several years, the proportion of all workers taking some form of leave is likely to be sizeable. However, there is a notable difference in leave-taking by eligibility, with 16 percent of those who are eligible for FMLA taking leave compared to 10 percent of those not eligible for FMLA. It is also important to note that a minority of leave is to care for a new child—only 21 percent of leave takers fall into this category. On the other hand, a slight majority of leave takers (55 percent) take leave for their own illness and 18 percent take leave to care for a parent, spouse, or child. Close to half of employees (48 percent) receive pay while on leave, mainly through paid sick leave, vacation leave, and personal leave, while 17 percent receive partial pay and 34 percent receive no pay (note these figures apply to all family leave, not just parental leave). Not surprisingly, low-income workers and those taking longer leave are less likely to receive pay, and the second most common reason for returning to work, after no longer needing leave, is the inability to afford leave (reported by 40 percent of employees who take leave). Nevertheless, most employers seem to have a positive or neutral view toward FMLA. A large majority (85 percent) of employers report that it is easy to comply with FMLA, and only a very small number (2 to 3 percent) of employers report confirmed or suspected misuse of FMLA.

There have been recent attempts to pass paid parental leave at the national level, most notably in the form of the Family and Medical Insurance Leave Act (known as the FAMILY Act), but they have thus far failed. In 2013, Democratic Senator Gillibrand and Representative DeLauro first introduced the FAMILY Act. When they reintroduced the bill in 2015, it was referred to the Committee on Finance in the Senate and moved to the Subcommittee on Social Security in the House, but never made it out of the Republican-controlled committees. Most recently, on February 7, 2017 Senator Kirsten Gillibrand reintroduced the FAMILY Act to the 115th Congress.[19] The FAMILY Act would provide up to twelve weeks of paid leave for the birth or adoption of a new child, to care for a sick child, partner, or parent, or to care for oneself. Workers on leave would receive 66 percent of their wages, up to a maximum of $4,000 per month. Funding for the program would come from a small tax of 0.2 percent of wages collected from employers and employees.[20] The main difference between FMLA and the FAMILY Act is that the FAMILY Act would provide *paid* leave. Eligibility and length of leave (twelve weeks) are the same under both policies.

While President Obama was unable to pass paid family leave under his administration, he gave an executive order in January 2015 that allowed up to six weeks of paid parental leave for federal workers. Under this order, federal agencies were required to let their employees use sick leave to care for a newborn or newly adopted child. It did not necessarily create new leave, as federal employees have access to sick leave, but it did allow federal employees to use sick leave for a new child and to advance sick leave days if they had not accumulated six weeks. The Presidential Memorandum included the following statement:

> Men and women both need time to care for their families and should have access to workplace flexibilities that help them succeed at work and at home. Offering family leave and other workplace flexibilities to parents can help achieve the goals of recruiting and retaining talent, lowering costly worker turnover, increasing employee engagement, boosting employee morale, and ensuring a diverse and inclusive workforce. Yet, the United States lags behind almost every other country in ensuring some form of paid parental leave to its Federal workforce; we are the only developed country in the world without it.[21]

Here we see that President Obama finds it alarming that the US is so out of step with the rest of the world.

State-Level Policies

In addition to the states that have broadened FMLA coverage, eight states have passed laws establishing their own paid parental leave programs, and four of these are currently in effect. As with other policies, there are stark differences in parental leave policy among states.[22] As Seymour Martin Lipset, an influential American sociologist, argued, the historical absence of a monarchy and the prominence of individualism in its creation means Americans are less deferential to government.[23] Many believe that politicians, especially those at the national level, cannot know what is best for them. These are the same arguments that have been made around issues as diverse as education, abortion, and same-sex marriage. Passing parental leave at the state level has not been easy, but strong local actors have been involved. Below, I highlight the policies passed in California, New Jersey, Rhode Island, New York, Washington, and Massachusetts.

California

California was the first state to introduce paid family leave, with the passage of Paid Family Leave (PFL) in 2002. As with FMLA, this policy covers care for newborn and newly adopted/fostered children, called bonding claims. Like FMLA, it also covers care for a spouse, child, or parent with a serious medical condition—instances called caring claims. Unlike FMLA, it from the start included registered domestic partners and, in 2014, added siblings, parents-in-law, grandparents, and grandchildren as eligible ill family members. This program offers up to six weeks of leave, and until a recent increase, it was paid at approximately 55 percent of wages. It is based on State Disability Insurance. Individual employees have rights to Paid Family Leave, so both mothers and fathers can take six weeks of paid leave.

Efforts to pass paid family leave began in the late 1990s, when State Senator Hilda Solis introduced a bill that required the Employment Development Department (EDD) to conduct a study on the costs of expanding state disability insurance benefits to individuals on family leave. When the study was released in 2000, it showed that family leave could be covered under state disability insurance for an increase of as little as a 0.1 percent of the state payroll tax. State Senator Sheila Kuehl introduced Senate Bill 1661 in February 2002. It originally included twelve weeks of paid leave (parallel to the amount of unpaid time offered by FMLA) and cost-sharing between employees and employers. While the bill garnered major support among Democrats and work-family organizations, business groups lobbied against it. After negotiations, the bill reduced leave to six weeks, deleted the employer contribution, and allowed a requirement that employees use up their vacation time (up to two weeks) before obtaining state benefits. This last requirement does not apply to new birth mothers, who can claim pregnancy-related disability insurance. Once these changes were made, the bill was approved quickly and signed into law by Governor Gray Davis on September 23, 2002. PFL went into effect on January 1, 2004, when the state started withholding 0.9 percent in payroll tax, and the EDD processed claims starting on July 1, 2004.

Parental leave claims must occur in the first year after the birth or placement of the child, and there was a waiting period of seven days before benefits could be paid (though this could overlap with an employer policy if the employer required use of vacation time first). In 2016, Assemblyman Jimmy Gomez introduced a measure, and Governor Jerry Brown signed the law, that amended PFL to increase benefits and eliminate the seven-day waiting period. While the initial law included paid leave at a rate of 55 percent of the employee's weekly wages, there was a recent increase in the percentage of pay offered to those on leave. As of January 1, 2018, workers whose wages are close to the minimum wage are eligible for 70 percent of their wages while on leave, while those with higher wages are eligible for 60 percent of their wages. The maximum benefit as of 2019 is $1,252 per week.

California's PFL goes well beyond the federal policy, so how has it done? The evidence so far suggests the program has been successful in increasing parents' use of leave while having minimal impact on employers. Between 2004 and 2009, the number of claims per one hundred live births increased from twenty-four to 30.[24] Furthermore, between 2009 and 2010 and between 2015 and 2016, the total claims paid increased from 180,675 to 233,113, and the percent of bonding claims filed has remained high at 88 percent, with the remaining 12 percent being caring claims.[25] Another hopeful sign is that the percent of "male bonding" claims has risen from 23 percent in 2007–2008 to 35.5 percent in 2015–2016.[26] In a quasi-experimental study of the program, researchers find that Paid Family Leave increases fathers' leave-taking by 50 percent for leave alone (while the mother is at work), and by 28 percent for concurrent leave (at the same time as the mother).[27] Nevertheless, there remains a gap in how much leave men and women take: while men take a median of three weeks of bonding leave, women take a median of twelve weeks of bonding leave.[28] Though studies thus far are limited, the evidence suggests that Paid Family Leave has had a positive impact on children and families through increased breastfeeding and time with children.[29] In terms of employer effects, Ruth Milkman and Eileen Appelbaum, authors of *Unfinished Business: Paid Family Leave in California and the Future of U.S. Work-Family Policy*, suggest that employers are quite satisfied, with approximately 90 percent of the 250 California firms in their study saying the law had a positive effect or no effect on outcomes such as productivity and morale.[30]

Unfortunately, California's paid family leave still lacks job protection. While those who are covered by FMLA and PFL can take paid leave under the latter and have it protected under the former, workers who are not eligible for FMLA may have to take paid leave under PFL without the guarantee that their job will be available upon their return. Incredibly, employers are not obligated to tell employees that there is no job protection.

New Jersey

New Jersey's Family Temporary Disability Leave law (commonly known as Paid Family Leave) went into effect in 2009, five years after California's Paid Family Leave. As in California, there is no requirement for a minimum number of employees at a workplace (as there is with FMLA) and it is completely funded by a payroll tax and administered through the state's Temporary Disability Benefit program. New Jersey's Paid Family Leave also provides up to six weeks of leave. While the pay is two-thirds of an employee's normal rate, which is higher than in California (except for low-wage workers), the maximum pay is $650 per week in 2019, much lower than in California. As with California's policy, there is no job protection, which means that employers that are not covered by FMLA (those with fewer than fifty employees) may decide not to hold a job for someone on leave. In 2017, State Senate President Steve Sweeney co-sponsored a bill to expand paid parental leave in New Jersey, but it was vetoed by the governor at the time, Republican Chris Christie. With Phil Murphy, a Democrat, taking over as governor in 2018, a new bill has been introduced, which increases leave length from six weeks to twelve weeks, increases the percent of pay from two-thirds to 90 percent, and raises the maximum benefit to $1,195 per week.[31]

According to a report issued by the Center for Economic and Policy Research (CEPR), the number of Paid Family Leave claims in New Jersey increased from 14,127 in 2009 to 29,456 in 2012. Bonding claims make up 82 percent of claims with the other 18 percent being family care claims. Unlike in California, there has been no notable increase in men's bonding claims with men representing 12 percent of bonding claims in 2009 and 2012.[32] Little research has been done on this policy, though an early study showed positive views of the program but limited awareness of its existence.[33]

Rhode Island

Rhode Island passed legislation called Temporary Caregiver Insurance in July 2013. It went into effect January 1, 2014, five years after New Jersey's policy and ten years after California's. As with these states, Rhode Island's law builds on its Temporary Disability Insurance program. With a payroll tax just above 1 percent, workers are able to take up to four weeks of leave at a 60-percent wage replacement, with benefits set at a minimum of $98 per week and a maximum of $852, as of 2019. Unlike the policies in California and New Jersey, Rhode Island's policy provides job protection, similar to FMLA. Currently, State Senator Gayle Goldin and State Representative Christopher Blazejewski are pushing for a bill that would increase the length of leave to six weeks in 2019 and eight weeks in 2020.[34]

An early study of Temporary Caregiver Insurance shows that many workers have benefited from it, but awareness remains an issue. About half of workers in Rhode Island are aware of Temporary Caregiver Insurance, with lower awareness among Hispanics and low-income workers. Women make up the majority of Temporary Caregiver Insurance leave-takers (84 percent compared to 16 percent of men). While 92 percent of mothers taking Temporary Caregiver Insurance use all four weeks of leave, only 68 percent of fathers use the maximum time. Furthermore, Temporary Caregiver Insurance users seem to benefit in other ways as they are more likely to report an increase in income and fewer work absences as well as longer time spent breastfeeding and more well-baby visits.[35]

New York

The official website of the state of New York boasts that it has "the nation's strongest and most comprehensive Paid Family Leave policy."[36] The policy was passed in 2016 and came into effect on January 1, 2018, to be phased in over three years. In 2018, it provided eight weeks of leave at 50 percent of pay with increases to ten weeks of leave at 55 percent of pay in 2019, ten weeks of leave at 60 percent of pay in 2020, and twelve weeks of leave at 67 percent of pay from 2021. Maximum pay is based on a percentage of the state average weekly wage, which is currently $1,296; for example, an employee who makes more than the

Figure 1.1. New York State Paid Family Leave advertisement.
Source: Courtesy of r/actuallesbians

state average will receive $713 or 55 percent of $1,296. While employers cannot require employees to use vacation or sick leave, they may allow employees to use this leave in combination with family leave to achieve their full salary. Like the other states, New York is funding this program with an employee payroll deduction. Like Rhode Island, New York's policy provides job-protected leave. It is more generous than other existing policies in a couple of ways. First, it currently provides the longest leave (though Washington and Massachusetts will provide twelve weeks when their programs begin; see below). Second, it covers part-time workers and coverage is not dependent on citizenship or immigration status.

Figure 1.1 shows one of the government advertisements for the policy that are posted in public places, including on the subway. The message is clearly inclusive as it depicts a lesbian couple with their baby and states: "All parents deserve time to bond with a new child."

Washington

In 2007, Washington State passed the Family Leave Act, which parallels the FMLA in providing twelve weeks of job-protected leave. Due to a shortage in funding, it never went into effect. However, recent efforts have brought new life to paid leave in Washington, where benefits will begin January 1, 2020. Since Washington does not have a TDI program similar to the other states that have passed paid leave, its legislators have created a new system based on the state's unemployment insurance program.[37] The new system combines a payroll tax and employer contributions. The premium is 0.4 percent of earnings, with employers paying approximately 37 percent (though they can choose to pay more). Businesses can substitute their own plans as long as they are at least as generous as the state law. Small businesses (fewer than fifty employees) do not have to pay in, but their employees still pay 63 percent of the 0.4 percent premium. All private sector employees are therefore covered.[38] When the program begins, payment will be 90 percent of average weekly wages for those who earn 50 percent or less of the statewide average; the formula is a bit more complicated for those who earn more than 50 percent of the statewide average weekly wage.[39]

Massachusetts

Massachusetts passed paid family medical leave (House Bill 4640) in June 2018. This policy, set to take effect in 2021, will cover up to twelve weeks of parental leave to bond with a new child in the first year after birth or adoption as well as leave to care for oneself or a family member with a serious health condition. In addition to spouses, children, and parents, family is defined to include domestic partners, grandchildren, parents' in-laws, grandparents, and siblings. All Massachusetts employees will be eligible regardless of hours or amount of time in employment. It also covers self-employed workers who opt for coverage and former

TABLE 1.1. Summary of state-level policies

	Year passed/ in effect	Length of leave	Level of pay	Maximum pay per week	Job protection
California	2002/2004	6 weeks	60–70%	$1252	No
New Jersey	2008/2009	6 weeks	66%	$650	No
Rhode Island	2013/2014	4 weeks	60%	$852	Yes
New York[a]	2016/2018	10 weeks	55%	$1,296	Yes
Washington	2017/2020	12 weeks	Up to 90%	$1,000	Yes
Massachusetts	2018/2021	12 weeks	Up to 80%	$850	Yes

[a]As of 2019. When fully implemented in 2021, NY will provide 12 weeks at 67% pay

employees who have been out of employment for twenty-six weeks or less. Employees must wait seven days before receiving wage replacement. Benefits are calculated at 80 percent of weekly wages up to a maximum of 50 percent of the state average weekly wage, plus an additional 50 percent of weekly wages up to the maximum of $850 per week. An employer payroll tax of 0.63 percent of employee's wages will fund this program. Employers with twenty-five or more employees can deduct up to 40 percent of the contribution from employee's wages for medical leave and 100 percent of the contribution for family leave. Employers with fewer than twenty-five employees are not required to pay premiums.[40]

Other State Initiatives

Several other states are considering family leave legislation. In summer 2019, Connecticut and Oregon passed paid family leave that will go into effect in 2022 and 2023, respectively. Hawaii is commissioning a study of how paid family leave could be implemented, setting the stage for a possible floor vote.[41] Arizona introduced a measure in May 2016 that mandates a report with a cost analysis for a family leave program by July 2020. Several states, including Arkansas, Colorado, Florida, Nebraska, New Mexico, Virginia, and Wisconsin, have introduced bills that have failed, died, been tabled, or been indefinitely postponed. These bills have mainly been introduced by Democrats.

Table 1.1 shows recent advances in state-level policies. To summarize, of the fifty US states, the four top-listed here have a paid family leave policy in effect (California, New Jersey, Rhode Island, New York); four more have passed paid leave scheduled to go into effect over the next four years, as shown here for Washington (in 2020) and Massachusetts (in 2021). Scheduled but not listed are Connecticut (2022) and Oregon (2023). All of these states are considered politically liberal, with higher proportions of Democrats than Republicans. As of January 2018, only 21.4 percent of the US population is fortunate enough to be living in a state with paid leave.

Beyond the National and State Levels

States are not the only governments taking matters into their own hands. Some cities around the country, such as Pittsburgh and Austin, are starting to provide paid parental leave to city employees.[42] In January 2016, New York City Mayor Bill de Blasio signed a personnel order that provides paid leave for maternity, paternity, adoption, or foster care to those who work for the city, numbering around 20,000 employees. The order provides six weeks of leave at 100 percent of salary, and this can be extended to twelve weeks if combined with existing leave. The policy was funded by canceling a planned managerial raise and capping vacation at twenty-five days.[43]

San Francisco introduced paid leave for all new parents, which went into effect on January 1, 2017. This policy goes beyond California's Paid Family Leave by offering one hundred percent of pay for six weeks and requiring employers to account for the difference between state and city policy. In other words, while the state policy provides sixty to seventy percent of pay, the city policy requires employers to pay the remaining thirty to forty percent of a worker's salary. This policy gradually applies to more and more workplaces. At its start, it applied to companies with fifty or more workers, but as of 2018, it applies to companies with twenty or more employees. San Francisco's law means that a national company with a branch in San Francisco must provide the remaining amount to cover full pay, regardless of what its policy is at its headquarters or in other branches. A report from the city controller shows that the policy would increase parents' wages from an average of $743 per week to $1,351 per week. In fact, the upper limit for total benefits from the state and employer is $2,133, which means that those who earn less than approximately $111,000 per year would receive full pay for the six weeks of leave.[44]

The District of Columbia (Washington, DC) passed the Universal Paid-Leave Amendment Act in April 2017, effective July 2020. The policy will provide eight weeks of paid leave for the birth, adoption, or fostering of a new child, as well as six weeks to care for a sick family member. All full-time and part-time private-sector workers who are employed in Washington, DC are eligible, regardless of residence, as long as they spend at least 50 percent of their work time in the District of Columbia. Benefits will be determined differently depending on wages. For workers who earn up to 150 percent of the D.C. minimum wage, pay will be 90 percent of their average weekly wage rate. For workers earning more, pay will be 90 percent of 150 percent of the minimum wage plus 50 percent of the difference between the worker's average weekly wage and 150 percent of the minimum wage, up to $1,000 per week.[45] Unlike policies in other cities, a business tax will fund this leave policy. There will be a one-week waiting period. Job protection is not guaranteed for those who work for smaller employers (those with fewer than twenty employees). Like the states that have passed paid family leave laws, the cities that have followed suit are left-leaning, with Democratic mayors.

Company Policies

Netflix received considerable attention in August 2015 when it introduced "unlimited" paid leave for salaried "streaming" employees—those who work in the company's streaming division—during the first year of their child's birth or adoption. The company later revised the policy to include more employees for shorter periods of time. In the last few years, several companies have introduced or expanded their family leave policies. In the first months of 2018, five companies introduced new or revised parental leave policies.[46] In this section, I focus on recent changes to company policies, as outlined by the National Partnership for Women & Families, in order to illustrate some similarities and differences across these policies in their aims and goals. Most are focused on improving their companies and doing better business in some way, but many also take stronger stances by molding policies that will improve gender equality.

Access to paid leave varies considerably by industry, with 37 percent of finance and insurance workers and 33 percent of information workers

TABLE 1.2. Employer policies by length of leave offered

10 weeks	12 weeks	14 weeks	16 weeks	18 weeks	20 weeks	>20 weeks
Airbnb	BP America	Kering	Bank of America	3M	Amazon	Adobe
CVS	CarMax	LL Bean	Citi	Capital One	IBM	American Express
Hilton	Choice Hotels	Nestle	Ernst & Young	GoDaddy	Microsoft	Deloitte
Lowe's	Coca-Cola	Nike	Facebook	Hasbro	Twitter	eBay
Walmart	DOW Chemical		Honest	Lyft		Etsy
	Gap		IKEA	Starbucks		Mozilla
	LinkedIn		Levi Strauss			Netflix
	Sallie Mae		Mastercard			Spotify
	Whirlpool		PayPal			
			Pinterest			
			Procter & Gamble			
			Shell			
			Vanguard			
			Zillow			

Source: National Partnership for Women & Families, http://www.nationalpartnership.org/

having access to paid leave compared to only 5 percent of construction workers and 6 percent of leisure and hospitality workers. Those working for larger companies are also more likely to have access to paid family leave—23 percent of those working for companies with 500 or more employees versus 9 percent of those working for companies with fewer than one hundred employees.[47] On top of all this, there is a great deal of movement between jobs, with the average American worker having a tenure with their current employer of only 4.2 years, which makes it less likely for people to have paid leave.[48] Overall, access to paid leave reflects the broader inequality in the American labor force and society more generally, with more educated workers and those with higher incomes also having better leave benefits. Table 1.2 shows employer policies by length of leave offered.

Leading by Example

Our employees are the lifeblood of our organization. This new policy represents an investment in them and their families, but more than that, it's simply the right thing to do.
—New York Presbyterian Hospital, May 2017[49]

In April 2016, Twitter introduced twenty weeks of paid parental leave, doing away with differently structured leaves for primary and secondary caregiving. The company's Vice President of Inclusion and Diversity, Jeffrey Siminoff, made the following notable statement: "The goal of this change was to expand how we think about parental leave. Primary caregiving is something that's hard to define . . . We want to lead by example and by doing so we can influence the decisions of others."[50] While many companies that offer paid leave distinguish between maternity and paternity or primary and secondary caregivers, Twitter saw the importance of removing labels and restrictions on different types of parents and families.

Making Up for a Lack of US Policy

Some companies are explicit about the lack of paid parental leave in this country. In August 2015, Adobe senior VP Donna Morris stated: "Caring for yourself and your family at home helps you be your best at work. But in the US, government mandates for paid leave are currently slim to nonexistent. That means companies must navigate the tough balance between supporting employees during major life events and meeting business goals." Stonyfield Farm made the following statement when announcing its twenty-four weeks of paid parental leave: "The US is tragically behind the rest of the world when it comes to acknowledging all of the benefits that come along with having a caregiver home when a child is introduced to the family. It resonates throughout that child's life . . . *We're doing it because America is not doing it for us*" (emphasis added).[51] Hamdi Ulukaya, founder and CEO of Chobani (which means "shepherd" in Turkish), talked about how being a father influenced his efforts to better support parents in his own company. When announcing their new policy of six weeks of paid parental leave in

October 2016, Ulukaya released the following statement: "As a founder and a new father, my son opened my eyes to the fact that the vast majority of workers in this country don't have access to paid family leave when they have a new child. That's especially true when it comes to manufacturing and that needs to change in this country and Chobani needed to be part of that change."[52]

Still other companies bring their European influence to the US. For example, Spotify was developed in Stockholm and offers twenty-four weeks of paid parental leave. In 2015, its Chief Human Resources Officer, Katarina Berg, announced: "This policy best defines who we are as a company, born out of a Swedish culture that places an emphasis on a healthy work/family balance, gender equality and the ability for every parent to spend quality time with the people that matter most in their lives."[53] Statements like these demonstrate how companies seek to express themselves more than as businesses but also as shapers of culture. In Spotify's case, it explicitly acknowledges the importance of gender equality as well as time off for new parents. All of these companies noted the absence of US policy and their determination to make up for what the US lacks in parental leave policies.

Balancing Work and Family

It's something we felt was so necessary in order to be family-friendly and to make sure our employees have the resources they need to balance family, finances and coming back to work.
—M&T Bank, September 2015[54]

More and more companies are touting their family-friendly policies, including paid parental leave. OppenheimerFunds introduced parental leave in January 2018, noting that their company "recognizes the importance of work/life balance and offers rewarding career opportunities, while providing programs and benefits that recognize family and personal needs." Others are more specific about the importance of having children and spending time with them. For example, FMC Corporation, a chemical manufacturing company, introduced its policy in October 2016 with the following statement: "The ability to balance work while caring for loved ones or welcoming a new baby to the family has become increasingly important. FMC is proud to be at the forefront of employers that are introducing progressive parental and dependent care benefits that help employees lead successful careers and raise great families." At the same time, Levi Strauss & Company emphasized the particular significance of having a child: "We recognize that one of the biggest life events for any man or woman is welcoming a new child, and we decided that we wanted to build on our support to our employees during this important bonding time. We know, and research has proved, families do better when parents are able to have the support and flexibility to cherish these important moments."[55] Noting that having or adopting a child is "one of the biggest life events" and that these moments should be treasured, this statement explicitly places value on children and family. Other companies similarly highlight the importance of family time:

> At Choice, we know how difficult it can be to achieve work/life balance and we are committed to providing our valued employees with the support they need. The time we each have to spend with our loved ones is never enough, and I'm proud that our company plans to give us all a little more of it.
> —Choice Hotels International, September 2016

> At IKEA, we believe time with family and friends is so important for a healthy work-life balance and a happy and productive workforce. This benefit, which applies to all parents, will give our co-workers the opportunity to spend more time with their families when welcoming a child.
> —IKEA, December 2016[56]

IKEA, another Swedish-based company, acknowledges the role of family and friends, or those who add to one's "life," in creating a positive work-life balance while also singling out time to spend with a new child. Choice further remarks on the feeling, noted by many, that we can never have enough time to spend with the people we love. According to a 2017 Pew Research Center poll, almost half of all parents of children under age eighteen say they spend too little time with their children, and for fathers this rate is 63 percent. Pew also asked the main reason for spending too little time with kids and it is not surprising that work is the main culprit.[57]

Some companies also raise the issue of choice in an effort to show the false dichotomy between choosing work and family. In January 2015, Intel made this statement: "At the end of the day, it's about creating a work environment and culture that says you're balancing an intense work life with a great family life . . . The days where you had to choose one or the other, we want to put that behind us." Likewise, Schneider Electric states: "We're committed to promoting a favorable work environment where our employees have more control over their work and personal life responsibilities. Our refined family-leave policy ensures our employees have more paid time off when they need it, allowing them to avoid having to make a choice between work and their family." BASF, a chemical company, is more explicit in their December 2016 statement: "We all have times when we need to be able to pause work and put family first. I'm happy to say that because of BASF's approach to leave, our employees don't have to choose between being there for the people they love and making a difference at work."[58] Here we see employers not only acknowledging the importance of family but recognizing that most people see family as more important than work and, in fact, need to prioritize family when having a new child.

Some executives even bring up their own experiences as parents. John Mingé, president of BP America, said the following in May 2017: "Becoming a new parent is an exciting and life-changing experience. As a father, I know how important it is to have as much time as possible with your new arrival."[59] In this way, he relates to his employees, sharing their view of the uniqueness of the role and the importance of having parental leave. In September 2017, Dan Springer of DocuSign said: "As an executive who has taken time away from my career to raise my two teenage sons as a single father, I've seen first-hand the value of spending time with, bonding with and caring for one's children—it's personally enriching for both parent and child." Springer's experience as a single father was obviously influential in getting parental leave at DocuSign. He also speaks to the particular difficulties of being a single parent: "Even though I conceptually knew it, even though I had lived that as the child of a single mother, until I found myself trying to balance the two, you just can't understand it. You kind of have to live it to feel the pressure you feel trying to do both jobs well."[60] Perhaps more executives should be single parents!

Though some of his company's policies have been unpopular, Mark Zuckerberg, founder and CEO of Facebook, has been a poster child for parental leave. When his second child was born in August 2017, he took one month off for the birth and then the entire month of December. He was spotted with his family in Hawaii and left the following message on Facebook: "At Facebook, we offer four months of maternity and paternity leave because studies show that when working parents take time to be with their newborns, it's good for the entire family. And I'm pretty sure the office will still be standing when I get back." That statement makes it clear not only that family time is important but also sets the example that even the top person in the company is not absolutely necessary all the time for the company to keep functioning.[61]

Diversity, Inclusion, and Twenty-First Century Families

There's no one-size-fits-all approach for parents balancing family and work every day of their lives. That's why our benefits have to reflect the diverse needs of IBM families. That's why, today, we're dramatically expanding our family support options to meet the increasingly diverse needs of twenty-first century parenting . . . It's important for IBM to reinvent family-friendly programs to address the needs of today's parents.
—IBM, October 2017[62]

Companies also increasingly focus on promoting diversity and inclusion in the workplace. In their June 2017 announcement of sixteen weeks of paid leave for all parents, a Pinterest spokesperson stated: "Diversity and Inclusion are woven into the fabric of our culture" and emphasized the importance of responding to employee needs. With the potential to expand benefits, they noted that part of "growing our culture" is to ensure that "all employees and their families feel represented and supported." Likewise, Procter & Gamble's recent statement emphasizes diversity and inclusion: "Our expanded benefits recognize the diversity of P&G families, the diverse needs of P&G families, and our commitment to full inclusion and support, both personally and professionally, during what is an undoubtedly special moment for our employees."[63]

As part of these efforts, there is recognition that families take many different forms. LinkedIn's website states: "At LinkedIn we celebrate the fact that families today are formed in many different ways. And we want to provide resources and support for all of our employees and their families."[64] Without explicitly saying so, LinkedIn leaves room for lesbian and gay families and single-parent families as well as shared parenting, regardless of gender. The following statements go one step further by explicitly including fathers and adoption:

> We are especially proud of the changes instituted today because they underscore our strong support for the modern-day family, no matter what shape that family takes. In addition to the obvious benefits for mothers, our new policy is also a great stride forward in terms of fathers' and adoption parents' leave.
> —Johnson & Johnson, April 2015

> We realize becoming a parent happens in different ways for different people. In fact, families come in all different shapes and sizes, from becoming a new parent as a biological mother or father, through adoption or perhaps through foster care or legal guardianship, and we want to support and celebrate that diversity.
> —Scripps Networks Interactive, June 2016

> We value the role that all parents play in raising children, so want to make sure mothers, fathers, same-sex partners and adoptive parents all have an opportunity to care for and bond with their newborn or adopted child.
> —Hasbro, April 2016[65]

These companies recognize that parental leave is not simply about heterosexual couples having children and mothers caring for those children; they allow for the fact that same-sex couples and single parents may have children and that any individual parent may care for a child.

Gender Equality

The inclusive policies described above often mention fathers, which is a nod to gender equality. More and more companies realize that gender equality is not simply about hiring and promoting women in the workplace. As long as women are the ones who are expected to care for children, inequality will be maintained both at home and at work. Encouraging men to take parental leave and focus on their families is a good way to support fathers having more time with children, but it is also a way to ensure a more level playing field for men and women at work. The acknowledgment that parental leave is critical for men as well as women is rather new. Jessica Alba, founder of the Honest Company, explained their paid parental leave policy (sixteen weeks) in September 2015: "You need to take that time also to bond with your baby; it's also important for men to bond with their babies." In December 2017, Legg Mason Human Resources Chief Patricia Lattin announced that the financial services company would offer twelve weeks of paid parental leave by stating: "It shouldn't matter if you are the mother or father. We felt it was important to equalize these policies. We needed to update our policies to look the way families look today." Ernst & Young also note that their sixteen weeks of paid parental leave "empowers all of our parents—men and women—to take advantage of this special bonding time with their child before returning back to work."[66]

Some companies focus on achieving gender parity through these policies. For example, David MacLennan, CEO of Cargill, a food production company, stated: "We believe inclusive teams deliver value, and we are committed to doing the important work to make gender parity a reality." Other companies insist on removing gender or creating gender-neutral policies. In December 2015, the Nation noted simply that "parental leave is a critical benefit for both women and men at our growing company, and will be offered on a gender-neutral basis." In April 2016, Coca-Cola released the following statement: "Fostering an inclusive workplace means valuing all parents—no matter their gender or sexual orientation. We think the most successful way to structure benefits to help working families is to make them gender-neutral and encourage both moms and dads to play an active role in their family lives." This was part of an effort to make working at Coke more attractive to millennials and also to work against gender bias in the workplace, which is more likely to occur when women are seen as potential parents who might take leave while men are not.[67] Constellation Brands released the following, similar statement in March 2017: "The expanded parental leave policy helps . . . build an inclusive environment that supports both working moms and dads by removing gender from the equation. We're confident that these enhanced benefits will allow the time needed to bond with their children so that when they return to work, new moms and dads will be more productive and successful."[68] By removing gender as a factor, these companies intend to promote greater understanding between men and women and ultimately gender equity.

Table 1.3 shows my classification of employer leave policies according to the gendering of their policy. *Gender equal* is parental leave only, with no mention of maternity/paternity leave. *Gender modified* is equal parental leave of at least six weeks plus maternity leave of six to eight weeks. *Gender unequal* is for those companies with more than two times the maternity leave as paternity or parental leave. *Gender neutral*

TABLE 1.3. Employer policies by gendering of policy

Gender equal	Gender modified	Gender unequal	Gender neutral gendering
Activision Blizzard	3M	Amazon	Adobe
Airbnb	Accenture	Blackstone Group	Anheuser-Busch
APCO Worldwide	American Express	BP America	AXA
Bank of America	BASF	Broadridge Financial Solutions	Barclays PLC
Blue Cross and Blue Shield of North Carolina	BCG	Capital One	Bloomberg L.P.
Bristol-Myers Squibb	CA Technologies	CarMax	Campbell Soup Company
Chobani	Citi	Children's National Health System	Cisco
Crowley Maritime Corporation	Coca-Cola	Choice Hotels International	Credit Suisse Group
Ernst & Young	Constellation Brands	The Container Store	Danone
Etsy	Deloitte	CVS	DocuSign
Facebook	Discovery Communications	Dollar General	First Data
Gap Inc.	Duke Energy	DOW Chemical	Goldman Sachs

(continued)

TABLE 1.3. Employer policies by gendering of policy (*continued*)

Gender equal	Gender modified	Gender unequal	Gender neutral gendering
The Honest Company	Ecolab	Eagle Mine	Hometeam
Klarna	Exelon	eBay	JPMorgan Chase
Legg Mason	FMC Corporation	Fidelity Investments	M&T Bank
LinkedIn	GoDaddy	Fifth Third Bank	Morgan Stanley
Lyft	Hasbro	First Tennessee	Nestlé
Marks Paneth	IBM	Hilton Worldwide	New York-Presbyterian Hospital
The Nation	IKEA	Intel	Procter & Gamble
Netflix	Levi Strauss & Co.	Johnson & Johnson	RaceTrac
Pinterest	L.L. Bean	KEEN Footwear	RB
Spotify	Mastercard	Kering	Rio Tinto
Stonyfield Farm	Microsoft	Land O'Lakes	Sallie Mae
SurveyMonkey	Nike	Lowe's	Schneider Electric
TD Bank	Nordstrom	Mozilla	Scripps Networks Interactive
TIAA	NVIDIA	Noodles & Company	Transurban**
Twitter	OppenheimerFunds	Vanguard	Wells Fargo
USAA	PayPal	Whirlpool	XL Catlin
	Protective Life	Yum! Brands	
	PwC		
	Shell		
	Starbucks*		
	State Street*		
	TJX Companies		
	Unum		
	Walmart*		
	WEX Inc.		
	Zillow		

Note: Discovery Communications offers twenty to twenty-two weeks of maternity leave and twelve weeks of parental leave. NVIDIA offers twenty-two weeks of maternity leave and twelve weeks of parental leave.
* Starbucks offers eighteen weeks of maternity leave and twelve weeks of parental leave for non-store partners and six weeks of parental leave for store partners. State Street offers maternity and parental leave for birth parents but only four weeks of primary-caregiver leave for adoptive parents. Walmart offers four more weeks of maternity leave than parental leave (ten weeks versus six weeks).
** Transurban only offers primary-caregiver leave.

gendering is for those companies that offer primary and secondary-caregiver leave, which creates categories that generally label mothers as primary caregivers and fathers as secondary. Etsy, Netflix, and Spotify are the only companies that offer long parental leave that is equal for all parents (Twitter also fits in this category, if we include companies with 20+ weeks of parental leave).

Gendered Employer Policies

Unlike the companies that seek to promote gender equality through gender-equal policies, many companies have separate maternity leave and paternity leave policies. These policies signal an essential difference between female and male employees. Some maternity leave policies provide six to eight weeks for birth mothers with the expectation that it takes that long to physically recover from giving birth. Examples include Deloitte (twenty-four weeks of maternity leave for birth mothers and sixteen weeks of parental leave for other parents), Duke Energy (twelve weeks of leave for birth mothers and six weeks of parental leave for other parents), Fifth Third Bank (ten weeks of maternity leave and four weeks of paternity leave), GoDaddy (eighteen weeks of leave for birth mothers and twelve weeks of leave for other parents), Hasbro (sixteen to eighteen weeks of leave for birth mothers and ten weeks of leave for other parents), Levi Strauss & Co. (fourteen to sixteen weeks of leave for birth mothers and eight weeks for other parents), Mastercard (sixteen weeks of maternity leave and eight weeks of parental leave), Microsoft (twenty weeks of leave for birth mothers and twelve weeks of leave for other parents), Nike (fourteen weeks of leave for birth mothers and eight weeks of leave for other parents), Walmart (ten weeks of maternity and six weeks of parental leave), and Zillow (sixteen weeks of maternity and eight weeks of parental leave). Hilton Worldwide offers ten weeks of leave to birth mothers and two weeks of parental leave to other parents. While eight weeks is in range of medical necessity, the additional two weeks marks a stark difference between birth mothers and other parents. Like Hilton, Land O'Lakes also provides ten weeks of maternity leave and two weeks of parental leave. Their press release notes that they are at the forefront in terms of benefits. Intel provides twenty-one weeks of leave for birth mothers and eight weeks of leave for other parents. They also provide funds for adoption expenses, fertility treatments, and expenses related to freezing eggs, sperm, and embryos, suggesting they want to support employees' desires to have children. Yet, the length of maternity leave is 2.5 times that of parental leave.

In the following subsections, I focus on gendered parental leave policies. This can happen through marking differences between maternity and paternity leave, seemingly gender-neutral policies that target primary versus secondary caregivers, and policies that specifically apply to women/mothers and exclude men/fathers. While having any policy is bound to help at least some people, policies that treat men and women differently, particularly those that reinforce female employees' roles at home, will likely harm women and the broader goal of gender equality in the longer term.

Maternity versus Paternity Leave

Several companies make a distinction between maternity and paternity leave. In their efforts to be inclusive of women in the workplace, they are highlighting gender differences and traditional assumptions about women as caregivers. This ultimately sets up women as working mothers and men as workers. Who would you want to hire? Blackstone Group, a financial services company that offers sixteen weeks of maternity leave and only two weeks of paternity leave, highlights the significance of their policy for their female employees. Their press release in April 2015 states: "The financial services industry has historically *struggled to recruit and retain women,* but by instituting robust policies that support working mothers and all employees as they integrate their work and family responsibilities, we hope to *help make asset management a more attractive industry for women*" [emphasis added]. The Container Store's website, updated in December 2017, indicates: "We are committed to ensuring that *our mothers* can strike the perfect balance between work and family life. This belief exceeds that of many other companies that are much larger than ours, and is in keeping with our philosophy of providing outstanding benefits to our employees."[69] The focus on mothers in the first sentence contrasts with the focus on employees in the second sentence, but these statements are in line with the company's different policies for birth mothers (eight weeks) versus other parents (two weeks).

Dow Chemical's chief medical officer, Dr. Catherine Baase, cited medical evidence in announcing the company's new policy in January 2016. Baase stated: "A twelve-week global minimum maternity leave policy supports Dow's Health Strategy and the recommendations of global medical experts for a balanced family life and a focused, productive employee, as well as adequate time to ensure that a child's wellbeing is properly provided for when the mother returns to work."[70] Dow provides twelve weeks of maternity leave for birth mothers, two weeks of parental leave, and four weeks of adoptive parental leave, clearly emphasizing the importance of birth mothers. The focus on ensuring the child's well-being after mothers return to work also suggests that fathers have a limited role in child's well-being.

Eagle Mine provides twelve weeks of maternity leave and two weeks of paternity leave. Because the company includes adoptive parents under both maternity and paternity leave, it makes a clear distinction between mothers and fathers. The inclusion of adoptive parents in maternity leave suggests that leave is not about medical needs but about caring for new children, which apparently does not include fathers (biological or adoptive). In March 2017, Eagle Mine's general manager stated: "We don't ever want our employees to be faced with the difficult choice of whether to stay home during those first few months with their child . . . Not only is paid leave a woman's issue, but it's a global economic issue."[71] There are two points. First, the statement refers to helping employees so that they do not have to choose between their job and their child. The company's policy, however, only provides two weeks of paternity leave and therefore does nothing to help ameliorate fathers' choices between work and family. Second, the statement also explicitly presents paid leave as a woman's issue. When I first read this, I was expecting it to say something along the lines of, leave is not only a woman's issue but a man's issue, too, or a parent's issue. By stating that it is also an economic issue, because of the importance of attracting and retaining good employees, the company missed the opportunity to include fathers.

An extreme example of differences between maternity and parental leave is Kering's policy. Kering, a luxury group that owns brands including Gucci and Yves Saint Laurent, offers fourteen weeks of maternity leave and only one week of parental leave. The irony is that the company's CEO, Francois-Henri Pinault, made the following statement: "This initiative, which is particularly close to my heart, reflects our enduring commitment to promoting equality between men and women throughout their careers, whatever their personal circumstances."[72] Nevertheless, men are relegated to one week of parental leave unless they are part of a gay couple. It is not clear to me in what world fourteen weeks is equal to one week. Furthermore, the focus on helping women balance families and careers, without a corresponding policy for men, is not as helpful as Pinault thinks. When leave is so different for women and men, women become the workers who are seen as the ones who take off time from work, the ones who are not as committed to their jobs.

Primary versus Secondary Caregivers

Several companies distinguish between primary-caregiver leave and secondary-caregiver leave. Often, they make the argument that this language is an attempt to be gender-neutral. However, creating two categories of caregivers creates two different classes of parents. One class of parents, the primary caregivers, would seem to be more important in this scenario. They are the ones who will stay home and care for newborns and likely take on the majority of the responsibility for caring and raising children. The other class of parents, the secondary caregivers, are not as important and can make do with taking a couple of weeks to help the primary caregiver settle in. In addition, the companies that distinguish between primary and secondary-caregiver leave tend to provide much more primary-caregiver leave than secondary-caregiver leave. For example, Wells Fargo provides sixteen weeks of primary-caregiver leave and four weeks of secondary-caregiver leave and M&T Bank provides twelve weeks of primary-caregiver leave and two weeks of secondary-caregiver leave (both include adoptive parents). One of the companies with the largest difference in leave policies is Credit Suisse Group, which offers twenty weeks of primary-caregiver leave but only one week of secondary-caregiver leave, while proclaiming it has a competitive program. It is important to note that it allows secondary caregivers to take up to nineteen additional weeks of unpaid parental leave, which suggests they realize that all parents may want/ need to take leave—but fails to provide a realistic (paid) opportunity to do so.

RB, a consumer goods company whose brands include Lysol, Mucinex, and Enfamil, presents another example of an extreme difference between primary-caregiver leave (sixteen weeks) and secondary-caregiver leave (one week). It is interesting that they note that the decision regarding this program was "an important one, particularly for our employees residing in the US." This suggests the company's awareness of the lack of paid parental leave in the US. At the same time, the company presents their employees with a choice—they can be either a primary caregiver (assumed for mothers but proven for fathers) or a secondary caregiver. Similarly, JPMorgan Chase, a financial services company, provides sixteen weeks of primary-caregiver leave and two weeks of secondary-caregiver leave. Even so, their January 2016 statement includes the following: "A lot of people in our demographic are having children, and [our policy] is something that just helps support them at these critical moments that take place in life."[73] While the use of "people" denotes a more general policy, there is a large difference between sixteen weeks, which could be very supportive, and two weeks, which is not very supportive of this "critical moment."

Companies that make a distinction between primary and secondary caregivers often frame this as a gender-neutral policy. First Data, for example, makes the following statement: "We are thrilled to announce our new gender-neutral paid parental leave policy that puts families first. At First Data, we believe that cultivating an environment where everyone can thrive professionally without sacrificing essential family obligations ultimately creates a more productive, long-serving and loyal workforce." First Data provides twelve weeks of primary-caregiver leave (including adoptive and foster parents) and two weeks of secondary-caregiver leave. This policy has the potential to be more gender-neutral as it is not tied to birth mothers. However, it still creates a large distinction between primary (more important) parents and secondary (less important) parents. Citi also touts its gender-neutral policy: "We recognize that families and parental roles evolve and that our policies should evolve to support those changing needs. To that end, we are pleased to announce our enhanced parenting leave policies to support Citi parents, regardless of gender, in caring for and building a bond with their newborn and newly adopted children."[74] Since Citi offers sixteen weeks of maternity leave and eight weeks of secondary-caregiver leave, it appears that gender is still very much factored into its policies. The language from its statement suggests that families might evolve—perhaps a nod toward gay and lesbian couples—and that parental roles might evolve—perhaps a nod toward working mothers and more-involved fathers. Yet neither of these family types would be fully supported under this policy. Both members of a gay couple and more involved fathers would both need to rely on the secondary-caregiver leave. Danone food company labels its policies "primary-caregiver leave" and "secondary-caregiver leave," but it explicitly provides eighteen weeks of leave for birth mothers, which leaves only two weeks of secondary-caregiver leave for men who partner with birth mothers. Note that adoptive parents who identify as the primary caregiver get fourteen weeks of leave, which is likely meant to be taken by mothers and gay fathers.

Other companies are more explicit about their equation of primary caregiving with mothers. Goldman Sachs, an investment banking company, and XL Catlin, an insurance company, explicitly identify mothers as primary caregivers and fathers as secondary caregivers by labeling their leave policies "maternity and primary-caregiver leave" and "paternity and secondary-caregiver leave." In a June 2015 statement, Goldman Sachs offered its rationale: "we have a number of employees where both spouses or partners are working and in order to provide opportunities for them to balance both their work and personal lives, it was important to provide individuals the opportunities to spend more time with their families."[75] The mention of partners and the inclusion of adoptive parents in both policies suggests an attempt to leave open the possibility of a gay father taking maternity and primary-caregiver leave, but the assumption still exists that mothers will take this leave unless there is some unusual circumstance.

Hometeam, a health company focused on in-home care, equates caregivers with mothers. Its director of communications and policy states: "We believe that caregivers should have the same benefits as those in the corporate office. We felt like maternity leave should absolutely be included in that." Even though the company labels its policies "primary caregiver" and "secondary caregiver," the emphasis on maternity leave makes it clear that it will be women who are expected to use the primary-caregiver leave. This is more problematic because of the difference between primary (twelve weeks) and secondary (two weeks) caregiver leave. Likewise, Procter & Gamble distinguishes between maternity leave, secondary-caregiver leave, and adoptive parental leave. Although it offers sixteen weeks of maternity and adoptive parental leave, it only provides four weeks of secondary-caregiver leave. By default, biological fathers can only fit into the secondary caregiver category.

Perhaps these policies can be seen as a step forward. Surely, they are good for some employees and often do leave open the possibility that any parent can be a primary caregiver. The policies that distinguish birth mothers, however, clearly make the distinction between the person having the baby and other parents. The policies that include adoptive parents in both primary and secondary caregiver categories suggest any person can be a primary or secondary caregiver, but they also implicitly rule out the idea that two people may parent equally. Why do families have to choose?

Maternity Leave/Primary Caregiver Leave Only

While less common, a few companies offer only maternity or primary-caregiver leave. These companies obviously do not feel as though paternity leave is important. Nestlé offers fourteen weeks of maternity and primary-caregiver leave. While men can use this policy as primary or adoptive parents (assuming there is no mother in the picture), their June 2015 statement makes it clear that the policy is intended for mothers: "This policy will help us better support mothers and their families in our sites across the world and reinforces our support for exclusive breastfeeding during the first six months of a child's life."[76] Not only does this statement mention mothers without mentioning fathers, but it specifically mentions support for exclusive breastfeeding, a stance that could alienate mothers who bottle-feed. Not to mention that fourteen weeks is not actually six months, meaning the policy will not even cover the period mentioned in their statement (though they also allow employees to take an additional twelve weeks of unpaid leave).

Transurban, a transportation company focused on toll roads, offers sixteen weeks of primary-caregiver leave. Although this policy is not restricted to birth mothers, it implies that only one parent needs to take leave to care for a new child. Their March 2017 statement also sends mixed messages about gender and parental leave: "We have to keep working on inclusion of women in this environment, but they have to move away from being viewed as women's issues. For us to really harness the true available talent, we have to have policies truly embracing of flexibility and inclusion."[77] This statement suggests that parental leave will help attract and retain more female employees, yet it also attempts to broaden the policy to be more inclusive of other parents.

While these policies may be a starting place, under the assumption that something is better than nothing, we need to include all parents, which means men, too. These types of policies operate under the outdated breadwinner-homemaker assumption in which one parent stays home to care for the child (the mom) while the other carries on working (the dad). These policies not only exclude men, but they actually make it more difficult for women to advance in the workplace.

Obstacles to Taking Parental Leave

In order to understand the potential effects of parental leave policies on fathers, I talked with fathers about their experiences with leave. Even when men "technically" have access to time off, they often feel pressure to take less time. For example, Julian,[78] a thirty-three-year-old father of two from California, talked about his supervisor and work environment as not being amenable to employees taking a lot of leave. He explained:

> I would say maybe a couple of things I think: one, is more just my direct supervisor doesn't really take much time off if at all so we'll come in on Saturdays and things like that, it's not like scheduled working hours so I just didn't quite feel comfortable being like "hey, can I take three weeks off." I had the time technically. I think I had enough time to take over a month off at that point if I wanted to, but I just feel like it's frowned upon at the workplace.

While Julian had enough paid days to take more than a month of leave when his second child was born, he only took two weeks. His supervisor clearly modeled working excessive hours, which created a situation in which workers could not even take off time they had accrued for something as significant as a new child.

Finn, a physician and father of one, took off two weeks when his child was born. However, he wanted to take additional time by working a part-time schedule for several weeks. He thought this would be better than taking complete leave since he acknowledged that "there's not many people who can cover what I do and I felt a little pressured into being here more than I needed to, or wanted to I should say." His supervisor, who was also his friend, did not understand or ignored Finn's request. As Finn relays:

> Well, we discussed it a little bit and then he came by when I was still off right after my son was born. And I said, well I know it's going to be tough to cover my position. What if I do some partial days in a couple of weeks? I should have said I will be back to work on Tuesday, the whatever. I think that would've been a better way to approach it. Instead of asking I should've just said this is what I will do.

The dynamics of their working relationship and friendship did not bode well for Finn taking extended leave as his boss felt comfortable visiting him at home and complaining about his absence. In fact, Finn continues: "My supervisor had a temper tantrum and called me on a Monday and wanted to know why I wasn't here. We discussed me working partial days and that would be starting the next day and that was not . . . I felt pressured to come to work." Not only did his supervisor object to Finn's preferred leave and schedule, but he continued to harass him while on leave about coming back. Others face similar pressures. Gabriel, who worked part-time at a movie theater while attending school, described the pressure he faced from his boss to return to work:

> My boss called the next day and my son was in the incubator. The boss asked if I was coming to work today. With part-time work you don't get any benefits, you don't have paternity leave at all. I didn't know what to do at that point. I was obviously really emotionally unavailable for work in every sense. So I told him I couldn't come in. I didn't know if they were going to fire me. It definitely made things more stressful, thinking my son could die, I might be fired over it, and it was really upsetting.

Gabriel was dealing with every parent's worst nightmare, a sick child. And yet his boss was pressuring him to return to work while his son was still in the hospital. While he clearly chose to stay home so he could be with his sick child, he also feared the real possibility of losing a job he needed in order to be able to pay for family expenses.

Perhaps the worst-case scenario is what was experienced by Mateo, an unemployed father who took eight weeks of parental leave while working as a lab technician in northern California. The short version of the story is that Mateo took parental leave and was fired. The long version is a bit more complicated. After taking several weeks of leave under California's PFL and the federal FMLA, Mateo wanted to continue taking time off through these programs by working four days a week and taking each Monday off. He told me about the numerous meetings he had with different supervisors, who did not seem keen on the idea. Mateo describes the situation:

> I was kind of scared to ask for FMLA. My priority was my son, to make sure I can provide as much care for him as possible because they grow up so quickly. I don't care if they get pissed off. I went to [my boss's] office one day and I asked her about it. She was really busy. It was urgent for me to tell her so I could get the thing signed and start taking the Mondays off. She was very displeased about it. Just her body language and verbally what she said. And I was like, "wow that's not cool." I was pretty upset about it for a while, but I thought, "I know my rights. I'm still going to take it. If they were to retaliate because I take time off, they're not allowed to do that because it's protected. It's an act." So one month after that protected one-year thing, I lost the job. So I think that had a lot to do with it. But they're not going to go, "this is the reason." They found other reasons to get rid of me and some of those other things were inaccurate and false. We can use this and this and this as a witness. I was like, "wait a minute, those guys like me." To this day, I saw someone at the grocery store who I worked under. They were like, "yeah man we're still pissed off."

While Mateo relied on California's PFL and his accumulated time to take paid leave, he needed FMLA for the job-protected aspect of family leave. He conveyed his fears and yet went ahead with taking leave because he thought it was very important for his child and he thought he was protected by the law. However, after time had elapsed, he was fired. He is confident that he was fired because he took leave and not based on the "inaccurate and false" reasons they provided. Yet, he felt he was unable to fight against his employer and was looking for work when we talked. Men's increasing participation as parents might help force a change.

There are other gaps in access to and utilization of parental leave related to class, race, and family status. More educated mothers and fathers are more likely to use parental leave.[79] For fathers, occupational prestige is associated with taking leave, with those in high prestige occupations being 68 percent more likely to take two or more weeks of parental leave than those in low prestige occupations.[80] Those in higher status jobs and those with higher incomes are more likely to receive family leave benefits while the majority of those with lower incomes do not have access to paid leave.[81] White parents are more likely to take parental leave than black and Hispanic parents.[82] Married mothers are more likely to take parental leave than single mothers.[83] LGBTQ individuals are less likely to have access to paid family leave and "continue to experience the collateral consequences of narrow family definitions in local, state, and federal policy."[84] This may be particularly true for gay men, who clearly do not have the option of maternity leave. LGBTQ individuals may also face obstacles because they are less likely to be married and more likely to be low-income workers.[85]

The Politics of Stalemate

As mentioned earlier in the chapter, there have been recent attempts to pass paid parental leave at the national level, most notably in the form of the FAMILY Act, but they have failed thus far. The National Partnership for Women & Families finds that 78 percent of voters support having a national law to establish paid family and medical leave. While support is greatest among Democrats (93 percent), a majority of Republicans (66 percent) and Independents (77 percent) also favor a paid leave policy. Much of this support may be due to individuals' recognition of the great financial strain that comes with taking unpaid leave. The same study finds that 71 percent of voters indicate that time off to care for a new child or an ill family member would likely create financial hardship. The Pew Research Center conducted a more extensive survey following the 2016 elections, from mid-November to early December. It also found majority support for paid family and medical leave. However, support varies based on reason for leave, with 85 percent supporting paid leave for workers who have a serious health condition and 67 percent supporting paid leave for workers to care for an ill family member. There is more support for new mothers than fathers (82 percent versus 69 percent) to take parental leave.[86]

There is general agreement that paid parental leave is a good thing and that the government should provide leave for new parents. Elias, a fitness trainer in Texas, notes: "it would be nice if there was just a more mandated one to where you get paid, you know three weeks, four weeks, you know . . . I think those first few weeks are just *crucial* especially for the little one . . . it's just like you wanna be there for them, you don't want to be worried about getting back to work." Rodrigo, a videographer in Texas, is also supportive of parental leave policies that enable fathers to take leave:

> And the father's role, a father being present in a child's life, for companies and government, start them off in that life of making them get it, and saying you have to be back at work the day after. I think it sends an automatic message that work is more important than family. And so if we can tell society and realize why family is important I think it creates a better society all together. And so the importance of the father in that role and the father being able to be there . . . I think a society adjustment needs to happen for people to understand and for fathers to understand, officials to understand the importance of a father in the whole parenting scheme.

In California, where almost all working parents have access to paid family leave, fathers argue for higher rates of pay:

> I think the government should help assist and pay for even those first two weeks, I think that's kind of an extenuating circumstance. It's not a vacation, it's not a thing that you can really . . . And it happens a couple times in your life, you know, and so it's hard. I've luckily been able to save up, but especially in a, your wife gives birth and they're unable to go back to work, and you're on a single income so it's hard to take that time to bond and I think the way our society is you obviously have to work and make a living and provide for your family so it's that hard balance of how much

time do you take and how much time can you actually afford to take. Especially in California, it's not the cheapest place to live, so.
—Iker, age 30, engineer

Anyways the government, well the only thing I would like to see in the government is if you are going to offer paternity leave then pay 100 percent. It's very hard for somebody that makes not even a grand a month and then you only make 500 a month and your rent is 600. What are you going to do? Shake their hand, tell them, you know, I'm really sorry about it. There's different things the government could do to cover expenditures that we are not doing.
—Roman, age 29, athletic trainer

I wanted to be off as much time with them as possible, but I didn't want to deplete all my time off at work because we wouldn't be able to afford if I just went off the radar at work for twelve weeks. We couldn't live on 60 percent of my check. I had 300 hours of sick time at the time. I burned half of it, 150. So that was close to the month. So yeah, I burned all my sick time.
—Kye, age 30, police officer

While these three fathers represent different economic situations, they all argue for more pay in order to make parental leave more feasible for fathers.

Since it is clear that most people on both sides of the political spectrum support paid leave, why has the US not been able to pass this measure at the national level? One reason may be the low relative importance placed on paid leave. A Pew survey conducted in early January 2017 finds that paid leave is a top priority for only 35 percent of adults, lower than twenty other issues, including terrorism, the economy, education, jobs, and health care costs.[87] It may be that Americans do not see how paid parental leave fits into larger issues of employment protection, maternal and child health, and long-term stability for families. Another reason may be disagreement over how paid leave should be implemented. For example, among those who support paid leave for new mothers and fathers, about three-quarters say pay should come from employers rather than federal or state governments. However, only half of adults surveyed think the federal government should require employers to provide paid leave while the other half think employers should be able to decide for themselves.[88] A third reason may be perceptions about the impact of a paid leave policy on businesses. While an overwhelming majority of Americans (94 percent) think access to paid leave would have a very positive or somewhat positive impact on families, 57 percent think it would have a somewhat negative or very negative impact on small businesses and attitudes are split on the impact on employers more generally.[89] This is related to a fourth reason, which is the particularly strong emphasis on individualism in the US. As Brad Harrington, executive director of the Boston College Center for Work & Family, states, "People would prefer to try to keep taxes low, let individuals be responsible for their own care, and that's sort of become the accepted value system in the US."[90] While many parents struggle to balance work and family, most do not necessarily see it as a government issue but rather an individual or couple problem that they themselves need to solve.[91] Finally, Republican legislators do not favor programs that help working mothers or families, and do not seem to care that the US is an outlier on this and related issues.

Where Do We Go from Here?

"Duck, duck, duck . . . duckling!"

This is how Senator Tammy Duckworth announced her pregnancy on Twitter in January 2018. And the headlines abounded, with the *Chicago Sun-Times* breaking the news: "Tammy Duckworth is pregnant; will be first senator to give birth."[92] Duckworth was already in a select group, having given birth to her first child while in Congress (only ten representatives have done this), not to mention that she was the first Asian American elected to Congress from Illinois and the first disabled woman elected to Congress, full stop.[93] Senator Duckworth also made history by bringing her newborn to the Senate floor to cast a vote in April 2018.[94] Will Ducksworth's presence in the Senate motivate a change, perhaps the passage of the FAMILY Act, authored by Kristen Gillibrand (another one of those ten women to give birth as a US representative)?

During the 2016 presidential campaign, paid leave finally became an issue. Democratic candidate Hillary Clinton proposed a paid family and medical leave policy that would provide twelve weeks of leave to new parents and to those caring for sick family members. Paid at two-thirds of wages, this proposal was basically the same as the FAMILY Act. Meanwhile, Republican candidate Donald Trump's proposal, prompted by his daughter Ivanka, included only married mothers. Since the election, and possibly based on backlash for his exclusion of fathers, single mothers, and adoptive parents, Trump revised his proposal. In his proposed budget, Trump includes six weeks of paid parental leave, which would be open to birth and adoptive mothers and fathers. However, a major weakness of this proposal is that it leaves the details of parental leave up to the states. Because it would be based on state-level unemployment insurance programs, wage replacement would vary tremendously. Unemployment insurance benefits tend to be lower than average wages and are currently less than one-third of average wages in twenty-two states.[95] At these rates, many, if not most, new parents would be unable to afford to take parental leave.

The good news is that changes in federal social policies related to education, health, and families often occur at the state level first. Marriage equality provides an example of a policy that changed very quickly. In 2005, same-sex marriage was only legal in Massachusetts. By 2009, Connecticut, Iowa, New Hampshire, and Vermont legalized same-sex marriage. New York, Maine, Maryland, and Washington joined this group by 2012. By the time the Supreme Court ruled in favor of same-sex couples in *Obergefell v. Hodges* in June 2015, only thirteen states still had same-sex marriage bans. Paid parental leave is unlikely to move so swiftly, but the increasing attention to this topic and the developments occurring at the company level and state level indicate some progress and hope for a national policy in the future. Why is it so important that the US introduce paid parental leave? The next chapter explores this question by reviewing its benefits.

2

Parental Leave Is Good

It was a great experience to take those days off. To me, it's
the most important job in the world because you're molding them and how they're going to be. It's like once those
years are gone, it's gone. Once their infancy/toddler years
are gone, they're gone. They grow up and you wish you had
spent more time with them.

—Mateo, age 30

It seems obvious that paid parental leave is a good thing. The fact that
pretty much every other country besides the US has some paid parental leave
suggests as much. Mateo, quoted above, tugs on the heartstrings as he vocal-
izes a common feeling among parents. Children grow up. And it often
seems to happen so quickly. There is a very real sense among parents that
they want to spend as much time as possible with their children, particularly when they are little. According to a 2017 poll conducted by the Pew
Research Center, parents were split on whether they spend too little time
(47 percent) or the right amount of time (45 percent) with their children,
with very few indicating they spend too much time with their children. A
majority of fathers (63 percent) say they do not spend enough time with
their children and this is mainly due to work obligations.[1] This is despite
the fact that today's fathers spend almost three times as much time
engaging in child care as fathers did in the 1960s.[2] While one-quarter of
American adults think it is more important for new babies to have more
time to bond with mothers, 71 percent think babies should bond with
both parents equally.[3] At the same time, a slight majority (53 percent)
think that mothers are better at caring for new babies than fathers while
45 percent think that fathers and mothers are equally good at caring for
new babies.[4]

 While Americans subjectively recognize the need for time with infants, this chapter focuses on the objective benefits of paid parental

leave. Paid leave has numerous positive consequences for mothers, fathers, children, employers, and society. First, it offers women the opportunity to return to employment with little or no consequences for their jobs or careers. It allows mothers to maintain stable employment, build their careers, and minimize wage penalties. It also provides time to recover from the physical pain of birth and to have space for mental recovery. Second, paid leave offers men time to bond with their children and the ability to develop caregiving skills so they will be more equal parents and partners. It also has a positive impact on men's well-being. Third, parental leave is good for children's health and development. When parents have time with their infants, infant mortality is reduced and there is greater likelihood of breastfeeding. Children also benefit in the long term from increases in cognitive and social development. Fourth, parental leave is good for businesses. It allows companies to be competitive, particularly as more and more high-level employees expect good parental leave policies. It also allows for a more productive workforce, increases recruitment and retention, and improves company culture. Finally, parental leave promotes societal goals such as a strong economy and higher fertility rates.

Benefits to Mothers

Employment and Careers

Many parental leave policies are aimed at maintaining or increasing the rate of women's participation in the labor force. I take it as non-controversial that it is desirable to increase women's labor force participation. There is ample evidence from Europe that parental leave does increase female employment. Countries that provide generous parental leave have higher maternal employment rates.[5] Parental leave policies encourage female employment both before having a child, in order to qualify for leave and obtain a higher level of earnings to ensure higher maternity pay, and, after having a child, by securing a spot in the workforce upon returning.[6] Comparative research shows that maternal employment rates for women with children zero to six years of age are higher in countries with longer parental leave.[7] In an analysis of OECD countries, economist Willem Adema finds that family-friendly policies have a significant impact on women's labor force participation.[8]

Specifically, countries that spend more money on parental leave and child benefits have higher rates of women's full-time employment and lower rates of part-time employment.

In a study of seven European countries in the period 1969–1993, public policy professor Christopher Ruhm found that forty weeks of paid and job-protected leave entitlement would increase the labor force participation rates of twenty-five-to-thirty-four-year-old women by seven to nine percent.[9] This effect is smaller in a more recent study based on shorter leave entitlement. Using data from sixteen European countries in the period 1970–2010, this study found that a twenty-eight-week leave entitlement would increase young women's labor force participation rates by 2.5 percent relative to men.[10] Similarly, another study of thirty OECD countries in the period 1969–2010 showed a 2.5 percent increase in twenty-five-to-thirty-four-year-old female participation rates when leave was two years or less.[11] Under a new policy in Germany, mothers are not only more likely to take leave and care for their child during the first year, they are also more likely to return to work in the second year.[12] Job-protected leave provides reassurances that women can return to work after parental leave.[13] In contrast, leave that is "too short" may act as a disincentive for women to return to work.[14]

To our north, in Canada, a study of the effect of lengthening paid maternity leave (from a length of seventeen to eighteen weeks to one of fifty-two to fifty-four weeks) found that leave entitlements increase women's likelihood of returning to their pre-childbirth employer. Increasing the odds that women continue working for their same employer benefits women by decreasing the likelihood that they will (permanently) leave the labor force to care for their children and by increasing the likelihood that women will return full-time to their jobs rather than seeking new part-time jobs.[15]

What happens in the US? Unsurprisingly, many studies show similar results. An early study of women with private employer–based maternity leave, based on the 1988 National Survey of Family Growth, showed that leave increased the chances of women's return to work within a year of giving birth.[16] Social work professors Lawrence Berger and Jane Waldfogel compared the employment history of American mothers from twelve weeks before childbirth to fifty-two weeks after childbirth.[17] They found that 80 percent of mothers who had leave coverage returned to the same job post-childbirth compared to 63 percent of mothers who did not have leave coverage. Furthermore, mothers without leave coverage were twice as likely as mothers with leave coverage to not return to work within twelve months (23 percent versus 11 percent, respectively). Demographers Sandra Hofferth and Sally Curtin found that following the introduction of FMLA, women's post-childbirth employment and job retention increased.[18] In a more recent study, researchers found an increased probability of maternal employment both in the three months leading up to childbirth and in the nine to twelve months following childbirth among California mothers eligible for Paid Family Leave.[19] Another study of California and New Jersey finds that paid leave in these states increases women's labor force participation around the time of birth.[20] Economic effects may be particularly strong for women with lower socioeconomic status. In a study of California and New Jersey, women who had attained less than a bachelor's degree spent less time without a job in the year after childbirth.[21] These effects may be long-lasting as American women with access to paid leave are more likely than those without paid leave to remain employed four years after the birth of their child.[22]

This is a sign of investment or stability in employment. Paid leave is also associated with longer work hours.[23] In a study of California's Paid Family Leave, researchers found that this program resulted in a ten to seventeen percent increase in the average weekly work hours of mothers of toddlers (one to three years old).[24] Similarly, Charles Baum and Christopher Ruhm found that Paid Family Leave in California had a positive effect on weeks and hours worked two years after birth.[25] Estimates suggest that mothers who were employed at all during pregnancy worked 5.3 more weeks per year and two more hours per week, whereas mothers who were employed at least twenty weeks during pregnancy worked seven more weeks per year and 2.8 hours more per week when their child was two years old. A recent study using Census and American Community Survey data from before and after the statewide parental leave program in New Jersey finds a significant positive impact of the program on mothers' share of work hours relative to their partners' share of work hours. In other words, more mothers are participating in the work force as a result of New Jersey's paid parental leave policy. The impact is particularly strong for low-income mothers.[26]

Parental leave may also mediate the potentially negative effects of career interruptions on women's pay and career advancement. Parental leave allows for greater employment continuity, and continuity, especially full-time employment, has a positive impact on career advancement.[27] This is more likely to happen when women return to work for their pre-leave employer.[28] It is important that mothers are able to continue building their careers and reaping the rewards of their investments in education and job skills.[29] Women with higher education and more job experience are more likely to return to work full-time following childbirth.[30] British research shows that post-leave employment is more likely when employers provide maternity pay above government levels.[31] Another study found that parental leave had no effect on women's chances of obtaining a higher prestige position.[32]

Furthermore, loss of income may be minimized or avoided when women have access to paid parental leave.[33] Indeed, parental leave has long-term consequences on women's earnings.[34] We can see this most clearly in comparing Sweden to the US. Swedish studies show little effect of family on women's wages. For example, a Swedish cohort study shows that while time out of work has a negative effect on wages, taking time for parental leave has no significant effect on women's wages (other reasons, such as unemployment, do have a negative impact).[35] Meanwhile, in the US, there is a sizable wage penalty for motherhood, but time out of the labor force is not a large factor in this penalty.[36] In fact, returning to the same employer after leave results in minimal impact on wages after two years.[37] In California, where mothers receive paid leave and stay in the labor force, there is also a decrease in their poverty rates.[38] It is also important to note that men's parental leave can have a positive impact on women's earnings. One study of parental leave in Sweden found that each extra month of parental leave fathers take increases mothers' income by 7 percent.[39] This may be because fathers who are actively engaged with their children enable mothers to work more.[40] In sum, well-designed parental leave policies can help reduce income loss.

It is also important that employers implement policies in a supportive manner. Zara, a British mother who took nine months' maternity leave, explained that maternity leave policies not only allow for women to take up to one year of leave, but they also include flexibility in length of leave: "They're quite flexible here, I think. You have to kind of give an indication of whether you think you're going to return to work, but again, I don't think that's set in stone, and I had always intended to return so I ticked that box and said, yes, I will be coming back, and I think you have to give eight weeks' notice." This means that employers must be flexible for if, when, and how mothers return to work following leave.

While policies in general are good, policies that enable parents to share leave are most useful because they allow couples to put female partners' careers on par with male partners' careers. Daniel, a university lecturer in the UK, talked about how the parental leave policy influenced his decision to have a child. He and his wife felt fortunate to land lecturer positions at two different universities within commuting distance. After settling into their positions, they talked about having a baby, but they were hesitant to have a child before the new policy. In fact, they specifically agreed that they would not favor one career over the other. Around this time, the UK introduced Additional Paternity Leave, which allowed fathers or partners to share up to six months of the leave, starting at twenty weeks. As Daniel tells it, the policy had a direct impact on their decision to have a child when they did:

> One of the things that actually convinced us that it was a decent time to start having kids actually was the fact that the law changed and this was then an option because up until that point [my wife] was a bit wary about taking, you know, nine months of maternity leave when she wasn't in a permanent job because obviously, you know, the law says you can't be discriminated against for that but, particularly in a research environment, if you're not, if you're out of the game you lose, you lose stuff compared to your competitors and if you then look at research track records, when you factor in career breaks it's not so obvious that. Well, it isn't going to help and it might hurt. So [my wife] was always a bit wary about taking, you know, nine months or a full year off work. And so the fact that the law changed and we were able to split the leave did make a difference. It made us think that this was something we could do, and we hopefully wouldn't massively damage either of our careers and would also allow us to start a family. So that was basically it.

Daniel's wife returned to work after six months and has continued her research agenda with limited interruption. In fact, Daniel relayed that his wife was awarded a large research grant while on maternity leave. Because Daniel took leave directly after his wife and was in charge of the transition of their child into nursery before returning to work, his wife was able to carry out her research plans and forward her career.

Physical and Mental Health

A review of two decades of research shows that paid parental leave is associated with better health outcomes for new mothers.[41] Parental leave can contribute to both greater physical and mental health.[42] Most women need some time to recover from the physical toll of giving birth. Common post-childbirth physical ailments include fatigue, breast soreness, neck and back pain, and discomfort from an episiotomy or cesarean section.[43]

The physical benefits of parental leave may accrue even before birth. Recent public health research shows that over the past few decades, American women are more likely to be engaged in paid employment during pregnancy and to continue working later in pregnancy.[44] In fact, one estimate suggests that 37 percent of employed women do not take any leave before their due date. Parental leave policies may help women reconcile their health needs with their work demands. Women who live in states with parental leave policies are more likely to take prenatal leave.[45] This is good for maternal outcomes. Women who take leave before birth are less likely to have a cesarean section or other complications during delivery.[46]

Parental leave may also be important in improving the mental health of new mothers. A widely accepted statistic is that 13 percent of women experience postpartum depression.[47] While the highest risk of postpartum depression occurs within the first three months following childbirth, some studies suggest that onset may occur later, up to six months after birth, and that depression may continue after the first year, especially if untreated.[48] A study based on the Early Childhood Longitudinal Study–Birth Cohort in the US finds that mothers who have less than eight weeks of paid leave experience more depressive symptoms and poorer overall health.[49] In a study of first-time mothers in the Midwestern US, comparing those who took less than ten weeks versus those who took more than twenty-four weeks of parental leave, mothers who took longer periods of leave reported better mental health.[50] Another study confirmed that better mental health outcomes were associated with taking at least sixteen weeks of leave.[51] Based on a nationally representative sample of mothers, health economists Pinka Chatterji and Sara Markowitz found that each extra week of maternity leave decreased depressive symptoms by six to seven percent.[52] A follow-up study found that mothers who take less than eight weeks of leave are fifteen percent more likely to experience symptoms of postpartum depression.[53]

Another mental health outcome affected by parental leave is stress. Mothers who take longer periods of leave experience less stress.[54] Lower stress seems to translate into higher-quality mother-infant interactions.[55] In a sample of low-income mothers, sociologist Richard Petts finds that very short parental leave of one month or less is linked to greater parenting stress and a higher risk of depression.[56] Sometimes parents who experience high levels of stress respond by spanking their children. Mothers who took short leaves are also more likely to spank their child in the follow-up study, approximately one year after birth. As with economic consequences, parental leave may have long-term effects on mental health. A study of eight European countries examining the impact of parental leave legislation between 1960 and 2010 on older women's health found a significant impact of policy specifically on the mental health of older women. In particular, they claim that implementing comprehensive parental leave policies would result in a reduction of 14 percent in depression among women aged fifty years and older.[57]

As with income, fathers' use of leave may have an impact on their partners' health. A study in Norway shows that fathers' use of parental leave may reduce illness among mothers. When fathers take parental leave above the daddy quota, it reduces the likelihood of mothers taking extended sickness absence above sixteen days.[58]

Improving Gender Equality

Parental leave also promises benefits for gender equality, particularly related to intimate relationships and the division of labor at home.[59] Those policies that provide high paid, nontransferable leave are more likely to promote a more equal division of labor at home.[60] In an experiment studying the effects of the Norwegian introduction of four weeks of daddy quota, economists Andreas Kotsadam and Henning Finseraas observe 11 percent fewer conflicts over the division of household labor among couples who had their last child after the reform.[61] This is related to the actual division of labor, which is also more equal among these couples. This may be because individuals who share parental leave with their partner have a better understanding of what their partner experiences on a day-to-day basis.[62] Evidence from Spain shows that fathers who take parental leave spend more time in housework than fathers who do not take leave.[63] Another study shows that Swedish fathers who take at least 20 percent of parental leave days do more housework.[64]

Men who take long parental leave are in a unique position to reevaluate their notions of fathering and parenting. Educational scholar Thomas Johansson presents case studies of four Swedish fathers who took at least six months of leave.[65] They experienced changes in attitudes and behaviors in a way that was more accepting of gender equality and equal parenting. For example, these men avoided talking about fatherhood and instead focused more on the gender-neutral parenthood. They acknowledged how they themselves benefited from caregiving as they gained emotional intelligence and social competence. This may also affect marital relationships as we know that paternal engagement makes for happier partners and thus greater marital satisfaction and stability.[66]

Based on a quasi-experimental design assessing the impact of the 2007 parental leave reform in Germany, researchers find that the introduction of the fathers' quota had a positive impact on attitudes toward gender equality.[67] Likewise, research in Spain suggests that father quotas may bolster gender equality by increasing fathers' duration of leave and involvement in childcare and thus reducing the negative impact of motherhood on women's careers.[68] In the US, paternity leave is associated with lower relationship conflict and higher relationship satisfaction among employed mothers. Increasing fathers' use of parental leave has the potential to reduce gender inequality at work and at home. It is important to target men as early as possible before gendered patterns become engrained. Leave policies have great potential to enhance gender equality because they come into play at a critical time around the child's birth or adoption.[69] In sum, parental leave has the potential to change attitudes and increase sharing at home, which also fosters more satisfying relationships.

Benefits to Fathers

While fathers may not spend all of their paid parental leave caring for their child, one estimate based on time diary data suggests that coupled fathers who have the opportunity to take paid leave spend approximately 70 percent of their time off on childcare.[70] There is a positive relationship between fathers taking parental leave and father involvement.[71] Paternity leave is not only important for short-term involvement in child care but also promotes paternal engagement throughout a child's life. One reason is that fathers on leave develop a stronger bond with their child, just as mothers do. A second reason is that instead of mothers monopolizing caregiving expertise, fathers on leave build caregiving skills that last.[72]

Connection with Child

Fathers who take leave are more involved after the birth; leave facilitates father-child bonding which in turn promotes long-term involvement.[73] Evidence from Germany shows that the introduction of two "daddy months" in 2007 was associated with an increase in fathers' time spent in child care as long as thirty months after birth.[74] A study of eight industrialized countries using Multinational Time Use Study data between 1971 and 2005 found that access to parental leave and non-transferrable leave reserved for fathers both increase fathers' time in child care.[75] Findings are similar in the US, where fathers who take longer parental leave are more engaged in caregiving and developmental tasks throughout the first few years of their child's life, and this pattern extends to nonresident fathers as well.[76] Based on 142 fathers in Massachusetts, fatherhood expert Joseph Pleck found that fathers who took more time off work were more involved in child care later on.[77] Another small study of US fathers similarly found that parental leave promotes father involvement in caregiving tasks.[78] In addition to increasing father involvement with new infants, when fathers take parental leave they spend more time with their older children as well. Furthermore, the existence of parental leave policies themselves encourage active fathering and lessen the public perception that caregiving is feminine.[79]

Fathers on parental leave particularly value the opportunity to build a close relationship with their new child.[80] Fathers frequently mention the importance of bonding. In response to a question about the importance of taking time off, Finn, an American father, said: "Well, probably first and foremost, I was able to bond with my son." Another father adds: "So I think it's very important, I know I've heard and read things that say it's very important those first few weeks for that bonding time. So trying to spend that time with the kid." Daniel, the British father who used Additional Paternity Leave to share parental leave with his wife, is convinced that his relationship with his son is different—better—because of the time he spent with him during leave: "I think it really, had I not ever taken some time by myself with [my son] I think we would have had a very different relationship in the family than we do. I think both in terms of how happy we both are to do stuff, we have a very even distribution of parenting, but also [my son is] equally happy with either of us. . . . I think I have a relationship with him that I wouldn't have had otherwise." Daniel knows that other fathers have not developed the same relationship with their children. To further his point about his son being fine with either him or his wife, Daniel talks about how other wives in their circle of friends do not even trust their husbands to take care of their own child for a few hours. James, a British father who took the standard two weeks of paternity leave while his wife took nine months of maternity leave, demonstrates what can happen when mothers take much longer leaves than fathers:

> Two weeks was okay in a work sense that I wasn't away for too long. It's like any other two-week holiday. But I think, because now I find it really difficult in coming home and she reacts differently to my wife than she does to me then my consideration now is that maybe I would have liked to have four, maybe three or four weeks off, just a little bit longer so I'm not away from work for too long but I also have that extra kind of couple of weeks' time at home to bond with her that little bit more. But that's only really been a thought since she's been born and she reacts slightly differently to me than she does to my wife. But that's because my wife's at home with her all day. She's the one that has that time with her.

The contrast between Daniel and James' relationship with their children is stark and demonstrates the importance of building a relationship early on. Parental leave is the most direct way to make this happen. This can continue as fathers who take longer parental leave work fewer hours. Among a survey of 4,000 Swedish parents of children born between 1993 and 1999, demographers Ann-Zofie Duvander and Ann-Christin Jans find that fathers who took more than sixty days of parental leave work about 3.5 hours less per week than those who did not take leave.[81] In addition, parental leave can have lasting consequences as separated fathers who took at least fifteen days of parental leave are more likely to have frequent contact with their children than fathers who took less leave.

Caregiving Skills

In addition to bonding, parental leave offers men the potential to increase their "practical and emotional investment in infant care."[82] An early study of Norwegian couples found that sharing leave resulted in a more equal distribution of household work as fathers were able to develop skills during their leave.[83] In addition, when fathers take leave alone rather than with their partner they become more aware of their children's needs and the pace of home life.[84] Fathers who share parental leave also increase their competency when it comes to taking care of children.[85]

American sociologist Linda Haas and Swedish psychologist Philip Hwang have conducted numerous studies of parental leave and father involvement. They find ample evidence that Swedish fathers who take more leave are more adept at caregiving.[86] Specifically, longer leaves have a positive effect on time spent in child care on work days, involvement in caregiving tasks such as preparing food and taking the child to the doctor, and solo responsibility (taking care of their children alone while their partner is at work).[87]

Building caregiving skills is an important reason for men to take parental leave. When fathers take parental leave it allows them to develop skills such as changing diapers, feeding, burping, and the like, skills that often become "maternal" skills simply because mothers are typically the ones to care for infants early on.[88] Indeed, there is evidence from the Millennium Cohort Study of babies born in the UK between 2000 and 2002 that fathers on leave build these skills. A majority of fathers engaged in regular caretaking activities, but fathers who took leave are more likely to engage in these activities: they are 25 percent more likely to change diapers, 19 percent more likely to feed their child, and 19 percent more likely to get up with the baby during the night.[89] This is also the case in a study of American and Canadian fathers, which finds that fathers who take at least three weeks of parental leave develop parenting skills similar to their partners and are more confident in their parenting, which ultimately allows them to be co-parents, sharing parenting tasks more equally.[90] Daniel again notes how he behaves more like the mothers around him than other fathers:

> It's hard to tell whether this is just me or whether it's because I was looking after him myself, but I feel like I'm a bit more apprehensive than a lot of other fathers are about, you know, is he okay when I leave him, that kind of thing. When he's with other kids the same age I'm a bit more, yeah, I'm certainly more on edge. Partly that's because he's more mobile than other kids so he's much more willing and prone to damage himself (laughs) . . . So yeah, I notice that I'm, I think it did, the fact that I was able to take a leave it changed my relationship with him in a good way compared to if I hadn't.

Whether mothers are more apprehensive is up for debate, but the fact is that Daniel sees himself as developing skills and sensitivity to his child's needs that come not from being a mother but from spending time with one's child. In part, policies that provide fathers exclusive (non-transferable) parental leave and high benefit levels are associated with fathers' increased time caring for children.[91] It makes sense that parental leave would provide the opportunity for men to share parenting, and evidence suggests that shared parenting from the start increases men's confidence, parenting capabilities, and involvement with children.[92]

A study of fathers' leave-taking in relation to fathers' involvement shows a pattern across OECD countries in which fathers who take more leave are more involved with their children.[93] This is particularly the case for fathers in the US. At nine months old, American fathers who took two or more weeks of leave were two times more likely to change their child's diapers, 1.9 times more likely to help their child get dressed, 1.6 times more likely to help their child with eating, 1.5 times more likely to help their child go to bed, 1.4 times more likely to give their child a bath, and 1.3 times more likely to read books to their child compared to fathers who took no leave. Spanish sociologist Gerardo Meil, using the European Working Conditions Survey, also finds that fathers who take parental leave spend more time in childcare, and the longer the parental leave, the more active fathers are.[94]

Research shows that fathers who take more parental leave are not only more actively involved in daily childcare activities and better at these activities, but also more emotionally involved with caring for their children over time.[95] Increasing father involvement in childcare has many positive outcomes, with the most direct impact on child well-being, which is the focus of the next section.[96]

Health

Parental leave is even good for men's health! Swedish health researchers at Gothenburg University administered the Swedish Parenthood Stress Questionnaire to parents at six months and eighteen months after childbirth to study the effects of division of parental leave on parenting stress. The researchers found that fathers who shared parental leave equally (in which each parent took forty to sixty percent of the available leave) experienced less parenting stress than those who did not share parental leave equally. In particular, shared leave reduced feelings of parental incompetence and health problems.[97] In fact, researchers at the Karolinska Institutet in Stockholm find a link between paternity leave and lower mortality rates. Anna Månsdotter and Andreas Lundin examined the population of Swedish men who had a child in 1988–1989, their paternity leave in 1988–1990, and their mortality patterns in 1991–2008.[98] They found that men who took at least thirty days of parental leave experienced lower mortality rates than men who took less parental leave. Amos, an American father, conveys the sense of feeling good about taking more time off: "I tried to personally . . . I didn't want to, you know, just spend a week at home with my first ever child. I guess I was in the mindset that I didn't really need to be back at work. I felt good knowing if I gave myself a solid month at home. I just felt good about that." Roman, another American father, talked about the fun he has interacting with his son and how this time allows him to feel like a child again:

Maternity leave is great. I think most people associate maternity leave with moms . . . and dads typically you had the baby and then two days later go back to work. My advice to any dad out there is don't do that. Because your child, you know, the more they see you the more they will associate who you are. [My wife] says all the time that he favors me and that's because he sees me all the time. He will sit there while he is being held by her and smile at me. And you know he associates me with that. And as far as fathers you know getting more time, anything you can possibly do to interact with your child . . . You know interacting with him is good memories for him and you. I don't think anybody wants to be the dad who is sixty years old and watch their son have a son or their daughter have a son or daughter and why are you interacting with them like that oh I should have done that forty-something years ago. I personally love interacting with him, I love that it gives me a chance to be a child again.

Fathers who take more parental leave are more satisfied with the amount of time they spend with their children. For example, they are more likely to disagree that they should spend more time with their children or that they have missed important times in their children's lives.[99] Fathers themselves benefit by engaging in healthier behaviors and creating more ties to family and community. And in the end, men are just as capable of caring for children as women. It is the act of providing direct care for a child that increases one's capacity for caregiving. Fathers who engage in high stimulatory contact with their infants experience an increase in oxytocin, a hormone associated with parent-infant bonding.[100] Men's body chemistry reacts the same way as women's to close physical contact with infants. In other words, fathers show similar hormonal changes, and this means they can experience similar levels of bonding with their children.[101] Like mothers, fathers experience benefits to their health from parental leave.

Benefits to Infants and Children

Infant Mortality/Health

There is a good deal of research showing that paid parental leave is beneficial to children's health.[102] Paid parental leave is associated with lower infant mortality rates.[103] Based on sixteen European countries, Ruhm finds that more generous paid parental leave results in lower rates of infant and child deaths.[104] In an updated study, Tanaka confirms these findings, showing that paid leave has a significant negative effect on perinatal mortality (stillbirths and deaths within one week of birth), neonatal mortality (deaths within four weeks of birth), post-neonatal mortality (deaths between four weeks and one year after birth), and child mortality (deaths between one year and five years after birth).[105] Tanaka's research suggests that increasing paid maternity leave by ten weeks would reduce infant mortality more than 2 percent.

Economist Maya Rossin conducted the first study to look at the causal effects of FMLA on infant health and mortality. She found that "FMLA led to small increases in birth weight, decreases in the likelihood of a premature birth, and considerable decreases in infant mortality rates" but only for college-educated, married mothers.[106] Rossin speculates that this select group of women would be the ones most likely to have access to FMLA and have the resources to be able to take unpaid leave. It is therefore likely that paid leave would provide this benefit more widely.

Leave before birth or a reduced workload has been linked to a smaller chance of having a premature or low birthweight infant.[107] In addition, the availability of paid leave may increase immunization rates. In a study of Japan, researchers found that children of mothers who took parental leave were more likely to have received all recommended immunizations by thirty-six months.[108] A US study found that children are less likely to get preventative health care, such as "well-baby" visits and immunizations, during the first year when their mothers go back to work within twelve weeks.[109] Furthermore, other infant health effects include a 31-percent reduction in the chances of being overweight and an 18-percent decrease in the odds of experiencing frequent ear infections.[110]

Breastfeeding

Length of parental leave and duration of breastfeeding are positively linked.[111] Evidence from different countries shows that longer leave is associated with longer breastfeeding duration.[112] A Canadian study found that increasing the maternity leave mandate in Canada resulted in greater success in achieving critical breastfeeding thresholds and fewer accidents in the baby's first year.[113] A study of Ireland, Sweden, and the US finds that parental leave is related to higher rates and longer duration of breastfeeding. At six months, 73 percent of Swedish mothers were breastfeeding whereas only 28 percent of Irish mothers and 29 percent of American mothers continued breastfeeding this long.[114]

Meanwhile, a group of maternal and child-health experts suggests that delaying mothers' return to work could lengthen the duration of breastfeeding in the US,[115] which could be accomplished by introducing paid parental leave. A study of the effect of California's Paid Family Leave program on breastfeeding finds an increase of ten to twenty percent in breastfeeding at three, six, and nine months of age.[116] Another study of PFL found that not only did the likelihood of breastfeeding increase, but so too did the duration of breastfeeding, from an average of only two weeks before PFL to an average of twelve weeks after PFL—a sizeable effect.[117]

It is not only maternity leave that increases breastfeeding. Paternity leave also has a positive effect on breastfeeding. A Swedish study finds that infants of fathers who took paternity leave during the first year were more likely to be breastfed at two, four, and six months.[118]

Child Development

Among low-income American mothers, taking more than six months off work is positively associated with developmental activities, including telling stories, singing songs, and playing games, at one year of age.[119] A Korean study finds that paid maternity leave is positively related to infant development, including motor skills, communication, social skills, and problem solving.[120]

Public health researchers in the UK find a positive relationship between father involvement with infants and socioemotional behavior when the child is age 3. Specifically, children whose fathers were more involved in caring for them at nine months are less likely to experience hyperactivity, emotional problems, conduct problems, or peer problems at three years old.[121] Interestingly, parental leave may even affect processing of emotional expressions. In a study of fourteen-month-old infants, a team of psychologists observed infant response to different emotional facial expressions. When both the mother and father cared for an infant through divided parental leave, the infants were better able to process different emotions than when cared for by one parent.[122]

These effects can be long lasting. A Canadian study finds a positive association between parental leave and child development five years later. Kindergarten children whose parents took parental leave show higher scores on social competence and communication and general knowledge.[123] An evaluation of California's Paid Family Leave program found a significant impact on child behavior. Specifically, PFL is associated with a 58-percent reduction in the odds of ADHD in elementary school children.[124] On the other hand, social work researchers find that children are more likely to show externalizing behaviors, such as aggressiveness, defiance, and impulsivity, at age four if mothers return to full-time employment within twelve weeks of childbirth.[125]

Education

While the evidence seems more mixed with regard to parental leave and educational outcomes,[126] some studies show positive effects on children. Based on parental leave reform in Austria, researchers find a positive effect of maternity leave on children's educational outcomes among highly educated mothers. Specifically, sons of mothers with higher educational attainment score higher on reading and science standardized tests.[127]

In their study of four OECD countries, Maria del Carmen Huerta and colleagues find a potential link between fathers' leave taking, later paternal involvement, and children's cognitive test scores.[128] A longitudinal study of Norway finds that paternity leave is causally related to children's school performance. Specifically, when fathers take more wage-compensated leave, their child's lower secondary school exam scores (fifteen years post-leave) are higher. The researchers argue that parental leave results in increased paternal care and attention to child academics.[129] Another study in Norway showed that parental leave reform in 1977 had a positive impact on children's education and wages years later. Specifically, the decrease in the high school dropout rate was 2 percent and the increase in children's earnings at age thirty was 5 percent.[130]

Parental Leave Is Good Business

Many companies that offer paid parental leave note the ultimate positive effect not only on their employees but also on the company itself.
Netflix grabbed headlines when they introduced one year of unlimited
paid parental leave to salaried streaming employees in August 2015
(four months later they expanded their leave to include other employees though capped this leave between twelve and sixteen weeks). Tawni
Cranz, Chief Talent Officer for Netflix, stated: "Experience shows people
perform better at work when they're not worrying about home. This
new policy, combined with our unlimited time off, allows employees to
be supported during the changes in their lives and *return to work more
focused and dedicated.*"[131] Here we see that a generous policy, perhaps
the most generous in the US, is about good business practice. Netflix
sees the importance of keeping employees, particularly skilled employees, committed to Netflix. And in the process, they gained a considerable
amount of positive publicity.

Another example is Facebook, which offers sixteen weeks of paid
parental leave as well as six weeks of paid family care leave. Chief Op-
erating Officer Sheryl Sandberg states: "Companies that stand by the
people who work for them do the right thing and the smart thing—it
helps them serve their mission, live their values, and improve their
bottom line by increasing the loyalty and performance of their workforce."[132] While Sandberg mentions supporting employees, she is also
explicit about the benefits such policies create for her company. This
section focuses on benefits of parental leave to employers, including
competitiveness, productivity, recruitment and retention, and company culture.

Being Competitive

Etsy offers one of the most generous policies with twenty-six weeks of
paid parental leave that can be used non-sequentially over two years
post-birth or post-adoption. Their statement refers to parental leave as
"a competitive necessity:" "A generous, fully-paid parental leave policy
is a competitive necessity for a company like Etsy . . . We also wanted
to align our internal policies with the spirit of our marketplace, which

offers a more fulfilling, flexible way to be a creative entrepreneur" (March 2016). Statements like this are backed up by studies that show paid leave increases retention and productivity.[133]

Likewise, Bank of America was clear about the potential benefits of offering sixteen weeks of paid parental leave when they released this statement: "From our perspective, happy associates translate into happy and healthy clients. Happy clients translate into a healthy company. For us it's good solid business . . . We're competitive and we're toward the forefront. I'd hope other companies would follow."[134] This seems to be a common theme among financial companies. Note the statements of Bloomberg L.P.: "We wanted to offer our employees a parental leave policy that was best in class and competitive with our peers in the technology, finance and media industries" (April 2015) and Credit Suisse Group: "We certainly see this as a competitive program, and I think one of the things we are recognizing is that our competition is not just financial services. When you look at talent coming out of the big schools they are looking at firms that offer flexibility" (November 2015). Even smaller companies like First Tennessee are making an effort after seeing what similar institutions offer: "We noticed that other companies were offering more benefits than what we were. We still can't match everybody's— the military came out with twelve weeks off—but we've heard a lot about time-off and felt this was the right time."[135] This statement made in August 2016 comes after several financial companies introduced longer parental leave policies.

Survey research suggests that a good paid parental leave policy can make a company more attractive. Over three-quarters of employees with access to paid leave in a 2016 survey claimed that their employer's parental leave policy affected their decision to work for their current employer.[136]

General Performance

A senior VP at 3M noted how important their new parental leave policy was for "better performance at work. This change is an investment in our people and our company's success." Several companies that have adopted or extended parental leave policies mention expecting performance or productivity gains. For example, Crowley Maritime

Corporation's statement in July 2017 asserts: "Not only is a family-friendly environment valued by employees, it also makes our company better by increasing engagement, motivation and productivity." Likewise, AXA's statement follows: "A company where one can be both a parent and a professional, a company that trusts its employees and understands the importance of well-being in the workplace: that's a company that drives innovation and fosters creativity" (December 2016).[137] These companies think workers who have access to good parental leave will perform better and even have the potential to create new ideas, products, and systems.

Prominent in many statements is the idea that a company's employees are "the best," a "valuable resource," and that employees work hard and "make the difference." When Microsoft expanded its parental leave policy in June 2017, it released the following statement: "As we ask our employees to bring their 'A' game to work every day to achieve our mission, we believe it's our responsibility to create an environment where people can do their best work. A key component of this is supporting our employees with benefits that matter most to them." In January 2018, Walmart made the following statement: "Today, we are building on investments we've been making in associates, in their wages and skills development. It's our people who make the difference and we appreciate how they work hard to make every day easier for busy families."[138] Some statements seem like a promise to employees:

> We expect our employees to be their best and achieve remarkable outcomes for our clients, so we promise our employees to do our best to support them.
> —Attain, March 2017

> We believe our employees are the best in the business and we will continue to invest in programs and policies that enable them to be successful and that make Exelon their workplace of choice.
> —Exelon, December 2016

> Our people are State Street's most valuable—and valued—resources and we can't operate effectively as a company if our employees aren't fully

supported and thus fully focused while at work. Offering them adequate time to attend to personal and family needs without financial stress is smart business.
—State Street, January 2017

Vanguard's crew members dedicate their workdays to serving our clients and giving them the best chance for investment success. We have long been proud of our excellent benefits program and long tenured crew, so it is vitally important that we continue to support them at every life stage they experience during the time they work at Vanguard.
—Vanguard, September 2016[139]

Notice that these policy statements praise employees and emphasize supporting these valuable employees. At the same time, it is clear that the support is offered with high expectations for achieving "remarkable outcomes."

The evidence is clear that paid parental leave has a positive effect on engagement and productivity. Fully 97 percent of employers in a recent survey indicated either no effect or a positive effect of paid family leave on employee morale (80 percent positive, 17 percent no effect). Similarly, 93 percent of employers reported no change (23 percent) or an increase (70 percent) in productivity. This generally translates into higher profits for the company.[140]

Recruitment and Retention

Perhaps one of the most commonly cited reasons for offering paid parental leave is recruitment and retention of good employees:

These expanded benefits will help us attract, retain and inspire the best people.
—Accenture, March 2015

We aim to attract and retain the world's top talent and value a truly diverse and rich perspective from our employees.
—The Boston Consulting Group (BCG), September 2017

> We recognized that parental leave is a compelling benefit to attract and retain employees, so we took the necessary steps to give parents the time off they need . . . Our goal is to attract and retain top talent and we believe this approach helps us do just that.
> —Fidelity Investments, March 2016

> This is part of a series of actions that we are planning to implement in order to continue to recruit and retain the best talent and be a great place to work.
> —Hilton Worldwide, September 2015[141]

The public relations company APCO Worldwide noted the importance of their paid parental leave policy (twelve weeks) on recruitment. Their July 2017 statements reads: "To do the best work, you need the best people. To attract the best people, especially in a consulting environment where there are often intense pressures, it's important to do what we can to help create a good quality of work-life balance."[142]

Retaining good employees is as important as recruiting. There is evidence that paid parental leave increases retention. One study found that taking paid leave increased women's likelihood of returning to the workforce within a year by 93 percent.[143] Another study in California showed a higher retention rate for low-wage workers (those earning under $20 per hour) who used the Paid Family Leave program.[144] This pattern appears to be stronger when policies offer longer leave, and a number of companies have experienced this benefit first hand. For example, Google reduced its female turnover rate by 50 percent when it increased its maternity leave from twelve to eighteen weeks and Accenture reduced its female turnover rate by 40 percent when it expanded its paid parental leave from eight to sixteen weeks.[145]

This is also important for fathers. Gael, an American father, talked about the importance of having extra time off when his baby needed to stay in the hospital to clear up health issues. He decided to take his leave when his daughter returned home so he could maximize his time to care for her. He states:

> When [my daughter] got home from the hospital I took what I think I said turned out to be five weeks of continuous. . . . and if I had to go to

work, you know, two weeks after that, I would have been so exhausted and unproductive, whereas, you know, being able to take more time off, and then even still, I think I did like another week of partial leave because she still had a lot of appointments, and so I kind of eased into it instead of going back to work full-time right away. You know, that allowed me to get adjusted and, you know, not resent work.

Kye, another American father, talks about the importance of quality of life to productivity at work:

> I think an employer should be invested in the quality of life of their employee because I think that would directly reflect in the output and work environment that the employee's in. Like I said when I came back to work, the only thing I could think about was I don't want to be here. So now right off the bat my mental state is I don't want to be here. Where maybe if I came back and I was like, hey, the city stepped up. They gave me time to be with my kid. That was really great. Maybe my attitude would be different. Hey, they took care of me. I actually feel like they're interested and invested in my well-being.

The contrast between Gael and Kye is marked. Kye did not feel ready to return to work and thinks this had a negative effect on his performance. His example shows that not just mothers, but fathers as well, want to spend time at home with their new children. When forced to return before they are ready, this can affect how they feel about their workplace and employer. On the other hand, Gael acknowledges that he would not have been productive at work if he had to return after only two weeks. His ability to take a longer leave and ease back into work meant he did not resent his workplace or employer.

Company Culture

Companies often like to portray themselves in a particular light. This includes promoting a particular company culture. Some companies pride themselves on extra perks such as free meals, on-site fitness centers, meditation rooms, and fun activities such as foosball and ping pong. But all companies want a positive, welcoming culture because this makes the working experience more pleasant and ultimately creates more loyalty. In September 2015, Airbnb co-founder and CSO Nathan Blecharczyk made this explicit in his statement: "When the employer plays a role in helping employees achieve that goal [of balancing work and family], their employee's loyalty will increase, and the culture of the company will benefit immensely."[146]

A parental leave policy can help companies demonstrate their values and may improve morale.[147] On the one hand, these policies reinforce ideals surrounding home and family. Take IKEA's decision to cover all US employees, including store employees. As a Swedish company, there is a need to recognize the value of parental leave. They state: "The starting point for everything we do is our values and our vision, to create a better everyday life for many people. . . . Plus, we believe in taking time off. We're in the business of home, and we encourage people to take time at home." Likewise, NVIDIA states: "NVIDIA is committed to creating a culture and environment that allows us to focus on our most important responsibilities, both at work and at home." PayPal agrees: "Supporting our employees as they raise their families, care for their aging parents, or volunteer in their communities is one of the most important things we can do to build a work culture at PayPal that aligns how we work with what we aspire to achieve on behalf of our customers."[148]

On the other hand, companies can show that they value diversity, inclusivity, and equality through their parental leave policies. For example, American Express claims that it "remains deeply committed to our working families and an inclusive culture that supports all of our employees" (December 2016). This is particularly the case when their policies are gender-neutral, include same-sex couples, and cover adoption and surrogacy as well as birth.[149]

Benefits to Society

Paid parental leave is generally good for society, especially for the economy. As mentioned above, paid parental leave policies increase women's employment. While employment is good for women's individual well-being, having more individuals at work is also good for the economy. At a basic level, more women in the labor force means more people paying taxes, which allows countries to maintain more programs.[150] Women's employment can also provide a boost to the economy. One study, seeking to understand the potential impact of stagnant rates of women's employment in the US, found that if the US had experienced similar growth to Japan in female employment over the first sixteen years of the twenty-first century, this growth would have resulted in an $800 billion increase in GDP in 2016.[151] Another study showed that American cities with higher female labor force participation rates witnessed greater growth in median wages (for all employees).[152] This may be because paid parental leave increases workers' productivity.[153] In addition, paid family leave decreases unemployment and the use of public assistance funds.[154]

Parental leave policies can also promote fertility rates. An Austrian study shows that women who had their first child after parental leave reform were more likely to have a second child than those who had their first child before the reform.[155] Similarly, there was a 13-percent increase in the intended number of children following the announcement of paid parental leave in Australia.[156] Encouraging men's use of parental leave is also important. Research from Norway and Sweden finds higher rates of continued childbearing (for those with one or two children) when fathers take parental leave.[157]

Conclusion

This chapter examined the benefits of paid parental leave for mothers, fathers, children, and employers. First, paid leave has a positive impact on women's careers, increasing stability in employment and minimizing negative effects of time off on career advancement and income. It also improves women's physical and mental health, particularly in its reduction of postpartum depression. Second, paid leave is good for men as it allows them to spend time with their children, build up their caregiving skills, and focus on family, which is better for their overall well-being. Third, parental leave benefits children in terms of health outcomes, such as lower infant mortality and higher immunization rates. It also has potential longer-term benefits on academic and social development. Fourth, parental leave is good business. Companies that provide paid leave have experienced greater productivity, higher recruitment and retention, and better company culture. Fifth, parental leave is good for society, with positive effects on the economy and fertility. If parental leave is so obviously good for everyone, does that mean more is better? The next chapter explores this question by examining the negative impact of too much parental leave.

3

Too Much Parental Leave Is Not Good

Parental leave is a key part of promoting gender equality in the work-place. But is it possible to have too much of a good thing? It makes sense that women take maternity or parental leave when it is available, and, unsurprisingly, studies show that increases in the length of leave available result in women taking longer leaves.[1] What is less clear is how extended leaves affect women's employment and gender equality more broadly. We do know that women face greater difficulties in achieving career success in countries with more extensive parental leave policies.[2]

What is the optimal length of parental leave? Based on studies that examine women's return to employment, there is some agreement that five to seven months is optimal. In this chapter, I consider evidence that shows the negative effects of long parental leave. Most research focuses on women and is related to employment, advancement, and income. Some research also suggests that there are negative health consequences of long leaves, particularly related to depression and mental health. There is also evidence that men may face negative consequences of long leaves. All this helps in thinking of ways to optimize the timing and division of parental leave.

Could Parental Leave Be Harmful to Gender Equality?

Some argue that women will ultimately be disadvantaged by parental leave policies. For example, Baroness Ruth Lister, emeritus professor of social policy, member of the Joint Committee of Human Rights, and vice-chair of the Fair Pay Network, asserts that programs that pay for care (such as parental leave) without addressing inequalities in the division of labor could act as an obstacle to gender equality.[3] Drawing on feminist citizenship theory, which critiques the public-private (read: work/home) dichotomy and women's exclusion from public forms of citizenship, Lister describes the dilemma between equality-based claims to full citizenship in which women and men take on the same roles and responsibilities versus difference-based claims to full citizenship in which women and men comprise different roles and responsibilities.[4] Lister labels this dilemma "pendulum politics" because the popularity of each swings back and forth among politicians. Lister proposes an alternative model called the "carer/earner" model, in which both men and women take on employment and caregiving. She admits that more effort is needed to make the division of labor more equitable in the private sphere, and this will happen more readily if men become more similar to women, rather than vice versa. Furthermore, Lister suggests that "a more balanced gendered division of labour needs to be seen as an *opportunity* for men to become more involved in the work of care, rather than as a threat."[5] As such, Lister is a fan of the daddy quota common in Sweden and other Nordic countries.

Philosopher Nancy Fraser discusses the potential problems of a caregiver parity model, which attempts to value caregiving in the same way as paid labor.[6] Parental leave policies may be viewed as attempts to value caregiving. Yet Fraser suggests that "caregiving is unlikely to attain true parity with breadwinning" because of the gendered notions of caregiving as feminine and breadwinning as masculine and the differential economic value placed on these roles. Ultimately, she argues that women will still be marginalized: "By supporting women's informal care work, [the caregiver parity model] reinforces the view of such work as women's work and consolidates the gender division of domestic labor. By consolidating dual labor markets for breadwinners and caregivers, moreover, the model marginalizes women within the employment sector."[7] In other words, these kinds of policies could reinforce the idea that domestic work and caregiving are feminine practices at the same time as establishing a "mommy track" in the labor market in which employers expect women to interrupt their careers to care for children. These arguments are related to the idea that women need to take leave and figure out how to balance work and family while men who have children simply carry on working with limited leave and limited or no change to their work lives.

There are also two competing arguments for women's poorer outcomes in the labor market—the human capital argument and the signaling effect argument. The human capital argument is based on the idea that time away from work means an employee will miss that time to accumulate human capital and may indeed lose some of their skills.[8] This may be more relevant in today's economy, where techniques and technologies change quickly. Someone on leave during the introduction of new technologies will not be there to learn it and may be considered behind. On the other hand, there is the signaling effect argument. Under this theory, those who take leave, or at least long leaves, "signal" to their boss that they are less committed to work. Those who do not take leave or take shorter leaves are seen as more committed to work. However, both gender and the reason for the leave may affect how employers read the "signals." The next sections consider the evidence regarding leave, employment, career advancement, and the pay gap.

Women's Employment

Most research shows a positive effect of parental leave on maternal employment. However, long leaves may have the opposite effect, reducing the probability of employment.[9] For example, there is some evidence that leave of more than one year reduces the likelihood of returning to work.[10] A study of the extension of Canadian paid parental leave from twenty-five to fifty weeks showed a decrease in new mothers returning to work in the first year after childbirth.[11]

Much research shows a curvilinear effect of parental leave on women's employment. In other words, some leave is good, but at a certain point leave becomes excessive and detrimental. In an early study, Christopher Ruhm examined nine European countries between 1969 and 1993. He found that short periods of approximately three months of paid leave had a positive impact on employment-to-population ratios of women with little effect on wages.[12] However, longer leaves (e.g., nine months), though they increased employment, also decreased earnings. Examining seventeen OECD countries between 1985 and 1999, economist Florence Jaumotte found a marginal effect of parental leave on female employment, which peaks at twenty weeks.[13] Beyond twenty weeks, parental leave has a negative effect on female labor force participation. Economists Yusuf Emre Akgunduz and Janneke Plantenga calculated difference-in-difference models based on data from sixteen European countries between 1970 and 2010.[14] They focused on the effect of weighted leave, a combination of maternity leave and parental leave, on women's employment outcomes. They

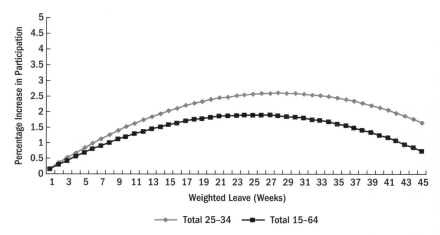

Figure 3.1. Length of leave and women's labor force participation. Source: Akgunduz and Plantenga, 2013; see figure 4 in this source

found that the optimal leave length for women twenty-five to thirty-four years old is twenty-eight weeks (see figure 3.1). After twenty-eight weeks, employment benefits decline. For example, parental leave of thirty weeks is associated with a decline of 1.5 percent in the proportion of women in high-level occupations and a decrease of 7 percent in women's high-skill wages. It peaks sooner and the benefits are smaller for the full sample of women aged fifteen to sixty-four.

Using the UK's Millennium Cohort Study, sociologists Colette Fagan and Helen Norman examine maternal employment following maternity leave.[15] They find that returning to employment within nine months of childbirth is critical to longer-term employment and career progression. Specifically, mothers who returned to work within nine months were significantly more likely than those who took longer leave to be in paid employment and working full-time three years after childbirth. Occupational class also plays a role. Mothers in managerial or professional positions before parental leave were more likely to be employed three years after childbirth regardless of leave length. In contrast, mothers who hold lower occupational positions are less likely to be employed and those who are employed tend to work part-time.[16] We know that part-time employment is associated with lower pay and fewer opportunities for career advancement.

In countries like Germany and the US, the length of time out of work has a negative linear relationship with returning to the same job. In other words, the longer women stay on leave, the less their chance of keeping their same job. In the US, highly educated mothers also have a greater likelihood of returning to their same job or one at a similar occupational level after family-related leave. This is because highly educated mothers take shorter leaves than less educated mothers, but it is also because they have better access to paid, job-protected leave. In contrast, these differences do not occur in Sweden, where policies protect employees on leave.[17] Furthermore, the relationship between length of leave and returning to the same job is not linear in Sweden. Rather, the chance of returning to the same job decreases only after three years. Therefore, women who return within three years have a high chance of returning to the same job. It is also quite common for Swedish women to make use of the "speed premium" by having two children within two and a half years. In these cases, parental leave pay is based on income prior to the first birth rather than the potentially lower income resulting between births.[18]

Women's Career Advancement

Some researchers argue that parental leave programs, on their own, increase the "motherhood-induced employment gap."[19] While job-protected, well-paid maternity leave may increase mother's employment following leave, it has the potential of having other detrimental effects on long-term economic outcomes as well. For one, long parental leave may reduce women's likelihoods of getting promotions.[20] This may be due to the fact that women miss opportunities for job training and other chances to build experience or other forms of human capital. These missed opportunities are likely to then impact women's earning capacity. In the US, even short leaves can have consequences for advancement, with women facing a greater risk of downward career moves.[21]

Two main factors create the negative relationship between leave and women's work success. One is human capital depreciation, in which skills decline or become outdated during long absences from the labor market. The other factor is statistical discrimination, in which employers decide not to hire or promote women more generally, based on the fact that many will take an extended maternity leave.[22]

Longer leaves reduce women's chance of upward mobility. However, this varies depending on the policy supports they enjoy. For example, in the US, making an upward move (measured by increases in occupational prestige) is 15 percent less likely for women who return to work between four and twelve months after childbirth compared to women who return to work before four months, and the likelihood of advancement is 24 percent lower for those who take more than a year off. Meanwhile, the negative effect of longer leave in Sweden does not hold until a woman takes sixteen months or more of leave.[23] Therefore, there may not be one answer to how long is too long. It seems that better policies ensure a delay in negative outcomes.

There is a negative relationship between state-funded programs such as parental leave and the percentage of managers and lucrative managers who are female. The US has one of the highest rates of female employment in managerial and lucrative-managerial positions while the UK and Sweden, countries with generous and lengthy state-funded leave, lag behind. For example, the rates of female employment in managerial and lucrative-managerial positions in the US are close to 80 percent each, while the corresponding rates are 56 and 30 percent in the UK and 43 and 41 percent in Sweden. On the other hand, the US has relatively low odds (under 10 percent) of female employment in female-typed occupations compared to the UK (19 percent) and Sweden (16 percent).[24] Paige, a thirty-two-year-old British researcher who took seven months of leave, relays her concern about taking such a long leave:

> Ideally, I would have, you know, if I could have taken a year but well. I think initially financially and secondary I was thinking it was sort of about work as well because when you're out of this type of work, research or that, for a year then it can be quite difficult to get back into the swing of things if you like, get back into what's happening, your current research field.

Paige took a shorter leave than she would have wanted, but the amount of leave she took falls near the peak optimum length for women's long-term economic prospects, according to Akgunduz and Plantega (see figure 3.1). Sociologists Hadas Mandel and Moshe Semyonov conclude:

We contend that family-friendly policies and employment practices assume the primacy of women's familial responsibilities. As such they are designed to allow women time off for the care of young children through extended maternity leaves and support of part-time employment. These policies, in turn, discourage employers from hiring women for managerial and powerful positions and foster women's attachment to female-typed occupations and jobs with convenient work conditions.[25]

They call this the "welfare state paradox" because policies such as parental leave, designed to promote gender equality, also act to inhibit gender equality. In the case of parental leave, we see that these policies encourage women to enter the labor force, but they also push them toward lower-paying, female-typed occupations instead of higher-paying, managerial positions.

Nabanita Datta Gupta and colleagues extend Mandel and Semyonov's argument by coining the term "system-based glass ceiling."[26] Here they refer to a system that is based on generous family-friendly policies and high levels of public sector employment. Since women in Nordic countries take more parental leave than men and are more likely to work in the public sector (over half of employed women versus one-fifth to one-quarter of employed men), the system encourages women to continue going into family-friendly public sector employment, which is also lower paying. This results in occupational segregation and a gender pay gap. Furthermore, the income ratio between women and men remained relatively stagnant in the last two decades of the twentieth century. Therefore, the glass ceiling is not necessarily an obstacle for individual women trying to advance in particular companies but a glass ceiling that limits women more generally. This is all to say that even Sweden and other Nordic countries have not completely figured out how to eliminate gender inequality.

It may also be important to consider women's subjective perceptions of the negative repercussions of parental leave on mothers' employment opportunities. The duration of a woman's career interruption is particularly important in forming these perceptions. Compared to women who take leave of up to six months, those who take medium leave (six months to two years) are 2.5 times as likely, those who take long leaves (two to four years) are 5.3 times as likely, and those who interrupt their careers for more than four years are over ten times as likely to perceive negative occupational consequences of their leave.[27] While long-term leave has negative effects on women's careers, there is also evidence that women's perceived negative consequences vary based on the policy context in which they find themselves. Emma, a thirty-year-old British office worker who took nine months, feels she may have been penalized for taking maternity leave:

> It's a bit uncomfortable because there were certain things that were promised to me before I left that have not been fulfilled now, and I wouldn't go as far, I don't think I would be taking it as far as saying it was because I went on maternity leave that I'm not getting these things now, but there's always that niggling thought in the back of my mind, if I'd not gone on maternity leave would I have got those things that I was promised and I would have carried on the job as normal. And I'm sure that, yeah, I'd like to think that I haven't been stopped from doing the things that were promised to me weren't stopped because I was on maternity leave because I took that break but I'll never know.

As Emma indicates, it is difficult to prove that her leave cost her job opportunities, but the timing seems to indicate this as a real possibility. Emma was promised a promotion shortly before she announced that she would go on maternity leave. Although she applied for the promotion while on leave, another employee was chosen.

Swedish women who take longer parental leaves have reduced odds of making an upward occupational move. Since non-family reasons for career interruptions do not seem to have the same effect on occupational mobility, researchers conclude that the negative effects of parental leave cannot be due to human capital depreciation but must be some kind of signaling effect, an indicator to employers that one is not as serious about work.[28] Using longitudinal data, Swedish demographers Marie Evertsson and Ann-Zofie Duvander ask whether parental leave is a benefit or a trap by focusing on women's leave-taking behavior and their occupational mobility.[29] They find that women who take parental leave for sixteen months or more are significantly less likely to advance in their careers than women who take shorter amounts of parental leave. This is noteworthy in that there only seems to be a negative effect for leave length that is above the average amount of time Swedish women take leave. In this sense, it may be that employers can speculate that women who take more leave than average are less committed to work.

A study of Sweden, Germany, and the US finds that the longer women are on parental leave, the lower their chance for an upward career move. While the relationship between parental leave length and downward mobility is not perfect, the conclusion is fairly clear that longer leaves are riskier in the sense that more women face the possibility of a downward move.[30] However, there is some difference depending on the overall leave policy context. For example, the negative effects of taking leave on women's career advancement occur immediately in the US, even after a short leave, whereas the negative effect does not appear in Sweden until parental leave surpasses fifteen months. While the more generous policy regime in Sweden buffers or delays the negative impact of leave, even Swedish women have better career prospects when they return to work earlier.

In addition, policy simulations suggest that parental leave policies aimed at fathers could increase women's employment. In other words, providing the opportunity to take long leaves often means that women take those long leaves and thus take a hit to their careers. But long leaves, divided more equally between partners, might not disadvantage women but may rather be beneficial. Human capital depreciation would be more even, and employers would need to expect that both men and women might take parental leave, removing a major reason for statistical discrimination. On the other hand, if women take longer leaves, which they do, employers may come to think that it is costlier to employ women than men.[31]

Gender Pay Gap

Parental leave may result in lower wages.[32] There is plenty of evidence that mothers experience a wage penalty[33] while men, particularly married, residential fathers, often experience a fatherhood wage premium.[34] In perhaps the most cited study on the motherhood wage penalty, sociologists Michelle Budig and Paula England find that each child is associated with a wage penalty of 7 percent.[35] Some of this penalty is due to the fact that women with more children have less work experience, but even after controlling for job experience, there is still a 5-percent wage penalty for each child. In the US, mothers who use work-family policies that result in fewer work hours or less time at the workplace also experience pay penalties.[36]

One cause of the gender wage gap is gender segregation in occupations. Women tend to work in more female-dominated jobs, which tend to have lower pay. Policies that promote women's employment may also result in greater occupational gender segregation.[37] Another contributor to the gender wage gap is career interruptions. Women are more likely to experience career interruptions, particularly family-related interruptions, and long maternity leave is a chief reason women face disadvantages in the work force.[38] There is evidence that the negative effect of motherhood on wages is at least partly due to loss of human capital during parental leave.[39] In particular, longer parental leave policies encourage longer career interruptions for women, which exacerbates the gender wage gap.[40] In addition to human capital depreciation, when employers expect women to have children and take leave, they are more hesitant to hire and promote women, a form of statistical discrimination. Employers may see long parental leaves as a "legitimate" reason to discriminate against women and favor men.[41]

Researchers from the Netherlands find a sizeable wage penalty from parental leave occurring as soon as during the first year.[42] More commonly, researchers find a negative impact of maternity leave on women's wages in the longer term.[43] Different studies find different penalties, but two studies from Germany suggest there are large penalties. One study shows that women suffer wage penalties of 0.4 percent per month of parental leave and 1.3 percent per year beyond the initial year of parental leave.[44] Another study shows that each year of parental leave decreases wages by 18 percent.[45]

Based on a study that followed the career progression of a group of health care administration graduates in the US, career interruptions that are seen as voluntary, such as parental leave, have a larger negative impact on long-term salary growth than career interruptions that are seen as involuntary, such as unemployment, or part-time work. The health administration researchers go so far as to recommend that workers continue with part-time work rather than take leave during times of greater family responsibilities in order to ensure that they suffer fewer negative impacts from career interruptions.[46] It would seem employers do judge those who take parental leave more harshly.

Furthermore, according to cross-national research, parental leave is more likely to have a negative effect on earnings in countries where there is greater support for more traditional roles in which men act as bread-winners and women as caregivers.[47] Some argue that the gender pay gap is due to the unequal division of family responsibilities. Using Swed-ish register data, economist Nikolay Angelov and colleagues were able to examine parents of first-born children and track their labor market activities before and after the birth of their child.[48] They found that the gender gap in wages increased after having a child such that mothers had 10 percent lower wages than fathers fifteen years after the birth of their first child. Sociologist Lynn Prince Cooke finds that motherhood pen-alties are similar across Australia, the UK, and the US for those in the upper half of the earnings distribution but wider in the US for earners in the bottom half.[49] These patterns are encouraged by the lopsided divi-sion of labor at home. With women, and especially mothers, doing more housework and childcare, they have less time to focus on their jobs.[50] Employers also expect women to place more priority on their families and this can affect hiring and promotion. This may extend to parental leave. Jennifer Hook, author of *Gendered Tradeoffs*, uses time-use surveys from nineteen countries to examine the effect of parental leave policies on housework.[51] She finds that women do more housework in countries with long parental leave. On the other hand, women do less housework in contexts where men have access to parental leave.

Problems with Long Leaves: The Case of Hungary

We can turn to Hungary for an example of the effects of long parental leave on women's employment. Hungary was ahead of the times when it introduced *three years* of paid maternity leave in 1967. Nevertheless, the goals of this extensive policy were to increase fertility and allevi-ate employment pressures, caused by a campaign for full employment of all adults. Even as other policies implemented under the communist regime were eliminated, the parental leave policy remained: "In place for over four decades, it has withstood several shifts in left, right and centre governments, the structural adjustment demands of the IMF, the explicit critique of the OECD and the World Bank, and the employment rate targets of the European Union."[52] In fact, after the fall of communism, family policies devoted to re-introducing traditional gender roles, termed "re-traditionalisation" or "re-familialisation," became popular. Gender studies scholars Éva Fodor and Erika Kispeter elaborate:

> While different in important details, each of these concepts suggests increased or ongoing incentives for women to leave the labour market and do unpaid care work in their homes, while noting rising obstacles to finding and holding on to paid employment. Indeed, post-state socialist politicians and public figures introduced a backlash against the communist slogan of women's emancipation; newly elected governments emphasised the differences between men's and women's "natural" roles and the patriotic importance of women as keepers of the hearth.[53]

These familistic tendencies were further promoted by fears of the demographic consequences of low fertility and the rise in extremists on the right. These policies, specifically paid parental leave of three or more years, exist in other Central and Eastern European countries such as Bulgaria, the Czech Republic, Estonia, and Slovakia and there seems to be a shift toward maternalism.[54] Here is where there is even a distinction between medium-length leave, which as noted above may encourage gendered occupational segregation and the pay gap, and extremely long leaves. The latter, which is defined as leave that is longer than two years, is likely to be even more detrimental to women. Potential consequences include exclusion from jobs, as employers refrain from hiring women of childbearing age in anticipation that these women will leave work for long periods of time to raise their children, and a higher risk of poverty.[55]

Hungary makes lots of top-ten lists when it comes to countries with the best maternity leave policies. Again, it is quite generous with maternity and parental leave extending to the child's third birthday.[56] With such generous leave, it may not be a surprise that most Hungarian mothers take parental leave, but perhaps the length is a bit surprising: the average mother takes 4.7 years of leave—more than 10 percent of a woman's working life![57] Unfortunately, return rates are quite low, with only one-third of mothers returning to their pre-leave jobs after finishing parental leave, which understandably reduces labor force attachment. Fodor and Kispeter's qualitative research shows that Hungarian women on parental leave are often actually working, as they are engaged in income-generating activities. Some work for small businesses run by friends or family; others work on farms in their rural towns. Yet others tutor children, wait tables at events, clean businesses, sell handmade clothing, and run workshops in their homes. Because this work is informal, it is also largely invisible. Fodor and Kispeter conclude that the extremely long maternity and parental leave policies are not in fact woman-friendly but rather exacerbate gender inequality. They suggest that the state is "complicit in the construction of mothers (and would-be mothers) as marginalized workers, while ostensibly offering them a chance, and expecting them to do the most they can for their children." Women therefore become an "invisible reserve army of labourers."[58]

Is the US Actually Better for Gender Equality?

Are American women better off without a federal paid parental leave policy? Silke Aisenbrey and colleagues suggest that much of the negative impact of maternity leave is due to statistical discrimination, which is different treatment of groups based on a group's "average" behavior.[59] If employers in countries with generous leave policies want to avoid the potential costs and hassles of female employees taking extended time due to maternity leave, they may simply choose not to hire women in the first place. They specifically point to the US as a country where women benefit from relatively limited statistical discrimination because there is no paid leave policy.[60] And their findings suggest a trend toward fewer women taking time out around childbirth—from 70 percent before 1987 to around half in the period 1988–1993 to less than 40 percent since 1993. Furthermore, American mothers return to work fairly quickly—65 percent return to work within three months and 75 percent within six months. Perhaps as a result of this, one study found that American mothers who remain in the labor force continuously do not face wage penalties.[61]

Sociologist Ann Shola Orloff describes the US as a "distinctive alternative gender regime."[62] While countless scholars have criticized the US for its lack of family policies, Orloff has claimed that "the US is a leader, not a laggard, in removing discriminatory occupational barriers."[63] She touts the US as a leader in gender equality when it comes to women's movement into management and professional jobs as well as into more "masculine" occupations.[64] Regarding parental leave, she acknowledges the highly problematic absence of paid leave. Yet she also claims the FMLA policy, with its gender-neutral language, contributes to "an understanding of caregiving needs that extends beyond mothers and children" and is "not limited by a maternalist or 'reproductionist' logic."[65] In this sense, sometimes less is more. An alternative gender regime that has fewer policies that focus more on gender neutrality may actually result in greater levels of gender equality at work and home.[66] Then again, this may be limited to women at the top. Research in the US shows no motherhood wage penalty for women with the highest wages.[67] Likewise, recent research shows no gender gap for the medium and high occupational prestige group. On the other hand, the gender gap is relatively strong for the lowest occupational prestige group, which suggests that gender equality is a white, middle/upper class privilege.[68] It appears that US policies may indeed encourage gender equality, but only for a select group.

Health Consequences

Most evidence shows that paid parental leave is beneficial for maternal health. However, public health scholar Rada Dagher and her colleagues find a non-linear pattern between time off and postpartum depression.[69] Using the Edinburgh Postnatal Depression Scale, which they claim is a better measure of postpartum depression than previous scales, they find: "on average, in the first postpartum year every additional day of leave results in a decrease in postpartum depressive symptoms until six months postpartum. After six months, the relationship reverses and every additional day of leave results in an increase in postpartum depressive symptoms."[70] In fact, figure 3.2, which illustrates their findings, shows that the predicted value of postpartum depressive symptoms at twelve months is at its lowest for those working again and at its highest for those still on leave. Shannon, a thirty-four-year-old British secretary and mother of one, talked about the importance of returning to work:

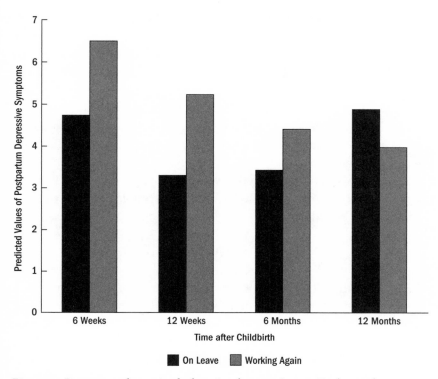

Figure 3.2. Postpartum depression by leave/work status. Source: Dagher et al., 2014; see figure 1 in this source

I was ready to go back to work. I needed something else. A lot of my friends had already started back at work. Had they still been off then it might have been different, but I felt that I needed something for me, you know, I couldn't, I didn't want everything to always be. . . . I notice you just get called Alfie's mum and I wanted my own identity back. I wanted to, I love being Alfie's mum, but I wanted to be Shannon again. Yeah, having something to come back to was important so I did want, I felt it was the right time. I don't know whether I would have, could have done it a month or so earlier, but I wouldn't want any more than that, no.

Shannon mentions the importance of getting her own identity back. Paid employment allows mothers to have an identity beyond "mother." It involves work tasks that help provide a sense of self. Social relations are also important. When mothers have other friends to socialize with while on leave, this provides much needed adult interaction. Even then, these interactions often center around their children. Returning to work allows mothers to have regular interactions with other adults about non-child-related topics.

Interestingly, a Korean study finds that women who take paid maternity leave experience more parenting stress than women who do not take leave. The researchers suggest that parenting an infant 24/7 may be more stressful than combining work and family.[71] This is consistent with Arlie Hochschild's notion that work can be a "break" from family.[72] Certainly working mothers may find support from interacting with co-workers or other adults.

Child Development

Generally, parental leave has a positive impact on child development. However, even in this area, there may be such a thing as too much parental leave. A Canadian study of kindergarteners found that parental leave of six to twelve months resulted in the best child outcomes. For example, kindergarteners whose parents took six to twelve months of parental leave scored higher on physical health, social competence, and communication than those whose parents took shorter or longer leaves. This pattern seemed to hold for girls and boys.[73]

Negative Impacts on Men

While most research has focused on the potential benefits and drawbacks of parental leave for women's employment and careers, men who take parental leave also face consequences. In fact, some research suggests that the negative association between length of parental leave and wage penalty is greater for men than for women.[74] Researchers have proposed that this pattern is due to a signaling effect:

> One might view the outcome as one in which men who are highly committed to their careers find it worthwhile to take little or no parental leave, while less committed men find it less costly to take time out. Employers, recognizing the correlation between men's leave-taking behavior

and their degree of career commitment, respond by penalizing those who take significant parental leave. The situation for women is quite different. Because the financial incentives to take one's legal entitlement of parental leave are so strong and because women have traditionally been the ones to take leave, virtually all Swedish women take substantial time off in conjunction with childbirth. Consequently, their leave-taking behavior cannot signal anything to their employers.[75]

Women taking parental leave is considered within the norm. We expect new mothers to take time off and perhaps to return part-time or not at all. But we do not (yet) expect the same from new fathers. Because men who take parental leaves (or, in the Swedish case, extra-long leaves) are not typical, they stand out. Basically, employers notice these men more. They then face judgments similar to the ones women have faced. If a man is an engaged father who takes time off, he is assumed to be less committed to work.[76] In fact, men who request family leave or quit work for family reasons face a "flexibility stigma" in which they are seen as more feminine and consequently earn less.[77] This goes back to our ideas about ideal workers being those who do not have any other commitments beyond work.[78] Julian, an American father, illustrates how these notions affect men's reasoning regarding employer's responses to men taking leave:

> I think the hard thing is and I don't know if its regulate-able or not if, like, even though, like, federally, technically, like, legally you have that time, your employer—even though it's, like, allowed it's not really allowed. So how do you really differentiate that and how do you kind of regulate that to say "hey, legally I have six weeks and I'm taking the full six weeks because I want to and I want to spend time at home with my family" and how do I do that and come back and not really be, like, you know, throwing myself under the bus wherever I work at, whomever it is. You know, I feel like it's more socially acceptable for that to happen with women than it is per se for men. And it's like it's there and it's available, but if you're not really comfortable using it then what's the purpose of it?

In this case, Julian is referring to the legally mandated California Paid Family Leave. Even though the law is gender-neutral, he points to the different view of women versus men taking parental leave. Indeed, an early study using data from Swedish company employment records estimated the earnings penalty to be 1.7 percent for women and 5.2 percent for men who took one year of leave.[79]

Studies from Sweden and Norway suggest that parental leave reforms, and particularly daddy quotas, may have a negative impact on fathers' earnings.[80] Norwegian labor economists Mari Rege and Ingeborg Solli examined the effect of the 1993 reform that introduced a four-week paternity leave quota in Norway.[81] Using registry data on fathers throughout the period 1992–2000, they found that "fathers, on average, earn 1 percent to 3 percent less as a direct consequence of the paternity-leave quota."[82] This effect continues through the study observation window or until the participant's child is five years old. Rege and Solli suggest three potential mechanisms for the decline in earnings. The first possibility is that fathers experience human-capital depreciation while on leave. They dismiss this explanation, since they find it unlikely that four weeks out of work, when they are not building work experience, would affect earnings over four years later. The second possibility is that fathers on paternity leave send a signal to their employers that they are more devoted to their family than their career and thus less committed, reliable workers. However, Rege and Solli also dismiss this explanation because of the extremely high uptake of paternity leave within the first few years of the reform. In other words, most fathers take the daddy quota so it would be hard to draw conclusions about work commitment based on uptake. The third possibility, and the one Rege and Solli find most plausible, is that fathers who take paternity leave become more involved fathers. Once leave is over, they may shift more of their time and effort to raising their child, which would result in lower earnings. So basically lower income is due to fathers choosing family over work.

This may be a self-fulfilling prophecy of sorts. A recent longitudinal study finds that men who expect that a longer leave would be associated with a forfeiture of qualifications or problematic due to trouble keeping up with the constantly changing work environment plan ahead of time to take shorter parental leave. Furthermore, those who have high leadership responsibility at their job are less likely to follow through in the event that they plan a longer leave than those with low leadership responsibility.[83] Managers are less likely to take leave than those not in managerial positions.[84] It may be that men in leadership positions do not see parental leave as a right as much as an indulgence when work allows. For those who feel that work demands are high, they may feel the expectations are for them to forego or take less leave.[85]

Other research suggests that men may be aware of the detrimental effects of long leaves, and this may in turn affect their decisions about leave. Swedish men who show a greater orientation to the economic dimension of work (salary and security) are less likely to take long leaves (twenty weeks or more). These men may be more aware of the economic costs of long parental leave. Since wage replacement is not 100 percent (it is about 80 percent) and men have higher incomes than women on average, there is greater potential for income loss among men.[86] In addition, these men may be more aware of the potential signaling effect and realize that their employers and supervisors will see them as less committed to work if they take parental leave.[87]

Labor economist Elly-Ann Johansson used longitudinal data to compare the effects of spouses' parental leave on earnings. She found that parental leave led to a decrease in future earnings for both spouses.[88] However, each month of parental leave was associated with 7.5 percent lower earnings for men compared to 4.5 percent lower earnings for women. Other research shows similarities in the penalty but differences in timing. Marie Evertsson followed Swedish parents from two years before to eight years after the birth of their first child.[89] She found that highly educated men and women both experience negative effects of parental leave on wages. When comparing the effects of twenty weeks of parental leave, the wage penalty was 0.6 percent for both women and men. However, Evertsson found gender differences in the effect of the amount of leave. Women's wage penalty works in a linear pattern—more parental leave results in greater wage penalties. For men, the wage penalty occurs quickly even with short leaves and does not increase much over time. So basically the bad news is that employers are judging fathers for taking any leave at all (they are not making less because their human capital has depreciated but because employers think fathers who take leave are not as committed to work). The good news is that the effect on women and men is similar, which is an indication of greater gender equality. Also, Evertsson suggests that given the minimal change in negative effect on men's wages, it makes sense for men to take more leave and to share it with their partners.

Conclusion

This chapter has examined some of the negative consequences for women and men of long parental leaves. Women who take long leaves risk long-term absences from the labor force. Even those who return to employment face reduced opportunities for advancement and lower pay. Contrasting the cases of Hungary and the US shows that very long leaves can result in severe limitations for women's success while the absence of leave may have a small silver lining. While career penalties seem to dominant discussions of the consequences of long leaves for women, there are also potential health risks, with women who take longer leave facing higher levels of stress and depression. Finally, men are not immune to the negative effects of long leaves. Particularly because men are expected to take shorter leaves compared to women, those who take leave often face backlash at work. The answer is not to have no leave but to consider a moderate amount of leave for both parents. Much of the negative impact of long parental leave may be due to the unequal division of parental leave and gendered expectations regarding women and men at home and at work. The next chapter focuses on the role of fathers as partners.

4

Fathers as Partners, Not Helpers

"Dads don't babysit (it's called 'parenting')."

This slogan, popularized by the US-based National At-Home Dad Network and now emblazoned on t-shirts, calls out the gendered language we often still use to talk about fathers. Babysitters are temporary caregivers who step in to help out the parents. But the fact is that fathers are spending more time with their children than ever before. In fact, American fathers today spend 65 percent more time with their children during the typical workday than they did thirty years ago.[1] According to the 2016 National Study of the Changing Workforce, about half of fathers in heterosexual relationships say they share caregiving responsibilities equally or take on a greater share of caregiving than their partner (about one-third of mothers say their partner shares or does more).[2]

This chapter examines gendered aspects of parental leave. While almost all parents who stay home with an infant for a period of time acknowledge how much work it is, suggesting that parenting has a learning curve, parental leave is often seen as a mother-centered activity. Much of the gendering is seen as natural, with an emphasis on breastfeeding and mothers as nurturers. The counterpart to this narrative is that fathers are seen as helpers or secondary parents. We know, however, that fathers who take leave and spend longer periods of time caring for children are highly capable of being equal partners and parents.

Leave Is Hard Work

"It was incredibly hectic and stressful and sleep-deprived, and of course, awesome at the same time. It didn't feel like time off, as all new parents know."
—Rufus, US father, age 37

Before getting into the gender dynamics of leave, it is important to note that almost all new parents talk about early days with their new child as a blur. American father Dante, age thirty-two, described the experience: "It was kind of a big blur because all the days intertwined. There wasn't really much sleeping. You have to wake the baby up every couple hours to feed, change diapers, prep any bottles or food. Everything just kind of mushed into one big day." On the other side of the ocean, British father Ishan provided a similar description:

> It's just a blur. It's just a complete blur. Because there's no set hours. He's getting up any time of day and night and you just . . . People are coming visiting obviously, which is what they do. You can't kind of remember having a conversation with them or anything like that. It's almost like you're just kind of sucked out of the world and you have no idea as to what's going on around you. But it just went so fast but felt so long. It's so weird. It's really, I can't, yeah, it was just bizarre. Everything is just focused around this little baby and nothing else. Yeah, it's probably the way to describe it, it's just the most shortest and the quickest time.

While Ishan took off three weeks of leave, a little more than average for British fathers, he aptly calls this time "the most shortest and the quickest time" in his attempt to capture his sense of fuzziness as it seemed a whirlwind of visitors in the midst of sleep deprivation. Another British father, James, who took off two weeks of leave, also expressed his feelings:

> The first two weeks at home. It was obviously a massive, a big change for us, to have somebody dependent on you for everything and to not get to. It was a little bit easier being off and being at home all day than it has been since I've come back to work. But those first two weeks were kind of very much a change in mindset and a change in routine and a change in pretty much everything, really. To have somebody dependent on you, like, say, all that time, it was difficult because we were trying to work out between the two of us as well how we would . . . It was quite easy during the first two weeks because we would just, we would both be up at the same time because we both wanted to kind of almost experience it in a way. And that was, that was okay. That was fine. But I don't know, it was, it kind of went with a bit of a blur really. It was very quick and it was very kind of hard

because you'd got a lack of sleep and you were kind of all your, you felt like
all your emotions were kind of a bit all over the place

The theme of lack of sleep is certainly repetitive, but James also touches
on this new sense of responsibility. The realization that his infant was
completely dependent on him and his wife was an awesome reality.
James also alludes to the fact that sharing this responsibility and the
care for their child was much easier when both he and his wife were
at home. Of course this was short-lived as James, like most British
fathers, returned to work after two weeks. Similarly, American father
Amos, a firefighter who took three weeks of leave, talked about changes
in responsibility and his role while at home: "It was a lot of worrying,
watching her sleep, making sure breathing was okay. Just real worried
about SIDS, worried about anything and everything. Her first couple of
weeks, there was almost no sleep." Amos talked about lack of sleep both
because his new daughter woke up every hour or two and because he
often watched her sleep. Many first-time fathers were surprised by how
hard paternity leave was. Kye, for example, a thirty-year-old American
father who took five weeks of leave, confided:

> I remember thinking up to it was going to be great. I'm going to be off for
> a month. I've never been off that long from work. And when I went back,
> I'm not going to say I was happy to be back, but the break wasn't at all
> what I thought it would be because I felt like even though I wasn't work-
> ing, I was still working. It was a different type of time off.

Kye's realization that parental leave was work reflects what many mothers have known all along. Parenting is a form of labor, one that is not
generally recognized or monetarily rewarded.

Mother-Centered Parental Leave

In my research on the UK, and to some extent in the US, a prominent
finding was the assumption that parental leave belongs to mothers. This
came up in interviews with mothers as well as with fathers. Both British
fathers and mothers place greater weight on women's needs and wishes
regarding parental leave, suggesting that mothers remain the primary

caregivers and fathers the secondary caregivers.[3] Mothers generally indicated that decisions regarding parental leave, particularly how much time to take, were up to them, and that their partners supported their decisions. For example, Amy, a forty-two-year-old manager who took the full twelve months, said: "He didn't care to be honest. He said as long as we can afford it do whatever you want." Likewise, Emma, a thirty-year-old administrative assistant, said she and her husband did not talk much about how much maternity leave she would take:

> Well, I don't know if we particularly discussed it as a couple. I think he's pretty much happy for me to do whatever I want, feel happy doing, and so you just kind of got on with it. I didn't want to take, I wanted to take as much as I could but after nine months it goes to no pay so we didn't want to live on no, just one wage so I stopped it after the nine months. But we didn't really have much, a great deal of discussion about it.

While there was some consideration of finances, Emma took nine months of maternity leave, which meant that several months were at a low pay rate. British mothers do not face the same pressures to be financial providers as British fathers do.[4] Paige, a thirty-two-year-old research associate, seemed to have a bit more discussion with her husband but still directed the conversation:

> He was very sort of amenable. We just sort of sat down, talked about it and just, because I suppose if I didn't feel ready then it was probably going to cause more arguments in the long run anyway, so, yeah, he didn't have any issues with it. He agreed sort of on the timing of it. And I think financially it was okay as well.

Paige took seven months of maternity leave in order to balance time with her newborn and still be able to return to work in order to carry on with her research agenda. Chloe, a thirty-three-year-old mother of one, explained how she and her husband came to the decision that she would take the full twelve months of maternity leave:

> We sort of felt that we'd probably be able to cope with doing the twelve months because we are deemed as, in our NCT group, as the readers and

we had read that the more time off that the mother can take to be with the child then the better, so that's what kind of instigated us to say, yes, let's go for the year.

The NCT is the National Childbirth Trust, a charity that supports parents through pregnancy, childbirth, and early parenthood, not only by distributing information but also by creating local networks, which often continue meeting after childbirth as mothers' groups. While this couple is highly educated, earn similar incomes, and strive to share parenting, they thought it would be best if the mother stayed home for a year while the father took off three weeks.

Mothers generally take more leave than fathers even when they make more money. This suggests that gendered ideals are strongly influential in maternity and paternity leave decisions. Lauren, a thirty-one-year-old mother of two, provides a good example of how gender can trump money. She recalls sticking to the original plan for her to take twelve months' maternity and her partner to take two weeks' paternity:

> I said, yep, I'll definitely be having twelve months off, unless something changes. And then my husband's job was reduced from full-time to three days a week. They went onto short time working because they were running out of work, and it was when all the building work started to dry up. Because that was drying up there was no electric work. But it was very lucky. My parents had a lot of work that they wanted doing so my dad paid him to do that and cash in hand so we were very, you know . . . We have been very fortunate.

As a senior advisor in her HR department, Lauren made more money than her husband before his hours were reduced and yet she continued her maternity leave for the full year even when her husband experienced problems at work and could have been available to care for their newborn and older child. It is unclear how they came to this decision given his involvement when on leave as an "active nappy changer" and more recently as the parent who routinely drops and picks up the children at nursery and school, fixes them food, bathes them, and engages in other household routines. In these cases, mothers' employment had little influence on fathers' leave decisions.[5]

Many of the fathers agreed that the decision was largely, or ultimately, left up to their partners, confirming the maternalistic orientation of the policy.[6] When asked how he and his partner decided how much leave she would take, Ishan, a thirty-four-year-old programming administrator and father of one, said:

> I think it's a case of how long she wanted to take and what we could afford. And we kind of worked it all out and everything that we needed to and the practicalities of it. And I think she was quite pleased to have a year out. I mean, I wouldn't say she was naïve about what it would entail, but there was kind of like a thought that it was going to be nice being away from work for a year and everything like that, almost like it would be a holiday. I'm probably selling her a bit short there, you know, not quite to that extreme, but I do think there was an element of that there. And yeah, I'll be honest. I thought that as well.

Ishan's wife took the full year of maternity leave, and his initial statement indicates that he felt this decision was up to her as long as they could afford it. Indeed, Ishan initially took a fairly casual view of maternity leave, as he agreed with his wife's expectation that it would be like "a holiday." While he did not maintain this attitude once his daughter was born, it does signal that he accepted the idea of his wife taking a year off work, much of it at low or no pay, while he only took three weeks, consistent with British patterns of gendered divisions of work and family.[7]

Mothers as Gatekeepers

In addition to taking a leading role in decisions concerning the length of maternity leave, women often have great influence on how much leave their partners take, even when the options for paternity leave are much more limited than those for maternity leave. Paige, the British research associate who took seven months of maternity leave, recalled asking her husband to take the second week of paternity leave:

> Well, I think it was a case of I was sort of saying, yes, please take them, and he was like, oh, well, I'm not sure whether I should, and I was like . . . Because I think what we, what he possibly wanted to do was to take the

first week immediately and then take the second week somewhere later on, which his work was flexible with, but I was sort of advocating for him to take them both together just because I thought, both selfishly for me, it was better for me to have him there at the beginning when we're still adjusting at that time.

Paige's husband contemplated saving his second week of paternity leave for a later time when their child would be more developed and potentially more interactive, but she talked him into taking the two weeks together at the very beginning. Paige explained that they have no family nearby and framed her pressure on her husband in terms of her own needs. Another British mother, Sita, a twenty-nine-year-old administrative assistant, relayed how her husband changed his mind about taking paternity leave:

> He wasn't going to [take paternity leave] initially but then he was like, no because then we did get to the house and everything and it was just, everything was new, and it was near Christmas time and everything, so he goes . . . Because if it snowed and the child within a few days would have to go to certain appointments and everything, you have to take them down, and because I had obviously just given birth, he goes, we don't know, and I'd had stitches and everything, he goes, no, no, I better take them off. It would just be a bit helpful with getting the child to and from the hospital or wherever.

After these considerations, Sita's husband took two weeks of paternity leave while Sita took the full year. These examples demonstrate the role of mothers as gatekeepers, which refers to instances in which mothers monitor and control how involved fathers are with their children. They also show that paternity leave is often seen not solely about fathers spending time with newborn children but also about helping mothers, so they can take on the traditionally maternal task of caring for children.[8] As gendered ideology seems to contribute to gendered differences in leave taking, leave and work decisions may also reinforce gendered ideology. The idea of mothers as "natural" experts is further strengthened when mothers stay home longer than fathers and plan to return to work part-time.[9]

Primacy of Breastfeeding and Mothers as Nurturers

Many fathers talked about their partners and the birth process as miraculous, and often saw themselves on the periphery of this incredible event. American father Iker described the following:

> [I want to] be the supporting role for my wife who's just kinda gone through this amazing experience that is really kind of indescribable, I mean you can't, you know, can't really put it into words how special it is, you know, just to see your wife go through that, the amount of pain and emotion that's all kind of involved with the birth process, so just trying to be a supporting role.

It is almost as if fathers like Iker feel the need to stand back in awe of the event. The consequence of this thinking is that it continues to affect how men see their partners and themselves. Supporting mothers' primary role as nurturer, many fathers talked about the importance of breastfeeding:

> As the father, it was a little different because that time with his mother—the whole nursing and just the nurturing aspect of being a mother, they spent a lot of time. So I was trying to be supportive and take him when I could and make dinner and clean the house and do all the little things I could while she recovered physically and also nursed and kind of took care of the health of the baby.
> —Iker, age 30, 5 days of leave

> Of course, you know, she would be the main caretaker because the baby had to be nourished and all that stuff. I was working more on the other stuff like cleaning up the bottles, arranging stuff, and occasionally you know, taking care of the baby when she needed rest. But you know, they need to be breastfed so often mostly it was my wife taking care of her.
> —Dai, age 37, 3 days of leave

Both Iker and Dai, who took five days and three days of leave, respectively, distinguish the roles of mother and father. Iker suggests he has a different role because he is the father while his wife as mother will take care of the baby. Dai suggests that it is a given that his wife would be the main caretaker for their child. They both help their wives by doing other tasks around the house, but they also make a strong connection between breastfeeding and caring for the baby as though breastfeeding means the mother will engage in all other forms of caring for their child. Likewise, Finn, a forty-seven-year-old father, says that things "just fell into place." While he helped by changing diapers, he says: "You know, mom had to feed him and take care of him because she breastfed him." While I concede the point that children who are breastfed need to be fed by their mothers (though there is also pumping and bottles), there is no reason that the person who breastfeeds automatically should be the one to be the primary caregiver. Often, this is used as an excuse.

British father Omar shared: "All my babies were breastfed so when I used to hold them and they were really small they used to cry an awful lot because they tend to sense mom because of the breast milk scent or whatever so yeah, it was just kind of helping change nappies, passing them over to mom, giving her a little bit of a rest, doing the odd bit of housework and stuff." Henry, another British father, explains: "being a man, I am unable to breastfeed so when he cries in the night it is her job and there's not much, we could give him a bottle but a lot of his reason for wanting to feed at night is for comfort so a bottle is very much second best. It's also time I think for my wife to bond more with the baby." The suggestion is that he could not comfort his son. While breastfeeding is certainly comforting, there are other forms of touch and comfort that fathers can provide as well as mothers. In the end, an emphasis on breastfeeding bolsters the idea that maternity leave is more important than paternity leave.[10]

Fathers also emphasized maternal bonding when talking about differences in maternity and paternity leave. British father Connor, who took two weeks of leave, talked about wanting more time off but not at the expense of his wife and her need to bond with their child:

> I'd always have preferred more. But it's a question of how much more because I think you have to have a . . . there has to be some time when you have a cut off, you know, the mother and child have to have more of a bonding process, I think, than necessarily the father and child because of what they've gone through for the previous nine months, you know, there has to be that. So I don't necessarily see the paternity/maternity leave

should be at the same level. I think another week or two would have been absolutely, would have been fantastic. But then you get to a point where I don't know, there's not much you can necessarily do, if that makes sense.

Connor explicitly says that paternity leave does not need to be the same length as maternity leave. Ishan, the programming administrator who took three weeks to his wife's twelve months, recounted: "I thought [my wife] was going to have another eleven to twelve months of this on her own so she needs to kind of just work it out and get on with it . . . There's nothing I could do, but I also knew that [she]'s got to get on with things and learn how to work things out." As sociologist Michelle Brady and colleagues note, fathers who emphasize a "physiology-focused" discourse tend to see themselves at a disadvantage in early bonding in comparison to mothers.[11] When fathers think mothers are more naturally suited to caring for infants, they are less likely to take parental leave or, when they do, to take shorter leave.[12] On the other hand, fathers who have a more egalitarian outlook, including beliefs in equal parenting, take longer leaves, and men respond to their partner taking shorter leave by taking more leave.[13]

Fathers as Helpers

Many British and American parents explicitly showed gendered expectations when they talked about maternity versus paternity leave. Fathers often thought they were less prepared or less able to engage in early bonding compared to mothers.[14] The sense that mothers were "natural" experts or that maternal bonding was more important than paternal bonding often meant that fathers saw their decisions to take less leave while their wife took more leave as being supportive partners.[15] Mothers, too, felt some resistance to increasing paternity leave if it would result in less maternity leave.[16] In this sense, both mothers and fathers "fell back" into gendered roles that emphasized the naturalness or ease of caring for mothers and earning for fathers.[17] Dominic, an American father who took five days of leave, labels himself as the helper:

When I was home it was, it was the first week. So a lot of it was being, doing the—it wasn't so much divided, it was more of me being the helper where [my wife] was mostly in bed and so I was just getting what she would need or even get [the baby] out of the bassinet and carry her to [my wife]. So just trying to make it as easy as possible with her during that time.

Levi, an American father who took only three days of leave, echoed this idea: "It was more of what she needs in the supportive role. If she needed a nap break . . . I'll be quiet and take care of the rest of the house. I'll be her supporting role wherever she needed." Iker, an American father who took one week of leave, told me that he felt "kind of helpless" because "the child's so dependent on the mother and just the physical nature of being a mother and giving birth." As such he viewed himself as taking on a "supporting role" in which he would do other household tasks and fill in the gaps where it was needed.

Finn, an American father who took two weeks, wished he had taken more time off. He talked about the benefits of being home: "Mom doesn't feel as overwhelmed. She feels like she's got a backup. I think that's big. My wife often says I don't think I could do all this without you. So that's a nice compliment. I feel like I'm doing the right thing." He feels good about doing the right thing—being backup for his wife—but this ultimately places the bulk of caregiving on his wife. Being a good father may also be framed as supporting the mother's leave as much as possible.[18] Interestingly, Gael, an American father who took off several weeks when his baby had some health issues, looked into the policy at his workplace because of his need for extra leave. He expressed surprise at what he found:

It was my impression that both the male and the female got six weeks of paid parental leave, and I—I was wrong. I found out through the process from my HR department that while the mom does get six weeks of paid maternity leave, the father only gets two weeks of paid paternity leave. The idea is that . . . that's what they need as medically necessary. It has nothing to do with the baby apparently. My two weeks are to take care of my wife . . . so I found it really interesting that it had nothing to do with the baby.

Gael had assumed that parental leave was equal for men and women because he thought the purpose of leave was to care for a new baby. That turned out not to be the case and even more surprisingly, his two weeks of leave was to care for his wife and not explicitly their baby.

The idea that fathers are helpers or secondary parents also arose when mothers talked about fathers returning to work after paternity leave. In the case of Amy, a British development manager who took twelve months of maternity leave, there was a sense that her husband was in the way. When asked about the possibility of her husband taking more leave, Amy responded: "Well, he probably would have taken all of his annual leave, but I didn't particularly feel the need to have him around. And the baby wouldn't settle with him anyway." While Amy's tone was a bit more dismissive than others, the idea that a father's return to work was welcome was more common than expected. Lauren, a British HR manager, confessed: "I think by the end of the two weeks I was ready for him to go back to work because he was just . . . I guess you're trying to find your feet in a routine with a new baby." These attitudes are consistent with mothers' resistance to increasing paternity leave if it means decreasing maternity leave.[19] Tex, an American oil worker, relayed this: "She's used to me being gone all the time and used to doing stuff by herself, so it was really up to her. Probably about the fourth or fifth day, I asked her: 'do you want me to stay here? Or what do you need?' and like probably about six days in, she was like: 'you can go back to work,' so, yeah." Men's decisions about returning to work often included reference to their partners. American father Elias relates: "I wanted enough time to be here to support my wife—to make sure she was feeling good before I went back to work. I didn't want to go back before she wasn't feeling in a good schedule, in a good routine with the baby." In all these cases, fathers act as helpers to ensure their partners—the mothers—are ready to take care of their babies on their own because the assumption is that fathers go back to work while mothers stay home and not vice versa.

Fathers Taking Leave, Fathers as (Equal) Parents

Prominent sociologist and gender scholar Barbara Risman posed the question of whether men can "mother" back in 1986. In her study of single fathers, Risman found that "mothering" is not limited to females. Instead, men without wives were able to respond to the situational demands of being single fathers and in fact responded with "strategies stereotypically considered feminine."[20] Risman also compared single fathers to single mothers and married parents and found that single fathers' parenting behavior is more similar to mothers than to married fathers.[21] An important point is that the structure of the situation matters. Even fathers who have not chosen to parent alone but find themselves in that situation become capable parents. Other research suggests that individuals learn how to parent "on the job."[22] Since Risman's classic study, other researchers have found that single fathers and stay-at-home fathers—those who engage in primary caregiving—are completely capable of responsible parenting.

Noted Canadian scholar Andrea Doucet returns to Risman's question in her book, *Do Men Mother?*[23] While her answer is not a definitive yes (she comes down somewhere in the middle, between difference feminism and equality feminism), she does find evidence that stay-at-home fathers are highly competent parents and that spending more time at home and in child-centered communities encourages fathers to cross borders and challenge gender binaries. Doucet also acknowledges that fathers need not be exactly like mothers to be good parents and caregivers. But time spent in direct and sole caregiving is crucial for developing parental skills.[24] Stay-at-home dads have similarly high levels of parental self-efficacy compared to mothers. Perhaps this partially explains the relatively high levels of relationship and life satisfaction among stay-at-home fathers relative to other men.[25]

A study using the American Time Use Survey found that single fathers spend similar amounts of time in primary caregiving and being accessible when their youngest child is six to fourteen years old as single mothers and married mothers (though less time when their youngest child is under six, but still more time than married fathers).[26] My previous research on single fathers in *Superdads* along with Roberta Coles' book, *The Best Kept Secret*, on single black fathers, show numerous examples of single fathers consciously choosing to take on a more active role and putting in the time to parent the best way they can.[27]

Sociologist Erin Rehel looks more specifically at fathers on paternity or parental leave in Chicago, Toronto, and Montreal. She finds: "The availability of an extended period of parental leave allows fathers the opportunity to gain a sense of the 'concerns' of parenting, many of which are invisible and therefore might go unnoticed by a father who is back at work . . . By sharing more than just tasks, partners become more equal co-parents than when one partner manages and delegates child care and related domestic labor."²⁸ Similar to Risman, Rehel argues that structure is important. Men need to be free of workplace responsibilities in the same way that women on maternity leave are. This is unlikely to happen in a one to two-week period. Rather, more extended leave time allows fathers to gain hands-on experience, which "challenges the perceived naturalness of women's superior parenting capabilities" and enables men "to move from the helper role to that of co-parent."²⁹ This theme comes up over and over again in varied country case studies of fathers on leave alone.³⁰

Daniel, a thirty-three-year-old British father, illustrates the benefits of fathers taking long leaves. He used the British Additional Paternity Leave policy to take three months of leave with his son after his wife returned to work. Daniel relays the following:

> I think, with hindsight, I think I'm very glad I did it. I think it really, had I not ever taken some time by myself with [my son] I think we would have had a very different relationship in the family than we do. I think both in terms of how happy we both are to do stuff, we have a very even distribution of parenting, but also [our son is] equally happy with either of us and I've seen other families where it's always been the mom and dad are very differently defined roles and if I know [my wife is] trying to arrange a night out in a few weeks with some of her friends, and some of the moms who their kids are eighteen months old and they're saying, well, I don't think I can really leave them with my husband for longer than a few hours because he's still not that, you know, he's never looked after them, and we don't have that kind of thing which I think is definitely a good thing, and also I get on really well with [my son]. I think I have a relationship with him that I wouldn't have had otherwise.

Daniel is clear that taking a long leave and spending time at home alone with his son changed their relationship in a very positive way. He feels more confident about his caregiving skills and is more in tune with his son's needs. He pities other families in which fathers are not capable of looking after their children because they simply have not had the experience. Most of all, he is proud that his son is "equally happy" with him and his wife. Daniel's story can be contrasted with that of James, who took the typical two weeks allotted to British fathers. James shows signs of regret regarding his decision: "now I find it really difficult in coming home and [my daughter] reacts differently to my wife than she does to me. . . . But that's only really been a thought since she's been born and she reacts slightly differently to me than she does to my wife. But that's because my wife's at home with her all day. She's the one that has that time with her." James is not alone. Other fathers regret not taking more time off, not being there for certain moments in their child's life, and not spending enough time in general. Expectations for fathers have changed, and most men do want to be more involved, so when they are not, they are more attentive to the differences in how they relate to their children, as is the case with James. But there are signs of progress and men like Daniel show that fathers can be equal parents.

This is even more apparent in the Swedish case, where many parents describe sharing parental leave as "self-evident." When asked about sharing leave equally, Astrid says: "this is how you do it" while Tom claims: "it's only oddballs and old-fashioned people who do not take daddy leave." Fathers emphasize the importance of spending time with their child, developing a strong relationship, and becoming a parent. For example, Danjel, a thirty-six-year-old shop assistant, says: "I learned to be a parent then, because I was fully responsible. You can be a provider without staying home with your child, but it's difficult to be a parent." Johan, an engineer, elaborates: "it's one thing to know and get it explained for you what a full day looks like, to experience it yourself." In other words, parenting is something you learn by doing, starting with parental leave. This ideology and the policies that make this possible are the focus of chapter 6.

Conclusion

There are some common experiences that mothers and fathers have when they are on leave with young children, and this includes being oriented around an infant whose needs must come first, which almost always results in a serious lack of sleep. At the same time, many parents talk about parental leave as mother-centered. Both fathers and mothers leave decisions about parental leave to mothers and often see maternal bonding as more important than paternal bonding. Naturalized views of parenting are encouraged by an emphasis on breastfeeding, which is often used as an excuse for mothers to take on all or most parenting tasks. This also feeds into the notion that fathers are mainly helpers and their time on leave is important to take care of their partners so that their partners can take care of their babies. While these narratives are still common, there are examples of fathers taking extended leave and making efforts to be equal partners. In these cases, it is clear that fathers can be good parents and partners. What lessons can we learn from the UK and Sweden? The next two chapters consider the development of parental leave policies in these countries and their potential impact on gender equality.

5

The UK Is Not a Good Model

I think in Britain certainly, not so much in [the public sec-
tor] but certainly in private sector, you hear stories of people
saying they don't want to hire women in their twenties into
that position because she's going to have a lot of time off. If
fathers were equally likely to have the time off then it would
be a case of, what are you going to do.
—Daniel, age 33, British father

Daniel, a married father of one child, seems to be an exception in the
United Kingdom. He was an early adopter of the new paternity leave
policy. He and his wife had the same education and training, and held
similar positions in two different organizations. They worked similar
hours and had similar career aspirations. And when they talked about
having a child, they talked about splitting leave and parenting as equally
as possible. In fact, the introduction of the Additional Paternity Leave
policy prompted them to move from talking about having a baby to
actually having a baby. While they initially intended to equally split the
nine months of leave available to them with at least partial pay, Daniel
ended up taking three months of paternity leave following his wife's six
months of maternity leave. Daniel was adamant that attitudes and policy
need to change. In his social circle, filled with highly educated men, he
was still an anomaly for taking so much paternity leave. He shared this:
"attitudes are not changing, you know, people don't think, people still
think it's unusual for fathers to take significant amounts of time off and
I think until it's equally likely that having a kid means either a mother
or father are going to be away from work that will always disadvantage
women career-wise."

When I went to the UK back in 2012 to study its newest parental
leave policy, Additional Paternity Leave, I went with high expectations.
I figured it was extremely unlikely that the US was going to adopt the

Swedish system of parental leave, but that there might yet be hope of adopting the British system. After all, we share so much in common—language, capitalism, Protestant influence, much music and popular culture. Here was a country with similar neoliberal ideology and they were saying, with their policy, that it was important to include fathers in plans for raising children. Fast forward a few years, and a couple of policy changes later, and I no longer really think this way. In fact, I think we should avoid the British pathway, and not just because of Brexit. On first glance, it looks pretty great for women, especially compared to the situation in the US. But there are some serious negative consequences of this type of policy.

There is still strong support in the UK for the male-as-full-time-breadwinner and female-as-part-time-carer model.[1] This is evident in the high frequency of full-time/part-time family households in the UK.[2] Further, British fathers' work hours are relatively long compared to fathers' hours in other developed countries,[3] perhaps due to the pressures on men to work longer hours to compensate for women's shorter hours and provide financially for their families.[4] And while it has become more difficult for British families to get by with a single earner,[5] the gendered division of labor persists as British fathers continue to work long hours with little increase in household work.[6] The UK has thus shifted to a one-and-a-half earner model, where men generally work full-time and women part-time. According to the Office of National Statistics, 70.8 percent of British women and 79.9 percent of British men aged sixteen to sixty-four years are employed. UK women have among the highest rates of part-time employment, with about 42 percent of women working part-time.[7] This can be compared to the OECD average of 25.8 percent.[8] One study found that British mothers are eight times more likely to work part-time than British women without children (the difference between mothers and non-mothers is much higher in the UK than in countries such as Finland, Denmark, and France).[9] On the other hand, full-time employment is particularly low, with less than 20 percent of British mothers working full-time.[10]

An astounding 44 percent of British mothers experience work interruptions for more than four years. Danish sociologist Anders Ejrnæs suggests that it is "the low level of paid leave and poor childcare provision" that "force a high proportion of British mothers to interrupt their employment for a long period and to engage in full-time caring in the childrearing years."[11] Perhaps as a result, the motherhood wage penalty, while present pretty much everywhere, is particularly heavy in Great Britain, both between mothers and fathers and between mothers and women without children.[12]

In this chapter, I review the UK's parental leave policy, including the development of maternity leave, the development of paternity leave, and efforts to shift to shared parental leave. I also consider workplace contexts and structures that continue to encourage women but not men to take leave. These gender distinctions are also reproduced in the gendering of family roles and the ideology that says leave belongs to mothers. Finally, I consider the policy limitations of current British parental leave policy.

What Is the Policy?

British parental leave policies lagged behind the rest of Europe through the 1980s and into the 1990s. Indeed, the UK was at the bottom of a list of Western European countries in a classification of father-friendly legislation in 1997.[13] Before 1999 and the rise of New Labour, maternity leave was spotty at best, varying from company to company. Laws did not necessarily protect, let alone benefit, pregnant women and mothers. Women were commonly made redundant (the British word for fired) for becoming pregnant or having children. Throughout the twentieth century, the UK was pretty flagrant about disregarding European trends in employment and parental leave policies and even blocked a Euro Commission draft directive that would have required a minimum standard for parental leave.[14] When they did follow directives, the UK generally went with the minimum requirements.[15] With New Labour coming into power in 1997, policies shifted to become more focused on family needs.[16] However, there appear to be long-lasting effects of the long period of lengthy maternity leave paired with limited paternity leave: "the legacy of a long mother-centred leave has been resilient and to some extent has hindered design innovation in the UK."[17] In fact, sociologist Karin Wall characterized the UK policy as a "short leave part-time mother policy model," which is on the lower end of European leave policy models.[18]

Development of Maternity Leave

The UK has the longest maternity leave compared to all other OECD countries. It offers a full year. But this statistic is not unproblematic. First, the pay is very low. While the first six weeks are paid at 90 percent of earnings uncapped, the following thirty-three weeks are paid at 90 percent of weekly earnings up to a maximum of £145 per week, and the last thirteen weeks are unpaid. According to the OECD, with the exception of the US (which has no paid leave), the UK has the lowest average payment rate across weeks of paid maternity leave, at around 30 percent.[19] Second, when access to parental leave is combined with maternity leave, the UK drops to near the bottom rank of the OECD countries (only Mexico, Switzerland, and the US are below the UK with no additional parental leave).[20] This is because the UK places all its eggs in the maternity leave basket, so to speak.

In 1975, the Employment Protection Act was the first legislation to include protections for pregnant women and maternity leave. Pregnant women could not be fired because of their pregnancy, and some employed women were also entitled to job-protected maternity leave. This included the right to eleven weeks of leave before childbirth and twenty-nine weeks after childbirth. However, it only included eighteen weeks of pay, with 90 percent of wages for six weeks and a low flat rate for twelve weeks. In addition, only about half of employed women were covered since eligibility required two or more years of full-time work or five years of part-time work. It wasn't until 1994 that this was extended to all employed women, in compliance with a European Commission Directive.[21]

When Labour was elected in 1997, increasing attention was given to maternity leave (as well as to paternity and parental leave). While efforts were made to introduce and encourage paternity leave, there was also concern about protecting maternity leave. In 1999, paid maternity leave was extended from fourteen to eighteen weeks and unpaid parental leave of thirteen weeks per parent was introduced. In Labour's first term, maternity leave was extended from nine to twelve months, while in the party's second term, maternity pay was extended from six to nine months.[22]

The current policy allows for fifty-two weeks of Statutory Maternity Leave, with the first twenty-six weeks being Ordinary Maternity Leave and the last twenty-six being Additional Maternity Leave. Mothers do not have to take the full fifty-two weeks, but they are *required* to take at least two weeks directly after their child is born (and at least four weeks if they work in a factory). While women are allowed to begin their maternity leave as early as eleven weeks before their due date, maternity leave automatically kicks in if a female employee takes off work due to a pregnancy-related illness in the four weeks before the due date or if she gives birth early. All female employees qualify for Statutory Maternity Leave regardless of their length of employment, hours worked, or pay. However, in order to receive Statutory Maternity Pay, female employees must earn at least £116 per week and have worked continuously for their employer for at least six months leading up to the "qualifying week," which is the fifteenth week before the due date. Employees taking maternity leave can change their return date but must provide at least eight weeks' notice to their employer. Employment rights, including job protection, pay increases, and accrual of holiday, are protected while on maternity leave. It is important to note that the UK still uses the term "maternity leave." Marian Baird and Margaret O'Brien note that "leave terms are cultural, and increasingly political, markers of policy intent."[23]

Development of Paternity Leave

When it comes to paternity leave, the UK is not the worst, but it is below average. With two weeks of paid paternity leave and eighteen weeks of unpaid parental leave, the UK blends in. However, the short two-week period of paid leave has an average payment rate at the bottom of the OECD countries with paid paternity leave.[24]

Social policy scholar Majella Kilkey aptly refers to the role of fathers in three phases of work-family policy development: "ambivalence towards fathers" (1998–1999), "the naming of fathers" (2000–2002), and "new opportunities for fathers" (2003–2005).[25] In 1999, unpaid parental leave of thirteen weeks per parent was introduced. While this policy was gender-neutral, it is often suggested that this policy reflected ambivalence towards fathers since there was not specific mention of paternity leave.[26] Fathers were explicitly written into policy with the introduction of paid statutory paternity leave in 2001. This type of leave, called Ordinary Paternity Leave (OPL), allowed fathers to take up to two weeks of leave paid at a flat rate. The leave could not start before the birth of the child, had to be taken at one time, and had to be taken within eight weeks of the birth. While fathers were explicitly named, expectations remained low and uneven. During this period, paid maternity leave was further extended from eighteen to twenty-six weeks and then from twenty-six to fifty-two weeks. By 2003, fathers' leave rights were only a fraction of mothers' leave rights, at fifteen weeks for fathers (combining two weeks of paternity and thirteen weeks of parental) and sixty-five weeks for mothers (combining fifty-two weeks of maternity and thirteen weeks of parental).[27] Mary Daly, a prominent sociologist writing on gender and the welfare state, asserts that the New Labour family policies that extended maternity leave and introduced paternity leave, while appearing to make substantial changes, also continued more conservative ideologies that emphasize a maternalist orientation, with family (read: mother) as the main care provider.[28] These policies were in alignment with the strong emphasis on the male breadwinner model in the UK[29] and did little to challenge the assumption of mothers as primary caregivers.[30] Indeed, at this point, maternity leave in the UK was well ahead of other European countries while paternity leave continued to lag behind,[31] falling in the bottom half of Ray, Gornick, and Schmitt's index of gender equality in parental leave.[32]

The current paternity leave policy in the UK offers one or two weeks of paid leave for fathers and partners for childbirth, adoption, or surrogacy of a child. While this is a very limited time, the policy requires fathers to use the leave all at once. Paternity leave cannot start before the birth and must be taken within fifty-six days of the birth. There is provision for time off for two prenatal or adoption appointments. Employees must notify their employers of their desire to take leave at least fifteen weeks before the baby's due date, known as the "qualifying week." At this time, employees need to provide information on the due date, whether they want one or two weeks of leave, and when they want to start their leave (this can be a general time frame, such as the day of the birth). In order to be eligible for paternity leave, employees have to have worked for the same employer for at least twenty-six weeks by the qualifying week. In addition to the required period of work, employees must be employed up to the birth date and earn a minimum of £116 per week in order to be eligible for paternity pay. Paternity pay is the same as maternity pay (following the six-week high-pay period), which is the lower of £145 or 90 percent of average weekly earnings. As with maternity leave, there are employment protections for returning to work, pay raises, and holiday time. Employment law expert Jamie Atkinson asserts that "there is a clear disparity between the ideal of the 'involved' or 'caring' father and the policies that have been presented to fathers."[33]

Efforts to Shift to Shared Parental Leave

British policy objectives have shifted over time. Initial parental leave policies aimed to increase women's labor force participation and reduce the number of children in poverty. As early as 2005, New Labour discussed plans to offer transferable leave, allowing mothers to transfer some portion of their maternity leave to their partners.[34] In 2011, Additional Paternity Leave (APL) went into effect. This leave ranged between two and twenty-six weeks above OPL. There were some notable restrictions with this policy. First, the leave could not start until twenty weeks after the birth or adoption. Second, fathers were only eligible for this policy based on unused maternity leave, which meant that the mother must have been eligible for maternity leave and then must have returned to work before the father could take leave. Both OPL and APL were paid at the statutory weekly rate, which was £138.18 per week until April 2015, or 90 percent of average weekly earnings (whichever was lower), the same as statutory maternity pay. At the end of the Statutory Maternity Pay period, APL was unpaid.

Peter Moss and Fred Deven, founding coordinators of the International Network on Leave Policies & Research, argue that this policy was "problematic, inscribed as it [was] with maternalist assumptions that make access to leave by fathers dependent on mothers transferring their entitlement."[35] They further suggest that long maternity leave of twelve months in the case of the UK is "hard to justify in terms of maternal and infant health." Two years into APL, the Trades Union Congress (TUC) reported that while an overwhelming majority (91 percent) of new fathers took some time off work following the birth of a child, less than one-third (29 percent) took more than two weeks at home, and, in fact, less than 1 percent of eligible fathers took APL in its first year.[36] One study of doctors found that only 3 percent used this leave.[37] Less than half of a percent of workplaces reported an employee taking the full twenty-six weeks of APL.[38]

After a 2009 report from the Equality and Human Rights Commission, there was support to reduce maternity leave from fifty-two weeks to eighteen weeks and in turn provide each parent with four weeks of paid non-transferable leave (similar to Nordic "daddy quotas") and an additional thirty weeks of parental leave that could be used by either parent (seventeen weeks of which would be paid with the remaining thirteen weeks unpaid, as in the current system). However, there was much resistance to the reduction in maternity leave, particularly among mothers' groups.[39] Paired with concerns about the recession, the Conservative party vowed to protect maternity leave and introduce flexible parental leave. This took the form of the Children and Families Bill in 2013 and became known as Shared Parental Leave.

The current system of Shared Parental Leave (SPL) went into effect in 2015, replacing Additional Paternity Leave, which had only been in effect for four years. Under this policy, maternity leave (fifty-two weeks) and paternity leave (one to two weeks) remain in place, but couples can share leave after two weeks if the mother transfers some of her maternity leave to her partner. To begin SPL, the mother must end her maternity leave and either return to work or give her employer "binding notice" that she will end her leave on a particular date. At that point, either parent can take the remaining leave, calculated as fifty-two weeks minus the number of weeks of maternity leave already taken (e.g., if the mother has taken twelve weeks of maternity leave, there are forty weeks of parental leave remaining). Statutory Shared Parental Pay is the same rate as maternity pay (except during the first six weeks, which are paid at 90 percent of earnings with no maximum) and paternity pay, which is the lower amount of either 90 percent of earnings or £145 per week. As with maternity pay, there is a maximum of thirty-nine weeks of shared parental pay (e.g., in the example above, where the mother took twelve weeks of maternity leave and there are forty weeks of parental leave left, there would be twenty-seven weeks of shared parental pay and thirteen weeks unpaid). Shared parental leave can be taken in up to three separate blocks (rather than all at once) and can be shared if both parents are eligible. And here's the catch: *The mother must be eligible for maternity pay or leave, adoption pay or leave, or maternity allowance.* This means that men who do not have female partners who are employed and eligible for maternity leave cannot use this parental leave.

In addition, the mother has to have been working continuously for the same employer for twenty-six weeks or more by the "qualifying week" (the fifteenth week before the due date) and must be employed by that same employer while on leave. The father/partner must also have been employed for at least twenty-six weeks and must have earned at least £390 per week in thirteen of the sixty-six weeks before the baby's due date. Employees who want to use shared parental leave need to submit detailed plans to their employer and can only make changes if they give at least eight weeks' notice.

Shared parental leave also differs from maternity leave in two important ways. First, as noted above, eligibility criteria include continuous employment for twenty-six weeks before the qualifying week, which in fact adds up to approximately forty-one weeks before the due date. Maternity leave does not require a set length of employment, though eligibility is similar for maternity pay.[40] Second, there is a large difference in pay between the first six weeks of maternity leave (90 percent of earnings with no maximum) and statutory pay received during SPL (the lower amount of 90 percent or £145 per week).

The UK-based Fatherhood Institute was critical of the Children and Families Bill because it did not in fact provide fathers with their own individual eligibility to take parental leave. Rather it still requires first that the mother/partner be eligible for maternity leave and second that she is willing to share the leave with the father.[41] In fact, the TUC estimated that 40 percent of new fathers would not be eligible for SPL.[42]

Sociologist Tina Miller asserts that a major problem with parental leave policy developments in the UK is policy makers' lack of attention to "the historical legacy of family arrangements." In other words, it is not enough to simply say that parents are equal and can share leave when mothers have historically been seen and treated as the primary caregivers. Because of this, "the apparently gender-neutral term 'parent' is still too often taken as shorthand for 'mother.'"[43] Shared parental leave is in fact tied to maternity leave as mothers must be eligible for maternity leave or maternity allowance and men's intention to take shared parental leave must include an explicit notice that their partners will return to work, thus indicating the mother's active consent.[44] This clearly demonstrates that the government still views mothers as primary and fathers as secondary parents. Atkinson argues that the SPL policy is in violation of EU law: "Member States cannot restrict the access of one parent to parental leave because of the employment status (or lack of employment status) of the spouse or partner of that person, which is exactly what the SPL scheme does in the UK."[45] Granted, Brexit means that the UK may choose not to follow EU directives, and some might think this was part of the reason for leaving the EU.

SPL does not encourage gender equality because it still relies on the primacy of motherhood. While the UK considered reserving leave for fathers, these plans were abandoned after considering potential costs to employers. Atkinson argues: "The government's retreat highlights the ambivalence that is at the heart of SPL: whilst it argues that parents should share childcare more equally, it remains unwilling to challenge the male breadwinner/female carer model by shortening maternity leave or by failing to make other policy changes."[46] Atkinson asserts that SPL is in breach of EU law because men can be refused access to parental leave and may be paid at different rates. To illustrate, Atkinson reviews a Greek case that went before the Court of Justice of the European Union (CJEU). In *Konstantinos Maistrellis v. Ypourgos Dikaiosynsis* (known as *Maistrellis*), a male judge was refused parental leave because his wife was not employed. Under the EU Directive, all parents must be given an individual right to three months (or more) of parental leave. This is intended for caregiving and as such the court reasoned that "the situation of a male employee parent and that of a female employee parent are comparable as regards the bringing up of children."[47] The court found the Greek law discriminated against the judge and was in breach of the EU parental leave directive. By extension, since SPL relies on mothers' employment, access is restricted for fathers or partners of birth mothers.

The only gender-neutral parental leave policy available to British parents is unpaid. Eligible employees may take up to eighteen weeks of unpaid parental leave for each child, up to their eighteenth birthday. This leave is available for the broad category of child welfare and includes spending time with children, making new childcare arrangements, and looking at new schools. Eligible employees can take a maximum of four weeks per child per year, unless granted an exception by their employer. In order to be eligible, employees must work for a company for at least one year and must be named on the child's birth or adoption certificate (or have parental responsibility). This is not available for those who are self-employed or in the "worker" category (agency workers, contractors, etc.) or who are foster parents. As with maternity, paternity, and parental leave, there is protection for employment rights, such as holidays and returning to one's job, during leave. Nevertheless, it is unpaid leave, and the additional eighteen weeks of unpaid parental leave is rarely used.[48]

Who Uses Parental Leave?

Based on the Maternity and Paternity Rights and Women Returners Survey conducted in the late 2000s, British women take an average of thirty-nine weeks of maternity leave, which is the full length of paid maternity leave (six weeks at 90 percent, thirty-three weeks at a flat rate). About 45 percent of mothers use some or all of the unpaid maternity leave period from forty to fifty-two weeks. Not surprisingly, these women tend to be employed full-time and have higher earnings than those who take fewer than forty weeks.[49]

While almost all British fathers take some leave around the birth of their child, less than 10 percent take more than the allotted two weeks of statutory paternity leave.[50] About half use statutory paternity leave only, one-quarter use statutory leave and other paid leave, 18 percent only use other paid leave, and only 5 percent use unpaid leave.[51] Other paid leave is generally holiday (vacation) or personal time. Some employers top up (provide replacement salary) but generally not for more than two weeks.

While "new father" ideologies were becoming increasingly popular at the turn of the twenty-first century, British men still showed a preference for being full-time breadwinners and part-time fathers.[52] While parental leave was available starting in 1999 and there was a cultural shift, most notably in popular publications, toward increased father involvement, few British fathers made use of their parental leave entitlement.[53] Sociologist Esther Dermott, in her study of new fatherhood and parental leave, classified British men's preferences into three types. The first type, called "parental leavers," were men who wanted to take longer leave and share parental leave with their partners. The second type, "paternity leavers," were those who were content with taking a short paternity leave. The third type were "no leavers," who did not see the need for leave as they identified more with work and saw childcare as the domain of mothers.[54] In later work, Dermott suggests that men may think about time commitments for being a "good parent" and a "good worker" in different ways and that involved fathering may not match up with more time with children in the way that it does for motherhood. Dermott further argues that "the role of the 'good mother' [is] defined similarly to 'good worker', where time equals commitment. The same association may not apply to men."[55] Sociologist Stephen Williams confirms that the breadwinner role has continued to occupy a central place in British men's understanding of themselves as fathers, even as fathers become more reflexive, contrasting their own ideas about fathering from those of their fathers.[56]

Workplace Context

British employers generally reinforce the idea that women are supposed to take long maternity leaves while men are supposed to take only brief leaves, providing more evidence that work organizations mediate the effectiveness of parental leave policies.[57] Employers clearly know and follow maternity leave policy, which makes the maternity leave process fairly straightforward for female employees. For example, Paige, a research associate who took seven months' maternity leave, described the process as easy and flexible:

> My experience of the filling out forms and expectancy about when you're going to return to work and everything, you know, has been quite easy compared to what I thought it would be and I mean, there's always the flexibility that if you decide, say I'm going to take six months, as long as you give them notice at least you know it's not set in stone. You can change it, or you can come back earlier if you want or you can sort of extend it, which I think is quite nice because you just necessarily don't know how long you want to take.

Holly, a thirty-four-year-old administrator who took nine months of maternity leave, also conveyed the ease and flexibility in the process:

> R: Yeah, had to go over and see HR to, just because, the maternity policy thing, had to go through that, so I went over and chatted to

one of the girls over there, but that was quite straight forward. It was just explaining what happens and what processes.

I: So no issues with you wanting to do the nine months?

R: No. Well, they don't actually ask you. They just ask if you're going to return and then they assume that you're taking the year off unless you tell them otherwise when you're on the maternity leave so I didn't have to say, I'm taking this time off, I should be back here this date. It's much more sort of fluid than that. They sort of assume you're taking the fifty-two weeks until you give them eight weeks' notice of your return.

These examples make it evident that employers start with the assumption that female employees will take the full year but that they may change their minds.

While the process is also fairly straightforward for men, employers sometimes set conditions on the flexibility they provide their male employees. When I talked to British fathers, many talked about the potential for workplace resistance, and this appeared to be a factor in their decision to take shorter leave. Omar, a thirty-two-year-old planning officer who took two weeks' leave, noted the standard practice at his workplace: "They ask you whether you want one week or two weeks. And they kind of ask you when the, if your child's not been born but when you'd like to take it. Would you like to take it immediately as soon as the child's born or would you like to take it a certain time period after the birth." When asked if he had ever considered taking longer than two weeks, he responded: "Not really, no, because I think . . . Wherever I've worked they've been quite good about it, two weeks, but then I could see if I tagged on some annual leave on the back of it so maybe a month or three weeks, yeah, I don't think anyone explicitly said it, but I think there might be some resistance to that." Even the possibility that his workplace would not be fully supportive seems to have been a deterrent. James, a twenty-six-year-old human resources administrator who took two weeks, explained the conditions of his flexibility:

I left on the day, the day she went into labor so they were very flexible in saying, just keep coming in every day until you need to be off so I left every day knowing that I'd done all my work in that sense. She said as long as you can go at the end of every day knowing you've kind of passed everything on that you need to, it's fine. You can go when you need to, which was good.

British employers have come to expect and plan for female employees taking a year of leave while they ask male employees to make sure everything is in order before leaving for two weeks.[58] This is also reflected in the attitude that from a work absence perspective, paternity leave is practically equivalent to a holiday. Henry, a forty-one-year-old research scientist, conveyed: "I said, 'Look, it's going to be soon.' I'm sure colleagues knew what I was doing so they were able to pick up any slack. But then it was two weeks. It wasn't really any different to going on holiday for a fortnight." James echoed this by talking about leave "like any other two-week holiday."

It is clear that men who go on paternity leave are expected not to disrupt the workplace or put an undue burden on co-workers. Omar felt there could be resistance to taking more than two weeks' leave. Henry talked of a "culture of presenteeism" that discouraged people from staying away too long. Even when it is not explicit, the expectation that there may be resistance or costs to taking more leave encourages men to take shorter parental leaves.[59]

Daniel, the thirty-three-year-old university lecturer who took three months using Additional Paternity Leave, made it clear that his absence did not affect others in his department:

> I guess the fact that I wasn't doing any, I didn't have any teaching responsibilities for the period I was taking off helped because I wasn't massively inconveniencing everybody. I wondered, would this, would the attitudes have been different if I'd taken leave and dumped a first-year lecture course on some other poor member of the department without warning? But as it happened that wasn't.

Employers do not generally replace male employees when they go on paternity leave. As a result, fathers often feel behind when they return to work. Connor, a forty-one-year-old human resources employee, showed some signs of resignation upon his return to work after two weeks of paternity leave: "it was very much come back in and you have to get on, you just have to get on and do it. Old school mentality, there's just work to do, you just have to do the job." Ishan, a thirty-three-year-old programmer who took three weeks of leave, mentioned his responsibilities at work when struggling with his return to work in the midst of troubles at home: "We both wished we could have had longer, but that was the most time that I could have had . . . it was really hard for me to go back, but there are obligations you need to fulfill sometimes." Fathers often do not want to be seen as uncommitted workers.[60] Ishan continued: "I really felt behind to be honest with you and there was an awful lot of stuff that I needed to catch up with and it was, yeah, I mean, it did feel like I'd missed a month, it really did. I think my colleagues did try and pick up as much as they could, but there's only so much that you can do with someone else's work load, really."

Because men are generally not replaced at work when they take paternity leave, this often means that either co-workers are left to take up the male employee's usual tasks or that the tasks pile up while they are on leave. This can result in dissatisfied co-workers as well as feelings of guilt for the employees on leave. Alternatively, it can create a burden that adds to a returning worker's stress levels. Even when workplace policies are supportive, there can continue to be a sense of disruption to the workplace.[61] New fathers may also have some concerns about retaining rights and responsibilities at work.

This can also make it seem like it is not worth it to take extra leave when the return is so overwhelming. This contrasts with the situation of most of the mothers I talked with, who indicated that their leave taking was expected and planned for by their employers. This is likely due to the extreme difference in amount of time between maternity leave and paternity leave, which is often exacerbated by the fact that female employees often try to use up their annual leave before maternity leave (or tack it on to their maternity leave) while male employees must save up their annual leave in order to use it for paternity leave. (Since annual leave continues to accumulate while women are on maternity leave, many women, particularly professional women who take longer leave, can extend their leave by a full month.) Part of this might be due to uncertainty among parents, and particularly fathers, regarding their rights to leave around the time of the birth of a child, in which case greater emphasis should be placed on educating parents about these rights.

Much of the reason, however, is also likely due to restrictions in the policy itself and a lag in employers' application of the policy. While more recent policies are aimed more generally at parents, in practice employers often see women as mothers (or potential mothers) while they tend to ignore men's paternity status. As Simon Burnett and colleagues suggest, fathers are often "ghosts" at work.[62] Fathers reported a sense that taking extended leave could potentially disrupt their workplaces even when this was not based on actual workplace policies.[63] While maternity leave is generally accepted and quickly approved for women, men often have a sense that they will be seen as less committed to their job if they take too much leave.[64] This perception may be due in part to the lack of male co-workers who take up leave.[65] Organizational change may be stalled by practices that marginalize fathers.[66] Again, these organizational assumptions can be linked back to gendered understandings of men as breadwinners and women as carers.[67]

The situation is more mixed when women return to work after maternity leave. Several mothers said their employers were not only flexible about the length of maternity leave but also about when and how they returned to work. Holly, the administrator who took nine months' leave, was replaced with a temp while on leave and had a smooth return to work:

> They're really quite amenable here, to things like that. They're quite, quite nice. They don't feel upset that you've got pregnant and you're leaving them in the lurch. They're like, oh, that's great. When you want to come back they say, oh, what do you want to do, as long as I suppose it's not too completely drastic from the norm they're quite happy . . . But yeah, everyone's been welcoming. There's been no issues or concerns. I've just come back and it's all clicked into place again.

Long leaves—and often a return that includes a shift to a part-time schedule—are the norm. Emma, a thirty-year-old customer relations manager, took nine months and then arranged a phased return to work:

> I came back, when I was coming back I wanted to do it, a phased return, so I used my annual leave because my annual leave had to be used either at the beginning or at the end of the maternity leave, and so I used it at the end. When I came back in May, I went part-time from May to July

to—using up annual leave that I'd accrued so I didn't come back full-time until July . . . they were fine with that, I think. I'm not sure. I think a colleague of mine wasn't sure that I'd be able to do that but he'd been looking at it from a paternity leave standpoint and said, I didn't think you could do that, coming back part-time. I thought you had to use it all in one chunk. And I wasn't sure at first whether I could use it, whether you had to use it all in one chunk, but they seemed okay with it. There were no problems.

Holly's and Emma's experiences contrast quite sharply with Connor's and Ishan's experiences returning to work. These cases suggest that employers tend to afford female employees much greater flexibility. The exceptions to this pattern came when replacements or co-workers did not complete the task fully or properly. For example, Shannon, a thirty-four-year-old secretary who took one year, had this experience: "It was very difficult to go back in and unfortunately the person who covered me didn't do a particularly good job of it and the academics who were, it was very controversial, the academics who were working on the course as well weren't doing a very good job either, so it was . . . I came back to quite a lot of mess and the first few months just seemed to me to be sorting out the problems of the last year." For the most part, even with changing policies, British employers still hold gendered expectations, and fathers seem to sense the potential negative impact of taking too much leave on their careers.[68]

This is confirmed in other qualitative studies of British men. Researchers from Lancaster University Management School found that men felt they were discouraged from using flexible working options even when a policy existed for "all parents." The fathers in their study thought their line managers saw them as economic providers and not as fathers. Sample quotes include: "they don't acknowledge men," "as a father you are completely out of the game," and "dads don't get the same focus, that flexible working is also for the dads."[69] Instead, the fathers in their study thought mothers were privileged in their workplace.

It's about the Money

Almost every parent I talked with mentioned the importance of financial considerations, even when talking about short periods of leave. In explaining why he took two weeks' leave for each of his three children, Oliver simply said: "it's to do with the differentials in pay and things like that. You know, you could just do the sums." Most men took two weeks off around the time of their child's birth, but even among this group it was common to take one week of paternity and one week of holiday, a pattern common among British fathers.[70] Connor, a forty-one-year-old father of one, fit this norm. When asked how he decided to take the two weeks, he responded: "Finances (laughs). The week was paid. The second week would have been back on statutory paternity pay and realistically we just couldn't afford to take that." For Connor and his partner, money was tight and played into both decisions regarding paternity and maternity leave. Yet Connor's partner took six months' maternity leave while he took two weeks total. This also happened with James, a twenty-six-year-old father of one, who took two weeks while his wife took nine months of maternity leave: "I wanted to take as much as was available, but obviously the pay was the main thing behind taking one week holiday and one week paternity leave." He continued: "We were already losing so much money with my wife being off that we couldn't . . . I don't think we could afford to be any less comfortable than we already were." Again, there is a stark contrast between the amount of time fathers take versus mothers. Much of this may be due to the pay gap between men and women. In James' case he was earning between £35,000 and £45,000 while his wife was earning less than £25,000 per year. When asked more specifically about sharing parental leave, James said: "But because again it was more of a financial thing, if my wife had been earning more than me then we might well have considered it. But for her to be earning so much less than I do, financially we couldn't consider it." Economic provision becomes a way of rationalizing leave decisions that are still often rooted in gendered discourses surrounding work and parenting.[71]

Even when female partners earn more money, however, men still take less time off. Ishan, a thirty-four-year-old father of one, took three weeks by combining paternity leave with holiday while his wife took the full twelve months of maternity leave. His wife earned more than he did, but Ishan still framed his decision about the amount of paternity leave in terms of financial reasons: "I think, to start off with, I knew the two weeks wasn't going to be enough, but that was the most that I could take because after that you can take longer, I think, but it's unpaid. And we just couldn't afford any longer than that." Henry, a forty-one-year-old lab manager married to a doctor, makes far less money than his wife. Nevertheless, he took two weeks with each of his two children while his wife took six months each time. Henry tried to explain what prevented him from taking off more time:

> The difficulty with that is due to the way my wife is paid, and her maternity payments aren't the standard ones that normal employees receive and so I would have had those . . . any subsequent time would have been unpaid, and because she wasn't getting paid anything like the normal amount that she would have expected in another occupation, if this follows. So we took the decision between us that I would return to work because otherwise the financial hit would have been too great.

Henry further explained that his wife's maternity pay was determined by the partners in her practice and that her boss was "notoriously tight fisted," which meant that her pay was significantly less than what they were accustomed to. While his wife was not compensated as much as they would have liked, it is not clear how he would have received lower payments than her. Indeed, with his income below £25,000 and hers at £55,000 or higher, it seems their "financial hit" would have been less if she had returned to work sooner while he stayed home.

Where Do Gay Couples Fit In?

It is not only mothers who are hurt by these policies but also fathers. Kiernan, a thirty-one-year-old educational administrator, told me of his struggle to get *maternity* leave from his company. He and his husband, Reece, were awaiting the birth of their child through surrogacy when I talked to him. As Kiernan notes: "I was always ready to have kids . . . I always in my mind had a vision of what my family would look like. I wanted a baby Reece." Kiernan walked me through the long process of finding a surrogate and how they finally "clicked" with Amber, a married mother of three, after meeting over several months to ensure that they trusted each other (since agreements are not legally binding, developing trust is critical). Kiernan and Reece were thrilled when Amber called to tell them she was pregnant. From the start, Amber has assured Kiernan and Reece that the baby is theirs and not hers. They go to appointments together and have discussed plans to submit paperwork to transfer parental responsibility and send the baby home with Kiernan and Reece that first day. Kiernan describes visualizing Reece with the baby as "the most beautiful thing in the world." While they were able to work through the complicated process of surrogacy, Kiernan said their plans to share care over the first year of their baby's life hit a roadblock when he looked into available leave at his workplace. Their ideal scenario was to share maternity leave by having Reece stay home two days per week and Kiernan stay home three days per week. When it looked like he might only get two weeks of paternity leave, Kiernan made it clear that that would not be enough time for what he thought would be a fundamentally life-altering change. Kiernan used a co-worker's pregnancy to negotiate more leave for himself. While he had been at the organization for longer and wanted to continue working after leave, another staff member who was unsure whether she would return to work received full maternity benefits. He saw this as unjust. Kiernan was able to negotiate for full pay for the first few weeks and pro-rated statutory maternity pay for the rest of the leave (he had to use his holiday first to attend prenatal appointments and for the first few weeks of leave, and they also took away tuition funding for an MBA degree they had been providing him). Kiernan concluded that "you have to pick your battles . . . legally these organizations don't have to do anything for us. Literally." Those who become parents via surrogacy are eligible for adoption leave (similar to maternity leave), but only one person in the couple can take the leave while the other can take paternity leave (one or two weeks). On the other hand, the gov.uk website clearly states that surrogates are eligible for maternity leave: "Every pregnant employee has the right to fifty-two weeks' maternity leave and to return to their job after this. What a birth mother does after the child is born has no impact on her right to maternity leave."[72] If we in the US follow the UK model, we will still be at the mercy of employer policies.

Conclusion

The most obvious restriction to British fathers taking leave is that the child's mother must qualify for leave. Paternity leave is thus literally attached to maternity leave. The imbalance in maternity leave and paternity leave creates a gap between mothers and fathers and encourages a more gendered division of work and family roles.[73] By limiting paternity leave and restricting parental leave, the UK supports right over duty,[74] which results in fathers taking the more limited, statutory paternity leave without considering more equal sharing of additional parental leave.[75]

While one could certainly conclude that something is better than nothing, the British system has negative consequences for gender equality. British women lag behind their European and American counterparts in several measures of employment and career success. Having a parental leave system that encourages women to take leave, and does not encourage men to do the same, creates real workplace barriers for women. It also shortchanges fathers.

While SPL has been in effect since 2015, there seems to be little increase in uptake. According to a survey of 200 British workplaces, only 1 percent of male employees used SPL in 2015.[76] In February 2018, the British government had a press release in which it estimated that while 285,000 couples are eligible to take shared parental leave each year, only about 2 percent use it.[77] Based on calculations using the average annual wage of £27,000 among women, women who use maternity leave can expect £7,449 in maternity payments based on six weeks of leave at £466 and thirty-three weeks at the statutory rate of £141. In contrast, men can expect only £282, based on £141 for two weeks. This amounts to a gender pay gap of 96 percent though both mothers and fathers may struggle to provide for their families with such low pay.[78] Some companies enhance pay, but this is much more common with maternity pay than paternity pay. A study of 341 companies in 2017 found that 95 percent of firms augment maternity pay but only 4.4 percent of companies augment paternity pay.[79] Even three years after SPL was introduced, a government study found that approximately half of people do not know the policy exists. Based on the low uptake and continuing lack of awareness, the government has started a campaign to promote use of the policy. Figure 5.1 shows an example of the ad, with the tagline "share the joy"; these ads appear online and on billboards around the country.

Figure 5.1. UK Shared Parental Leave advertisement. Source: UK Department of Business, Energy and Industrial Strategy and the Government Equalities Office, photography by Laura Lewis, https://www.lauralewisphotography.co.uk

The British policy may benefit by returning to discussions of non-transferrable leave, introducing extended paternity or parental leave, and boosting statutory pay. If the UK provides an imperfect example, perhaps Sweden will offer a better model. The next chapter focuses on the development of parental leave policy in Sweden and the country's simultaneous emphasis on gender equality.

6

The Swedish Model Is Great—But Not Perfect

Sweden is the best country in the world for women.
Business Insider, March 18, 2017[1]

In Sweden, men can have it all.
The New York Times, June 9, 2010[2]

Sweden is the world's finest home for families.
Wall Street Journal, July 15, 2018[3]

There is a lot to love about Sweden. It shows up again and again on top-ten lists for best parental leave policies and highest levels of gender equality. But Sweden also makes the top ten on lists for things like best healthcare systems and best countries for raising kids and even for being the happiest of countries (despite the cold weather).[4] The first time I went to Sweden, to Stockholm, it was May and I didn't take off my fleece the whole week. After meetings at Stockholm University, I would take nice long walks around Brunnsviken Lake, down through Östermalm, and to Djurgården. I could hear the joyful sounds of children at Gröna Lund, the local amusement park, but opted for the more peaceful pathways beyond Skansen and Rosendal. I was beginning to fall in love with that beautiful city. The second time I went, I tried swimming in the Baltic off a popular beach spot in Långholmen and wondered why the Swedish people even bother buying bathing suits. I had planned a more extensive stay with family in tow. We first stayed in Sollentuna, a place that my children still remember fondly, despite or perhaps because they had to trek through the forest to find the town and some pizza. We then headed into Stockholm and set ourselves up in an apartment on Drottninggatan, a major pedestrian street that stretches from Norrmalm to Vasastaden. My daughter was particularly pleased that there was an ice cream shop right next door. We made almost daily treks to

Humlegården, where my children played outdoor floorball with other youngsters. Growing up in New York, I was amazed that they just left the sticks and balls in a bin out in the open. The love fest continued as I returned to Sweden again and again. But it wasn't simply about outings to wonderful places like Umedalen Skulpturpark and Norrbyskär. After all, the purpose of my visits was to study gender and family dynamics in Sweden.

Sweden inspired me because it offered a vision of gender equality that I have not seen here in America. Sweden has consistently ranked at the top of the World Economic Forum's annual Global Gender Gap Index and is often touted as a model of gender equality. This is probably because gender equality is not simply a talking point in Sweden but a fundamental value that individual Swedes as well as Swedish institutions and government place as a top priority. We see this in something as basic as the Swedish language, which has its own special term for gender equality, *jämställdhet*. More recently, there have been efforts to use more inclusive language through the gender-neutral pronoun *hen*, and this seems to be well accepted in preschools throughout the country.[5] At the government level, Sweden has a Minister for Gender Equality and indeed all ministers are required to maintain a gender equality perspective throughout their work. This emphasis on gender equality has led to numerous legislation and policies that address gender equality, including paid parental leave.

The combination of generous parental leave along with policies and a general culture that value gender equality means that Sweden stands out as a model of success for countries that want to promote gender equality by implementing policies that help women in the labor force and men at home. In Sweden, the question is not whether fathers will take parental leave. The question is: how much parental leave will fathers take? Swedish fathers, often referred to as "latte pappas," commonly take three to nine months.[6] Of course, Sweden is not perfect, but we would do well to learn from its example. This chapter describes the development of parental leave policies in Sweden, from its pioneering introduction of parental leave in 1974 to its current model of reserving three months of leave for each parent in addition to ten extra months available for either parent. I then discuss Swedish efforts to promote gender equality and particularly the focus on promoting men's use of parental leave in order to encourage greater gender equality in the home as well as in the workplace. Finally, I provide some examples of Swedish parents from the research I conducted with Swedish collaborators. This ultimately will provide context for the lessons learned and policies proposed in the conclusion.

Development of Parental Leave Policy in Sweden

While there is a lot of attention given to Sweden's introduction of parental leave in 1974, the country has an even longer history of maternity leave that dates back to 1901, when the government introduced four weeks of unpaid maternity leave. In 1937, unpaid maternity leave was extended to three months and the leave was made job-protected so women could return to their same or a similar job. In 1945, unpaid maternity leave was again extended to six months. Ten years later, in 1955, after Sweden's baby boom (which ended before the baby boom ended in the US), the policy was amended so that, given nine months of pre-birth employment, the first three months of maternity leave were paid. All six months became paid leave (at 80 percent of earnings) in 1963.

The 1970s saw the transition from maternity leave to parental leave in Sweden. Starting in 1974, parents could share six months of job-protected paid parental leave. This was extended to 210 days (or seven months) in 1975 and 270 days (or nine months) in 1978. At this time, leave was paid at 90 percent of earnings and parents could take additional unpaid leave after nine months up until their child was eighteen months old. The 1980s saw further extensions and the introduction of paternity leave, beginning in 1980, when the government introduced ten days of paternity leave paid at 90 percent of earnings. Even at this time, the leave was gender-neutral, which meant that the "other parent" could take leave and receive benefits. At the same time, parental leave was increased from nine months to twelve months, with full pay for the first nine months and a lower, flat rate for the last three months. At the end of the decade, in 1989, parental leave was extended to 450 days, or fifteen months.

The 1990s saw the introduction of the "daddy" month. Until 1995, parental leave was available to either parent, but it was mainly women who used the leave. Starting in 1995, parental leave was given to individual parents, such that each parent received half of the leave, or 225 days. However, parents could transfer their leave to each other so that fathers typically could give their partners their leave. In order to encourage more men to take parental leave, the government introduced a "daddy" quota of one month. While the focus was on men using leave, the government balanced the "daddy" quota with the less well known "mommy" quota of one month. This month was non-transferable, which meant that it was only to be used by the earmarked parent. In other words, fathers could still give their partners 6.5 months of their 7.5 months of parental leave, but if they did not take the one month, they would lose it. In 2002, a second "daddy" month was added and parental leave was extended to 480 days or sixteen months.[7]

Not surprisingly, progress has been uneven. Political scientist Christina Bergqvist and colleagues have sought to understand why a policy designed to address gender inequality by extending the individual parental leave quotas failed in the mid-2000s. In 2004, the Social Democratic government formed a committee of inquiry to examine possible reforms of the parental leave policy. In 2005, the committee report "recommended a division of the parental benefit into three separate parts: five individual months for each parent, and five months that could be freely divided by the parents."[8] At the time, it seemed that most people in the party supported this legislation. Proponents talked about gender equality, removing the "women's trap" of discrimination in the labor market and encouraging fathers to take equal time with their children. Opponents to this change emerged, however, and while these opponents agreed with the goals of removing discrimination in the workplace and fostering father-child relationships, they were concerned about losing votes in the next electoral race to the center-right alliance. The reform ultimately failed because it took into account working-class families, who see shared parental leave as economically unfeasible.

In 2008, Sweden introduced a gender equality bonus, which provided an economic incentive for couples to divide parental leave. The more evenly couples split their sixteen months of leave, the greater the bonus. However, analyses seemed to show that the "daddy" quota was much more effective at promoting fathers' use of leave while the gender equality bonus had limited impact on the sharing of parental leave. The bonus was consequently eliminated. Shortly after the Social Democrats came back into power in 2014 via an alliance with the Green Party, plans for

Figure 6.1. Timeline of Sweden's parental leave policy

the third reserved month were announced. The third "daddy" month began in 2016.[9] Figure 6.1 summarizes the major changes in Sweden's parental leave policy over time.

Current Policy

Table 6.1 shows parental leave days broken down by type of leave for mothers and fathers. Note that even though I have labeled the columns "mother" and "father," the leave policy applies to all parents. At present, new Swedish parents each get 240 days of paid parental leave. Of the 240 days, 195 are paid at 77.6 percent of earnings up to a ceiling of SEK 447,783 or the equivalent of about $51,000 per year and the remaining forty-five days are paid at SEK 180 per day ($20.50). The wage-based days are split into reserved time and transferrable time. The reserved time is called *pappamånader* (father's quota) and *mammamånader* (mother's quota) even though the leave policy is gender-neutral so that two mothers or two fathers would also be eligible for the same amount of time. The forty-five days paid at the flat rate are transferrable. Parents can use parental leave until their child turns twelve.[10] There is considerable flexibility in the use of parental leave. Leave can be used all in one block or in up to three blocks per year. In the first year, both parents can take up to thirty days of leave together, a period called dubbeldagar (double days) though parents must use part of their 105 wage-based transferable days and not their reserved days. Parents also have the right to reduce their working hours up to 25 percent until their child turns eight years old. There is also temporary parental leave of 120 days per year per child in order to care for a sick child, and half of these days can be used to care for a preschool child if their caregiver is sick.[11]

Benefits are not restricted to citizens. All parents living and working in Sweden for at least 240 days before a birth or adoption are eligible. In addition, there is something called the "speed premium" in which parents who have a second child within thirty months of the first child

TABLE 6.1. Parental leave in Sweden (in days)	Mother	Father
Total days of paid parental leave	240	240
Wage-based	195	195
Reserved (non-transferrable)	90	90
Transferrable to other parent	105	105
Paid at flat rate (and transferrable)	45	45

receive benefits based on their wages before the first child. Since wages while on parental leave or just after parental leave are potentially reduced, due to working reduced hours, it is a way of encouraging second births.[12]

Recently, the government has proposed some revisions to the parental leave policy, including raising the individual entitlement to five months for each parent. Additional recommendations include extending full parental leave benefits to couples living together in which one adult is the parent while the other is the partner but not parent and allowing other non-parents (e.g., grandparents) to take up to thirty days of the allotted leave time.[13]

Gender Equality in Sweden

Sweden is known as much for its gender equality as for moose and IKEA. Attitudes in Sweden tend to skew heavily egalitarian. In fact, it is difficult to study gender ideology in Sweden since there is actually quite little variation in attitudes. Still, this egalitarian-minded country continued to become even more egalitarian in the 2000s as the idea of the male breadwinner became less and less palatable to Swedes.[14]

Sweden fits into the "earner-carer" model, in which there is high support for dual-earners and low support for traditional families.[15] There has been wide government support for gender equality and promoting women's participation in the workplace and men's participation in childcare.[16] Many classifications developed before 2000 focused on breaking with a traditional division of labor in which women stayed home and men went to work, to shift toward a dual-earner model in which both partners were employed. In the 2000s, however, there was increasing attention not only on getting women to enter and remain in the labor force but also on getting men to do more at home. Out of this arose policies that would support dual-carers, specifically with encouragement for men to engage in care work at home through paternity and parental leave.[17] Sweden stands out because they have a long history of supporting an earner-carer model, since the early 1970s.[18]

Relative to gender patterns in other countries, Swedish mothers have quite high levels of employment[19] and this is paired with lower proportions of time spent on care work.[20] Swedish fathers, on the other hand, take on a relatively high share of unpaid work and parental leave. Compared to British adults, Swedes view mothers' employment more positively,[21] which is consistent with the generally high levels of support for gender equality at home among both Swedish women and men.[22] It is notable that while Sweden has not achieved true equality, becoming a parent, a transition that often initiates more traditional attitudes and behavior in other countries, seems to have much more limited impact on support for gender equality or the division of household labor in Sweden.[23]

Over twenty-five years ago, sociologist Linda Haas wrote: "there is only one society whose policymakers have long advocated equal participation of fathers in child care—Sweden."[24] The idea that a government would set gender equality as an official goal and place importance on men's role as fathers as well as women's participation in the workplace is relatively new for many countries, but not for Sweden. Sweden has been at the forefront of parental leave policies, and its policies have emphasized the importance of including men from the beginning.[25] According to the International Social Survey Programme (ISSP), Swedish adults show a preference for moderate to long parental leave (at least five months) financed by the government. In addition, 70.5 percent of Swedes prefer that parental leave be shared equally between parents. This demonstrates norms that support social redistribution, gender equality, and the dual earner-carer family model.[26]

Gender equality is one of the main goals behind parental leave policies, particularly the inclusion of individual rights for fathers.[27] Even though fathers could take leave under the parental leave policy implemented in 1974, most fathers transferred their leave to their part-ners. Tommy Ferrarini's doctoral dissertation explored the incentive structures of parental leave legislation. He noted that "one official mo-tive for the reform was to achieve gender equality."[28] Furthermore, the shift to the "daddy quota" was a way to address the continuing gender inequality in take up of parental leave. In Sweden, the non-transferrable time was seen as a way to get more fathers to take more time, which was intended to boost their female partners' careers as well as their own par-ticipation at home, thereby equalizing the division of childcare.[29]

Linda Haas and Tine Rostgaard, social scientists with the Inter-national Network on Leave Policies and Research, suggest that four groups have prioritized gender equality in the development of parental leave policies in the Nordic countries. First, women have worked to-ward improving women's status through policy change. Second, men have also been active in campaigning for more individual entitlements, including the daddy days. Third, left-leaning political parties, includ-ing the Social Democrats, strive to lessen gender inequalities through policies. Fourth, there has been heavy reliance on social science data in creating and implementing parental leave policies. They conclude that "Sweden has the best record for fathers taking parental leave" and suggest that the father's quota is key to increasing men's involvement in care.[30]

Sweden is only one of two countries (Iceland is the other) that scores high on Helene Dearing's "Equal Gender Division of Labour" indica-tor.[31] This is based on length of parental leave, duration of well-paid leave, and the proportion of leave reserved for fathers. Sweden has high levels of gender equality. Researchers Rebecca Ray, Janet Gornick, and John Schmitt created an index to assess how generous and gender-equal parental leave policies were in twenty-one high-income countries.[32] Based on their index, Sweden is ranked number one, with a total of fourteen out of fifteen points. Sweden scores high on generosity and gender equality within parental leave policies, which suggests their policies are consistent with the "earner-carer" model, acknowledging the father's role as caregiver. Public policy experts Jana Javornik and Anna Kurowska consider parental leave as an opportunity structure and develop an ideal type to assess how well parental leave policies provide "real opportunity for equal parental involvement in the raising of children across gender and income lines."[33] They find that Sweden is the closest to achieving this ideal type. Indeed, Swedish fathers are increasingly taking parental leave and sharing responsibility for caring for young children,[34] and the introduction of the first "daddy month" had strong positive effects on Swedish fathers' use of parental leave. The second reserved month had a more moderate effect on fathers' leave, however.[35] It is still too early to evaluate the effectiveness of the third "daddy month."

Who Takes Parental Leave?

Demographer Ann-Zofie Duvander classifies the length of Swedish parental leave in the following way: short is less than forty-nine weeks for women and less than six weeks for men, medium is forty-nine to sixty-six weeks for women and six to twenty weeks for men, and long is more than sixty-six weeks for women and more than twenty weeks for men. About one-fifth of parents take short leaves (21 percent of women and 22 percent of men), 45 percent of women and 37 percent of men take medium leave, and 34 percent of women and 42 percent of men take long leaves. Furthermore, belief in gender equality is important as men with egalitarian views are 94 percent more likely to take more than twenty weeks of leave than men with less egalitarian views.[36]

The latest statistics from the Swedish Social Insurance Agency show that fathers take 28 percent of parental leave days, which is the highest level in Sweden's history and higher than every other country save Iceland (see figure 6.2). The highest rate of leave taking among fathers is 35 percent for those living in the northern Västerbotten region.[37] There has clearly been steady growth—Swedish men took twelve percent of parental leave in 1999 and 21 percent in 2007. While the numbers are still not equal, a 33-percent increase has taken place in the last decade alone.[38]

The "daddy quota" has had a huge impact on the proportion of fathers who take parental leave. Before the quota, fewer than half of fathers took any parental leave (44 percent) while after the quota was introduced, the proportion shot up to more than three-quarters of fathers

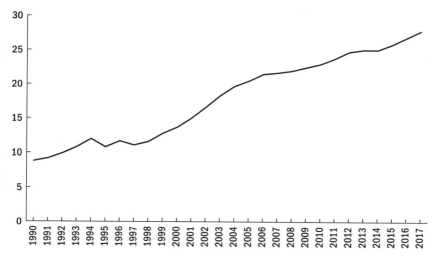

Figure 6.2. Percentage of parental leave taken by fathers in Sweden. Source: Haataja, 2009; Swedish Social Insurance Agency, 2017

(77 percent) within a few years. The effect was particularly dramatic for low-income and foreign-born fathers. And now almost 90 percent of fathers use at least some parental leave.[39] In fact, almost three-quarters of Swedish fathers took their full sixty days of "daddy quota" in 2007.[40] Looking at children born in 2008, the average number of parental leave days taken over the eight years of eligibility was 106 days for fathers and 342 days for mothers.[41] In a recent analysis of parental leave in twenty-nine countries, policy experts Marre Karu and Diane-Gabrielle Tremblay find that Swedish fathers take more parental leave days, on average, than fathers in other countries.[42] According to the Swedish Social Insurance Agency, men were 45 percent of recipients while women were 55 percent of recipients of parental leave benefits in 2016. Figure 6.2 shows the percentage of parental leave taken by fathers. While Swedish fathers took less than 10 percent of parental leave days in 1990, this number has increased consistently over time, so that in 2017 fathers took about 28 percent of parental leave days. The numbers are becoming more equal. For children born in 2013, 14 percent of couples split parental leave equally, which meant each parent took between 40 and 60 percent of leave.[43] Furthermore, in 2016, fathers took 38 percent of

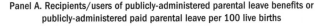

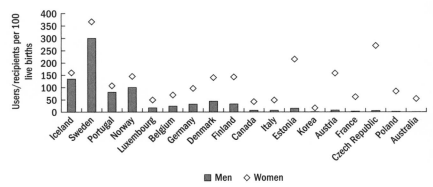

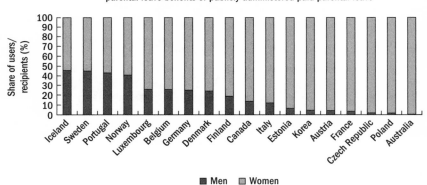

Figure 6.3. Parental leave users by gender. Source: OECD Family Database, http://www
.oecd.org/els/family/database.htm, latest data are from 2013, PF2.2: Use of childbirth
-related leave by mothers and fathers, chart PF2.2.C http://www.oecd.org/els/family
/PF2-2-Use-childbirth-leave.pdf

temporary parental benefit days to care for sick children, and there is
no gender difference in the number of parental benefit days taken for
children three years old and older.[44]

Figure 6.3 shows users of parental leave benefits (Panel A) and the
gender distribution of parental leave benefits (Panel B). According to the
OECD, Swedish men have the highest rate of parental leave users, with
just around 300 users per one hundred live births. Admittedly, Swedish

women also have the highest rate, around 367 users per one hundred live births. As a comparison, the rate for Danish women (140) is three times that of Danish men (44). Sweden, along with Iceland, also has the most equal gender distribution of users of parental leave benefits, with men making up 45 percent of users.

From Gender-Equal Men to Gender-Equal Fathers

Being an involved father, including staying home to care for infants, is "common wisdom" in Sweden. Education scholar Thomas Johansson asserts that gender-equal fatherhood means that fathers must "display their readiness to engage in childcare, their child orientation and their willingness to live up to an ideal of gender equality."[45] The idea of a "child-oriented masculinity," one that focuses on men as carers possessing both caring attitudes and behaviors, is prominent in Sweden.[46] This ideal is fostered by government campaigns related to gender equality and corresponding media attention.[47]

While broader discussions surrounding feminism and gender equality existed as far back as the 1960s, parental leave campaigns provided a visible emphasis on the promotion of women at work and of men at home.[48] Fatherhood scholar Roger Klinth suggests that earlier campaigns in the 1970s and 1980s often relied on more traditional notions of masculinity, promoting the idea of fathers' opportunity, rather than responsibility, to take leave. Further, campaigns advocated emotional benefits and professional gains for fathers. Figure 6.4 shows a government advertisement from the 1970s that featured Swedish weightlifter Lennart "Hoa-Hoa" Dahlgren, a clearly masculine figure. National as well as regional information campaigns during the 1990s and early 2000s promoted fathers' parental leave use to encourage shared responsibility for children.[49] The beginning of 2000 saw a shift in the understanding of fatherhood, in which similarity rather than difference in terms of men's and women's rights, capacities, and responsibilities came to be emphasized. By the mid-2000s, such campaigns advocated a framework of gender equality with fully shared responsibility.[50]

A study of parents in Stockholm found that when Swedish fathers took the full "daddy quota" but did not share the full amount of leave equally, "they were aware that merely doing one's duty was less than what was hoped

Figure 6.4. Swedish parental leave advertisement. This ad features
Lennart "Hoa-Hoa" Dahlgren, a top weightlifter in the 1970s.
"Barnledig Pappa!" is Swedish for "father on parental leave."
Source: Swedish Ministry for Social Affairs and Health

for—that is, such behavior falls short of the national ideal of caring—even
though it conforms to the minimum requirement."[51] This shows how normative gender equality is in Sweden. While Swedish men take a higher
share of parental leave than fathers in other countries, they still realize that
they are falling short when they take less than half of the leave.

Stories from Sweden

In my previous research with Anna-Lena Almqvist, we found that Swedish couples often worked together to arrange more equal leave-taking arrangements.[52] In these cases, women supported their partners' use of long leaves. For example, a participant named Lena shared the following about her and her partner's decision to divide parental leave:

> Firstly, I am such a person, I want to work and to meet people. Secondly, I think it's very important that Stefan [father] and Nils [child] are bonding . . . Then Stefan gets an understanding for how it is to stay at home. That I don't lie on the couch and are having a good time the whole day, but there are things to do. So that you get a better understanding for each other. That I go out and work and are away from Nils the whole day and miss him while I am at work, so we experience both sides. It's very important.

Lena is clear that she wants her partner Stefan to bond with their son and to experience the daily routine of staying home and caring for their child. At the same time, she is also clear that she likes her work and would not want to stay home for the full period of leave. This is consistent with other Swedish women's attitudes toward work and home, as very few believe being a housewife would be fulfilling.[53] Another Swedish mother, Lisa, said:

> I didn't think it was so fun to stay at home [on parental leave] and that became very evident for me when I was staying at home. The thoughts about work became even more intensive then . . . it's the same things the whole time. The house doesn't get nicer just because you clean it every day and the food maybe became better after you had made it five times, but there was no potential for development in the maternal role.

Yet another mother, Linn, said: "I have to admit that I have to work, otherwise I will climb up the walls." While these women want to be good mothers, they also have few qualms about sharing how important work is to them. In general, Swedish women rate work commitment high, and while there is a small decrease following childbirth, levels of work commitment bounce back and increase after a few years of motherhood.[54]

The discourse on equal partnerships, in which both individuals share work and family roles, is also important.[55] Women's focus on work also makes it more possible for fathers to take longer periods of leave.[56] Another example is Sandra, a head nurse. She talks about shared parental leave with a little more ambivalence than Lena, but still comes to the conclusion that it is important for their child and their relationship:

> I: Why did you share the parental leave?
>
> R: There are several reasons. But I have two children before and this was Per's first child. I stayed at home with Lena and Sandra, as are the names of my older children, all days except for the ten daddy-days . . . Now I feel that: "No, now when we are having a child together, me and Per, then I want him to be involved from the very beginning." I wanted him to stay at home to see what it's like to stay at home with a small child, because it isn't just "yes, we can rebuild the house at the same time, since Linnea is so young and mainly sleeps."
>
> I: This was before she was born?
>
> R: Yes. . . . But then I can say that I regret my decision. Why did I say that we should share the parental leave, I should stay at home, how stupid can you be? How could I be so stupid? One should enjoy the time with the little girl. But at the same time, I feel: "No, I should not be so 'mamaegoistic.'" I can see that today, when I talk with those who had children about the same time. Then when they started work after having been on leave for a year. . . . And the father hadn't been so much on leave, there are more conflicts or discussions in the couple. It's about the understanding.

As with Lena, Sandra feels it is important for her partner, Per, to stay home and learn the ropes. She has already had the experience of staying home for the full period with her first two children and realized that this was not very equitable. In efforts to build a more equal relationship with Per, she felt it was only right for him to stay home and be involved from the start. During her response to the follow-up question, Sandra hesitates a bit and questions whether this was the right decision. But she quickly realizes that this falls into a maternalistic trap. Her use of the term "mamaegoistic" is enlightening as it suggests that mothers who take more parental leave than their partners are seen as selfish in a way, caving in to ideas about the prominence of maternal bonding and basically hogging time with the children. This is clearly not equitable. In addition, Sandra mentions the potential conflicts couples who do not share leave have. She suggests that there is a lack of understanding between partners who do not share parental leave because they each only experience and thus understand a limited role. Her partner, Per, a maintenance worker, reinforces the importance of their decision to share leave:

> We only had it clear that I should be on "daddy-leave" too, also pretty early. It was also based on how it may affect the child. Linnea became much more "daddyish." When she was so young, all our friends' children cried when their father took care of them. But that has never been any [problem], she has spent a lot of time with me.

The contrast between Sandra's fear of being "mamaegoistic" and Per's clear pleasure in their daughter being more "daddyish" is illuminating. This egalitarian approach is in line with more caring masculinities, which support gender-neutral parenting[57] and in turn result in more father-oriented children.[58] Longer shared leave allows for more equal parenting, greater bonding time for fathers, and more satisfaction with time allocation.[59] Other research also supports these patterns. My recent research with Anne Grönlund shows that Swedish fathers actively work on displaying themselves as good fathers.[60] A key element to being a responsible father is sharing parental leave. One father, Daniel, stated: "I learned to be a parent [when I was on parental leave], because I was fully responsible. You can be a provider without staying home with your child, but it's difficult to be a parent." There is an interesting parallel between the American fathers I talked with and Swedish fathers. Many American fathers make a distinction between being a father, which anyone can do, and being a dad or daddy, which involves being present and actively involved with one's child. It is interesting that Swedish fathers use more gender-neutral language in making a similar point. Anyone can be a provider, but only those who are actively involved, and this includes taking a good amount of parental leave, can be a parent. This

sentiment is so widely held that another father, Tom, who shared parental leave equally with his partner, said: "Nowadays you are regarded as a
suspect person if you don't take parental leave and that is exactly how I
feel. It's only oddballs and old-fashioned people who do not take daddy
leave."

Conclusion

In any comparison of the US, the UK, and Sweden related to parental
leave and gender equality, Sweden is going to win by a mile. Sweden
was the first country to adopt parental leave back in 1974 and its current policy provides sixteen months of paid leave, with three months
reserved for each parent, a strategy adopted to encourage men to take
more parental leave. A sizeable minority, 42 percent, of Swedish fathers
take more than twenty weeks of leave. Swedish men are increasingly
taking on a child-oriented masculinity. Both mothers and fathers see
the importance of sharing parental leave and being equal partners and
parents. Nevertheless, Sweden is not equal. Fathers do not take as much
parental leave as mothers nor do they spend as much time on childcare
as mothers, and women still face some difficulties in career advancement.[61] Even with the most generous and gender equal policy in the
world, the Swedish government recently had an investigation of parental
leave that resulted in a government report recommending more focus
on equal sharing of parental leave between women and men. Specifically, the report, released in December 2017, recommends increasing
the non-transferable days, referred to as "daddy quota" days, from three
months to five months.[62] While Sweden might be the closest we come to
gender equality, there is still some work to be done.

Conclusion

The Six Month Solution

I think that our culture needs to grow up and acknowledge the fact that bringing up children and work cannot be
separated.
—Oliver, British father

Family medical leave, all that stuff should be a right. There's
no reason it shouldn't be.
—Finn, American father

When I set out to write this book, my ultimate goal was to find a good
parental leave policy for the United States. What do I mean by a good parental leave policy? I mean a policy that will not only allow for work-family
balance, but one that promotes gender equality. I want women to be equal
in the workplace, not penalized for taking time out. I want men to be equal at
home, as partners and parents. Oliver's sentiment suggests that it should be
obvious in this day and age that parents are often workers and workers are
often parents, regardless of gender. Finn picks up on this in his demand for
the US to adopt paid family leave. My perfect policy would provide adequate time and compensation for all working parents.

Where to start? It seemed like a no-brainer to start with Sweden, the
first country in the world to develop a parental leave policy (back in
1974). What can Sweden's example offer us? Is it the 480 days of parental
leave, 240 days for each parent? Is it the 390 days paid at almost 80 percent of wages? I think the most successful part of Sweden's policy, and
the part we should pay close attention to, is the "daddy" quota, reserving
three months of leave just for fathers. This is the policy that has made it
possible for greater and greater proportions of Swedish fathers to take
an equal share of leave.

It's not so simple. Sweden has relatively high taxes, up to 60 percent (though only about one-third of parental leave funds come from individual taxes; the other two-thirds come from an employers' fee paid to the government). As a side note, Swedes are quite content with their tax rates, probably because they get so much—childcare, free college education, health care, etc.[1] Still, Americans don't seem eager to pay higher taxes. Beyond the cost, Sweden's parental leave system is not perfect. Women still take more leave than men. Women also tend to be more concentrated into public-sector and lower-paying occupations. So maybe we need to think about reducing the length of leave and making all leave non-transferrable.

Given Sweden's political and social distance from the American situation, I wondered whether there might be a more suitable comparison for the US than Sweden. The United Kingdom presented itself as the closest parallel to the US in terms of economy and culture. The UK is not in the same league as Sweden, but it has what many would consider a generous maternity leave policy—fifty-two weeks total, of which thirty-three weeks include some form of paid leave. And the UK has recently made efforts to shift its parental leave to be more inclusive of fathers. The problem is that the UK's policy is not as generous or equal as it would first seem. Only the first six weeks of maternity leave are paid at a high rate of 90 percent of wages while the remaining 7.5 months are paid at a low flat rate. Furthermore, their Shared Parental Leave policy is actually rooted in maternity leave, which excludes a good proportion of fathers.

When we compare the US to the UK, we can ask whether it may be better to have no policy than a highly gendered policy. In the short term, we might opt for the gendered policy. After all, it would allow women to take a break from employment to have a child and ensure their own and their child's well-being over the first year. But I have to argue that in the long term, a gendered policy is potentially more damaging than no policy at all.

When we look at gendered policies, the impact on gender equality is clear: Gendered policies reproduce gender inequality. In the UK, a parental leave system that has historically been lopsided continues to be gendered even as it is called "Shared Parental Leave," as it in fact belongs to mothers. These policies encourage women to take longer leave than men, on average thirty-nine weeks compared to two weeks. This initial difference is extremely important in setting up and reproducing a system of inequality. When mothers stay home to care for children, they "get on with it," as many of the British parents I talked with told me. Caregiving becomes gendered. Mothers know how to feed, bathe, comfort their children. Fathers become secondary parents or "helpers." And these patterns don't disappear when mothers return to work. This system encourages women to work part-time. Along with the high costs of nursery, mothers are already equipped to care for children and so adjust their work lives around their family lives. This ensures that women experience less career advancement. And it all continues.

We might question the continuing attempt to achieve gender equality by helping women fit into workplaces designed for men, and specifically men who have wives at home to take care of all their home/family needs. We should be trying to create policies and workplaces that are better suited to human beings (who have lives outside work). The ideal worker type certainly doesn't benefit women, but it doesn't benefit many men anymore either. Instead of changing women and admonishing men, we should change workplaces. Regarding family-friendly policies such as parental leave policies, it may seem that a gendered policy (women get it, men don't) might help women in the short term. However, these policies inevitably hurt women and the broader aims of gender equality in the long-term. The research presented in this book shows this. Gendered policies encourage employers to treat women differently, which results in lower chances of hiring, promotion, etc. At least in terms of parental leave policies, the most effective policies are those that are gender-equal with incentives for men to take leave. In other words, we need to be encouraging men to change more than women.

The way to promote gender equality is to have gender equal policies. But what we also learn from looking at the case of Sweden is that gender equal policies with incentives for men to take leave are the most effective policies in moving toward gender equality. These policies increase men's use of parental leave and in conjunction make the division of leave more even between women and men. This also promotes continued sharing of caregiving and household work, which then supports more equal roles in the workplace.

The first step in creating opportunities for parents to spend time with their children is to provide paid parental leave. Yet we have seen that there are drastic differences in access to parental leave across countries and within countries. Sociologist Margaret O'Brien refers to growing up in "parental-leave-rich" versus "parental-leave-poor" households: "A privileged group of infants will commence life in parental-leave-rich households with high access to maternal, paternal, and financial capital. By contrast, another group of infants enter into disadvantaged parental-leave-poor households with comparatively less emotional and economic investment available in their daily life."[2] While policies have the potential to expand the number of parents included, there is also potential to exclude certain groups, particularly low income parents.[3] The good news is that we know that parents, both mothers and fathers, will increase leave-taking if provided the opportunity.[4]

In this conclusion, I consider the important lessons that the US, the UK, and Sweden have provided for understanding the relationship between parental leave and gender equality. These lessons also provide clues for developing a parental leave policy that will best promote gender equality in the workplace and at home. Throughout this book, we have seen the following lessons:

1. The US is way behind the rest of the world when it comes to parental leave
2. Parental leave is good
3. But not too much leave
4. We need to think of fathers as partners, not helpers
5. The UK is not a good model for parental leave and gender equality
6. The Swedish model is great but not perfect

The US Is behind on Parental Leave

The US is in a category by itself when it comes to parental leave, and not in a positive way. It is the only industrialized country without some form of paid leave and even when we expand the circle of comparison, we are only left with Suriname and Papua New Guinea as the other countries without any paid parental leave. This fact, in itself, should be enough motivation to pass a paid parental leave policy.

In chapter 1, we saw the development (or lack thereof) of family leave at the federal, state, and company level. It was a struggle just to get the Family and Medical Leave Act (FMLA) passed and signed into law in

1993. The compromises that had to be made then meant shorter leave of only twelve weeks and no pay. And over twenty-five years later, we still don't have paid leave! There are several shortcomings of FMLA. The most obvious is that it is not paid. This needs to change. Another limitation is that eligibility criteria, particularly the size of the workplace, mean that only 59 percent of American workers are even eligible to use this form of unpaid leave.[5]

We have seen some success in the states that have adopted paid family leave. California, the first state to introduce paid family leave, has seen an increase in employees taking leave to bond with their children, and the increase in men's use of bonding leave is particularly notable.[6] Based on a small payroll tax, this policy is especially helpful for low-income employees and, even from employers' perspective, this program has had a net positive impact on productivity and morale.[7] With states like New York, Washington, and Massachusetts coming out with their own policies, we have several models to choose from. And yet most Americans still rely on their employers for some form of leave. Etsy, Netflix, and Spotify all have generous policies that offer an equal amount of paid leave to all parents. But many companies follow more of a British model with more leave for mothers than fathers. And even more companies don't offer paid parental leave at all, forcing employees to use paid vacation or personal days or, even worse, to take leave without pay. The bottom line is that it is simply not fair that access to paid parental leave is so unequal across states and employers.

Parental Leave Is Good

We saw the benefits of parental leave for mothers, fathers, children, employers, and broader efforts for gender equality in chapter 2. One of the main reasons for developing parental leave policies has been to increase women's employment. Job-protected, well paid leave encourages women to enter and remain in the labor force throughout their childbearing years.[8] It is particularly important in encouraging women to return to their same employer after leave, which reduces the negative impact of career interruptions on future advancement and income.[9]

Another benefit of parent leave is better health outcomes for women, men, and children. Perhaps it is most obvious that parental leave improves infant health. After all, newborns can't take care of themselves.

Parental leave decreases infant mortality, death in the first year, at least in part through higher rates of immunization and breastfeeding.[10] Parental leave is also important for women who have given birth in order to have some time for physical recovery. Likewise, taking parental leave can reduce postpartum depression.[11] The fact that parental leave is good for women and children's health may seem like common sense, but it is also good for men's health. That's right. Parental leave can reduce fathers' health problems and may even lower mortality rates.[12]

Parental leave provides time for parents to bond with their new child. This is particularly important for fathers, who are often seen as secondary parents. When fathers take parental leave, they become more active parents, and they develop the skills and routine for long-term involvement.[13] People often assume that mothers are naturally good at caring for infants, but caregiving and parenting is a learning process. And it turns out that fathers who spend time with infants figure things out pretty quickly. When men are full parents, it also contributes to more gender equal and happier relationships.[14]

More and more companies are offering their own paid parental leave policies. While some might be motivated by altruistic reasons, the bottom line for most companies is that parental leave is good business. Several companies note the need to be competitive in introducing their parental leave. Others mention recruitment, retention, productivity, and company culture.[15]

In sum, parental leave makes for better maternal, paternal, and child health outcomes, better maternal employment outcomes, stronger connections between fathers and children, and better business. Parental leave, especially if shared equally between parents, has the potential to foster gender equality. It seems like a win-win-win-win situation.

But Not Too Much Leave

While parental leave has many benefits, there is a limit to these benefits. As we saw in chapter 3, there is such a thing as too much leave, which becomes detrimental to women and men's employment and women's health. Feminist philosopher Nancy Fraser argues that women are marginalized by policies that support women's caregiving because they reinforce the association of caregiving and domestic labor with women and breadwinning with men.[16] When women take extended leaves from employment, they are seen by employers as less committed workers. Even if this is accepted, these differences encourage the formal or informal establishment of a "mommy track," where mothers are assigned to positions with less responsibility and pay.

The evidence does suggest that long parental leave decreases women's employment.[17] In general, the longer one is out of employment, the more difficult it is to return to the same position or a similar occupational position. Those who are out of employment for long periods may miss training and updates and also signal their reduced priority on work. Even when maintaining high levels of maternal employment, such as in Sweden, taking long leaves can reduce the chances for women's career advancement.[18] Based on employment gaps and stagnant or downward career mobility, it is not surprising that long leaves are associated with lower wages, and in fact, may be a prime contributor to the gender pay gap.[19] Taken all together, research suggests that five to seven months is the optimal length of leave for women's employment outcomes.[20]

Long parental leave is not only bad for women's employment outcomes. It also has negative effects on women's mental health. Public health research shows that the protective effects of parental leave against postpartum depression stop around six months after childbirth. In other words, continuing leave after six months actually increases women's odds of experiencing depression.[21]

But it is not just women who suffer negative consequences of long parental leave. In fact, long parental leave may be even more detrimental for men's careers. While women are expected to take time off when they have a child, men are expected to carry on working after a week or two. Sweden is an exception though employers still expect shorter leaves from men than women. As a result, employers and co-workers may think male employees who take long leaves are not team players, and ultimately men's earnings take a hit.[22]

There is even some research that suggests unlimited leave is not good for children. When children are home with parents too long, they may not experience as much interaction with other children and learning environments. In this case, the ideal amount of parental leave is six to twelve months. Too much parental leave is associated with lower social competence, communication, and physical health.[23]

So what is the optimal amount of leave? Looking at employment, depression, and child development, it looks like six months per parent is the ideal.

Fathers as Partners, Not Helpers

When parental leave is different for men and women, it is all too easy to fall into gendered roles, with mothers as primary caregivers or nurturers and fathers as helpers or secondary parents. The UK has a history of very different parental leave policies for women and men. This has created a pattern of mother-centered parental leave, in which both mothers and fathers see parental leave as belonging to mothers. British parents convey that there is not much discussion about maternity leave because women decide how much time they want to take off and their partners simply agree. There is some reliance on the idea that women are naturally nurturers, and an emphasis on breastfeeding further encourages this ideology.[24] It allows, or requires, men to step back and take a secondary role. Both British and American men talk about supporting their wives. To be fair, fathers who are limited to one or two weeks of leave don't have many opportunities to develop caregiving skills, and certainly not to the level of mothers who take several months and potentially a year of leave.

If we view parental leave as a chore, we seem to be letting fathers off the hook. If we view parental leave as a special time for bonding, we seem to be excluding fathers. When fathers are left alone to care for their children, they do just fine. Individuals are not born knowing how to parent—they need to learn how to parent. When parental leave is mainly provided to women, women get to spend lots of time figuring out how to be mothers. But we often ignore this fact and instead assume that women are naturally good at caring for children. If we divided leave equally between parents, men would also figure it out. We already see this in countries like Sweden.[25]

The UK Is Not a Good Model

While the US and the UK share many similarities, the UK does not provide a very good model for parental leave and gender equality. Their efforts to achieve more shared parental leave have fallen flat in the face of the lasting effects of an imbalanced policy and the continuing gendering of current policy. The main problem is that maternity and parental leave policy development in the UK has been heavily weighted toward mothers. While the UK lagged behind much of Europe in its initial policy development and was often rebuked by the EU Commission for not following EU directives regarding parental leave, it quickly extended maternity leave in the late 1990s and early 2000s. By 2003, mothers had a right to fifty-two weeks of maternity leave while fathers had a right to only one or two weeks of paternity leave. It should be no surprise, then, that most mothers take long maternity leaves, which leads to long career interruptions and high rates of part-time employment. A shocking 44 percent of British mothers are out of work for more than four years while 42 percent of all British women in employment work part-time.[26]

The UK has recently been trying to change. In 2011, British leaders introduced a policy that allowed fathers to take additional paternity leave, starting at twenty weeks, for up to six months. In 2015, they introduced Shared Parental Leave, which allows couples to share up to fifty weeks of parental leave (after the first two weeks of maternity leave). This is definitely progress. In theory, a couple could evenly divide parental leave, with each parent taking twenty-six weeks of leave. Unfortunately, there are some problems. Perhaps the biggest is that not all fathers are covered. One UK government estimate shows that 40 percent of new fathers are not eligible.[27] This is because a father must be attached to a mother who is eligible for maternity pay or leave. Another big problem is that the pay is appalling, with the exception of the first six weeks, which are paid at a rate of 90 percent of wages. Let's say a father wants to take the second half of the year of parental leave. They would only receive thirteen weeks of pay at the low flat rate of £145 per week, and the other thirteen weeks would be unpaid. It shouldn't surprise us that only 2 percent of couples use shared parental leave.[28] The UK is fighting momentum. It is difficult to overcome such a large difference in parental leave. The good news for the US is that we are starting from scratch.

The Swedish Model Is Great—But Not Perfect

When I started my research, I thought Sweden was the dream. Certainly, I still think Sweden provides one of the best existing models for parental leave and gender equality. It is important to highlight the positive aspects of Sweden's parental leave system. Obviously, Sweden has had some practice in getting things right since it was the first to introduce parental leave back in 1974. A big part of the country's success is that it has been guided by an official goal of gender equality. Sweden seems perpetually ahead of the rest of the world in acknowledging that gender equality cannot be achieved simply by fitting women into the workplace, a domain traditionally dominated by men, but also fitting men into the domestic sphere, a domain traditionally occupied by women.

Sweden realized that its original parental leave policy was not effective in encouraging men to take leave. In response, Sweden introduced its first "daddy" month in 1995, and then proceeded to add a second "daddy" month in 2002 and a third in 2016. Setting aside parental leave for fathers—time that is lost if a father does not take it—has been instrumental in increasing men's use of parental leave. Almost all fathers take at least some parental leave, and fathers are taking an increasing proportion of leave over time. While Swedish men took 12 percent of parental leave in 1999, they took 28 percent of it in 2017, higher than every other country except Iceland.[29] Swedish fathers talk about a "national ideal of caring" and even speak of fathers who do not take leave as "suspect."[30]

Time after time, Sweden has scored at the top of indices of parental leave and gender equality.[31] How could we possibly improve on the Swedish model? For one, as we saw above, there is indeed such a thing as too much leave. We can ask whether Sweden offers too much leave, a total of 480 days. This is especially problematic if women take more than half, which in many cases means more than one year. A second issue is that the non-transferrable leave, or "daddy" months, is really effective at getting men to take their months, so why not split all leave days in half and reserve half of the time for each parent? Here is where the US actually might have something to contribute. While our federal parental leave policy is unpaid, it is an individual entitlement, provided to each employee (though we know many employees are excluded due to eligibility requirements). The point is that reserving leave for each parent, rather than each couple, is a better way to encourage both parents to take leave.

Policy Recommendations

Policy design is crucial. A recent study of Finland and Sweden sheds light on the relative importance of policy design. Researchers set out to understand why a much higher percentage of Swedish fathers take up parental leave compared to Finnish fathers. They decided to compare immigrants and native-born men in both countries. They found that men who were born in Sweden and immigrated to Finland had parental leave uptake rates that were closer to those of native-born Finnish men than to Swedish men in Sweden, whereas men who were born in Finland and immigrated to Sweden had rates that were closer to those of native-born Swedish men than to Finnish men in Finland. In other words, fathers who migrated were more similar to men in their destination country than in their country of origin. This suggests that the men were influenced more by the available policies than their origin culture.[32]

In considering parental leave polices, we might note the European Commission's recent proposal, which recognizes the importance of providing paid parental leave to both parents. In April 2017, this commission sought to repeal Directive 2010/18 and to introduce a new proposal. It is important to note that the objective of this new proposal is "to ensure the implementation of the principle of equality between men and women with regard to labour market opportunities and treatment at work." The two specific objectives related to the main objective are to increase the availability of work-family balance policies and to prompt men to make more use of parental leave and other family-friendly policies. As such, the proposal includes an increase in parental leave requirements to a minimum of four months of non-transferrable leave for each parent at relatively high compensation levels (minimum pay must be at or above the level of sick pay).[33] The proposal has gone through various steps, but it faces uneven support from stakeholders.[34]

We can now consider how the six lessons can inform development of a paid parental leave policy in the US. Based on lesson 1, we need a paid leave policy. This is a no brainer. It is impossible to believe that the US is right and all those other countries—every single one apart from Suriname and Papua New Guinea—are wrong. Now that we know we should have paid parental leave, how much leave should we have? Lessons 2 and 3 tell us that some amount of (paid) leave is good (lesson 2)—but not too much (lesson 3). The balance I recommend is six months of parental leave for each parent. Parents need time to care for and bond with their children. This is important for every parent and every child. But in looking at the potentially negative consequences of parental leave, six months seems to be a turning point. This is the case for women's employment. It is also the case for postpartum depression. It is the case for child development, as well.

Do we really need to give all parents, mothers and fathers, the same amount of time? Yes. Based on lesson 4, we need to include fathers as equal parents. When mothers are the only ones to take leave or take a great majority of the available leave, it ultimately hurts women's careers, stifles father-child bonding, and inhibits gender equality. When each parent takes six months, it will allow women to return to work and continue building careers that are satisfying and financially rewarding. It also takes the target off mothers by recognizing the importance of family for all employees. It is easy to see why employers might not want to hire and promote women when they are the only ones who take extensive time off work, but the same reasoning doesn't apply when both men and women are equally likely to take leave. When each parent takes six months, it provides fathers with the opportunity to build caregiving skills and develop a strong bond with their child, which will pay dividends for eighteen-plus years. When each parent takes six months, norms will change and society will come to accept that women and men are equally capable of doing it all.

What are some final tips from the UK and Sweden? Based on the UK model (lesson 5), it would not be wise to go down the road of developing maternity leave without paternity or parental leave. Even if that seems like a quicker, more feasible solution, this kind of gendered policy has long-term, detrimental repercussions for gender equality, setting women back in the workplace and restricting men's roles at home. The US has been pretty clear about gender-neutral policies. FMLA and all the state family leave policies apply to individuals regardless of gender. This is a good thing.

Based on the Swedish model (lesson 6), the US may want to limit the amount of leave and keep all leave as non-transferable. The first point is probably a non-issue. I do not hear anyone proposing one year of paid parental leave. The second point is also one that would already fit with American ideals.

I recommend:

1. Paid parental leave of six months for each parent.
2. Leave should be available to all employees, regardless of size of employer or time with employer. Part-time employees should get pro-rated benefits.
3. Leave must be job-protected, with guarantees for an employee to return to their same job or a similar job in terms of level and pay.
4. Leave should be well compensated, at a rate of at least 80 percent of pay.
5. All parents should be encouraged to take the full six months of leave. This includes resident and non-resident parents.

With leave of six months for each parent, couples or co-parents could take turns and be at home with their new child for up to one year in total. Six months is a good amount of time for individual parents to bond with their new children. It also means that new parents will not face the economic consequences of long leaves. Children will benefit from spending six months with each parent. In cases where there is only one parent (where no other parent is available, even non-residential), the policy should allow for leave to be taken by an alternative caregiver, such as a grandparent, aunt, or uncle, or used to fund child care.

Points 2–4 are important to cover all employees, make leave feasible, and minimize the economic impacts of leave. FMLA only covers 59 percent of American employees because of its restrictions. It is also important to ensure that new parents can return to their original or comparable job so that they are not penalized for taking time off. In order to allow more parents to take leave, it must be remunerated at a relatively high level. We already have models of successful state programs funded by small payroll deductions (amounting to less than one dollar per week). Many employees simply cannot afford to take unpaid leave or to take leave that only pays half of one's wages. Finally, there should be incentives for individuals to take leave. This policy can only promote gender equality if men and women both take leave. When everyone takes leave, it will become normalized as part of the workplace. There will be no reason to penalize women or create mommy tracks that offer less pay and opportunity for advancement. The good news is that non-transferrable leave is already built into the American system, since all of the existing leave provisions—unpaid FMLA and paid state leave policies—mandate leave for individual employees rather than couples or families. The FAMILY Act, introduced most recently in 2017, might provide a starting point since it would provide paid leave to workers in all companies. It could be phased in, so that the twelve weeks of leave would be increased to twenty-six weeks and pay would be increased from 66 percent to 80 percent over a few years. Funding models might come from state policies. In particular, Washington state funds its generous leave (paying up to 90 percent of average weekly wages) through a 0.4 percent employee and employer payroll contribution.

While I set out to find a solution to America's problem of the absence of a national paid parental leave policy, I think these recommendations could also help the UK and Sweden. Instead of having a shared parental leave policy that still actually works through the mother and maternity leave, the British government could offer a similar amount of leave but divided between two parents. There would be no maternity or paternity but rather simply six months of paid parental leave for each parent. The UK would also need to invest in better funding to make leave more feasible. For Sweden, I would suggest that all leave be allotted as non-transferrable. Any additional costs could be accommodated by reducing the total leave from sixteen months (or eight months per parent) to one year. With the six month solution, I think we can develop a paid parental leave policy that is not just okay but that is a model for other countries in its capacity to promote gender equality.

ACKNOWLEDGMENTS

This book has been several years in the making. It was inspired by my time in Sweden and the UK and aided along the way by many generous individuals, organizations, and institutions. Thank you to the many parents across the US, UK, and Sweden who took the time to talk with me or one of my colleagues about their experiences with parental leave.

Thank you to the Fulbright Program, the US–UK Fulbright Commission, and the University of Leicester for providing me the opportunity to spend time in the UK at a critical point in my evolving understanding of parental leave. The Department of Sociology at Leicester were wonderful hosts during my stay. Thanks especially to Ellen Annandale for supporting me throughout, as well as Jane Pilcher and David Bartram.

Thank you to Mattias Strandh for inviting me to Umeå University while I was planning this book. Special thanks to Anna-Lena Almqvist and Anne Grönlund for sharing Swedish interview data and collaborating with me on related projects. Also to Eva Bernhardt for first welcoming me to Sweden and Frances Goldscheider for introducing me to Eva and making all other connections possible.

Thank you to the International Network on Leave Policies and its many outstanding members, including Sonja Blum, Ann-Zofie Duvander, Alison Koslowski, Alexandra Macht, Gerardo Meil, Peter Moss, Margaret O'Brien, Richard Petts, and Michael Rush. Special thanks to Shirley Gatenio Gabel for shepherding me through our country note and my first meeting and Linda Haas for her valuable feedback and support. I am thrilled to be part of such an excellent group of researchers.

Thank you to Davidson College for the generous research support over several years through Davidson College Faculty Study and Research grants, the Clark Ross Academic Innovation Fund, and Dean Rusk travel grants. And to Mary Muchane and Beverly Winecoff for grant support. And to Brian Little and James Sponsel for help procuring images and Joe Gutekanst and the library staff for obtaining materials quickly. And to my fabulous sociology and GSS colleagues, including Natalie Delia Deckard, Joseph Ewoodzie, and Gerardo Marti. Special thanks to Amanda Martinez for conducting interviews in Texas and collaborating with me on a related project. Thanks also to my productive undergraduate research assistants: Molly Bair, Ashley Behnke, William Botchway, Nick Boyd, Jaela Cabrera McDonald, Breanna Davidson, Yashita Kandhari, Fabian Lara, Maria Mavrodieva, José Olvera, Mimi Schrimsher, Micah Turpeau, and Grace Woodward.

Thank you to the crew at NYU Press for always providing support at the right time, including my wonderful editor Ilene Kalish and her assistant Sonia Tsuruoka. And to Martin Coleman for editing and production and Mary Beth Jarrad for marketing savvy. I am also indebted to Isobel Bainton at Policy Press for encouraging me back at the ISA in Vienna.

Thank you to my amazing family for always being there—Fred and Lori Kaufman, Victor Jung, Frances and Robert Bell, Rick and Vee Kaufman, Kai and Suji Jung, John Bell and Hilary Spiegelman, Chris and Kindra Bell, and all the not-so-little ones, Aleksei, Noah, Hannah, Elliot, and Quinn. I wish my mom were here to tell all her friends, acquaintances, and strangers about my book. For my kids, Emily and David, who are the ultimate inspiration. Thanks for picking up and going to school at Avenue and Sir Jonathan and trudging along on all our trips. I hope there will be a six month solution in place if/when you ever have your own kids. And to Kevin, for reading every page, picking me up when I was down, and simply being the you.

NOTES

INTRODUCTION

1 Bureau of Labor Statistics. 2018. Employee benefits survey, access to paid personal leave.

2 Dagher, McGovern, and Dowd. 2014. Maternity leave duration and postpartum mental and physical health; Sundbye and Hegewisch. 2011. Maternity, paternity, and adoption leave in the United States.

3 International Labour Organization. 2014. Maternity and paternity at work.

4 Hennig, Gatermann, and Hägglund. 2012. Pros and cons of family policies for mothers' labour market participation.

5 Goldscheider, Bernhardt, and Lappegård. 2015. The gender revolution.

6 Aisenbrey and Fasang. 2017. The interplay of work and family trajectories over the life course; Hennig et al., 2012.

7 Newport. 2018. Democrats more positive about socialism than capitalism.

8 Moss. 2013. International review of leave policies and related research 2013.

9 OECD. 2016. Trends in parental leave policies since 1970.

10 Moss, 2013.

11 ILO, 2014.

12 World Bank. 2018. Women, business and the law 2018.

13 Moss. 2012. Caring and learning together.

14 O'Brien. 2009. Fathers, parental leave policies, and infant quality of life, 194.

15 Ibid.

16 Sainsbury. 1999. Gender, policy regimes, and politics.

17 Bernhardt and Goldscheider. 2006. Gender equality, parenthood attitudes, and first births in Sweden.

18 Sainsbury, 1999.

19 Aisenbrey, Evertsson, and Grunow. 2009. Is there a career penalty for mothers' time out?.

20 Dearing. 2016. Gender equality in the division of work.

21 OECD. 2017. Key characteristics of parental leave systems.

22 Esping-Andersen. 1990. *The three worlds of welfare capitalism.*

23 Laughlin. 2011. Maternity leave and employment patterns of first-time mothers.

24 Hernes. 1987. *Welfare state and woman power*, 15.

25 Orloff. 2009. Gendering the comparative analysis of welfare states, 314.

26 Fraser. 1994. After the family wage.

27 Ibid., 599–600.

28 Ibid., 612.
29 Borchorst and Siim. 2008. Woman-friendly policies and state feminism.
30 Rubery. 2015. Regulating for gender equality.
31 Crompton. 1999. *Restructuring gender relations and employment*; Gornick and Meyers. 2003. *Families that work.*
32 Thévenon. 2011. Family policies in OECD countries.
33 Gornick and Meyers. 2003. *Families that work.*
34 Bergqvist, Bjarnegård, and Zetterberg. 2016. When class trumps sex, 174.
35 The US declined from its rank of twenty-eight in 2015, likely due to its extremely low ranking of ninety-eight on political empowerment.
36 World Economic Forum. 2018. The global gender gap report 2018.
37 Center for American Women and Politics. 2018. Women in congress; The Local Sweden. 2018. In stats; OECD Family Database; World Bank. 2018. Proportion of seats held by women.
38 The Swedish Institute. Gender equality in Sweden.
39 Kaufman, Lyonette, and Crompton. 2010. Post-birth employment leave among fathers; Lyonette, Kaufman, and Crompton. 2011. "We both need to work."
40 My colleague Amanda Martinez conducted eleven of these interviews in Texas.
41 Kaufman and Bernhardt. 2012. His and her job; Kaufman and Bernhardt. 2015. Gender, work and parenthood; Kaufman, Bernhardt, and Goldscheider. 2017. Enduring egalitarianism?.
42 These interviews were conducted by Anna-Lena Almqvist and appear in the following: Almqvist and Kaufman. 2016. What work-family conflicts do fathers experience; Kaufman and Almqvist. 2017. The role of partners and workplaces.
43 These interviews were conducted by Ann Grönlund and appear in Kaufman and Grönlund. 2017. Displaying parenthood, (un)doing gender.

CHAPTER 1. THE US IS WAY BEHIND THE REST OF THE WORLD

1 June. 2016. Why is maternity leave so terrible in this country?
2 Rubin. 2016. U.S. dead last among developed countries when it comes to paid maternity leave.
3 Strauss. 2018. Paid parental leave elusive.
4 International Labour Organization. 2014. Maternity and paternity at work.
5 Bureau of Labor Statistics. 2013. Employee benefits survey.
6 Bureau of Labor Statistics. 2018. Employee benefits survey, access to paid personal leave.
7 Shepherd-Banigan and Bell. 2014. Paid leave benefits among a national sample of working mothers with infants in the United States.
8 Zagorsky. 2017. Divergent trends in US maternity and paternity leave.
9 National Partnership for Women & Families. 2017. New and expanded employer paid family leave policies; National Partnership for Women & Families. 2018. Leading on leave.
10 Karr. 2017. Where's my dad? A feminist approach to incentivized paternity leave.

11 Ibid.

12 Ibid.

13 Elving. 1995. *Conflict and compromise.*

14 Elison. 1997. Policy innovation in a cold climate.

15 Elison. 1997; Elving. 1995.

16 U.S. Department of Labor. 2000. The 2000 survey report.

17 Klerman, Daly, and Pozniak. 2014. Family and Medical Leave in 2012.

18 Institute for Child, Youth and Family Policy. 2015. Working adults who are eligible for and can afford FMLA unpaid leave.

19 Zillman. 2017. Kirsten Gillibrand is giving her paid family leave proposal its first Trump-era test.

20 Farrell and Glynn. 2013. The FAMILY Act.

21 O'Connell. 2015. Obama authorizes up to six weeks of paid parental leave.

22 See Cassandra Engeman's 2018 working paper "Time for care: A history of state leave legislation in the United States."

23 Lipset. 1997. *American exceptionalism.*

24 Zigler, Muenchow, and Ruhm. 2012. Time off with baby.

25 Employment Development Department, State of California. 2016. Disability Insurance (DI) and Paid Family Leave (PFL) weekly benefit amounts.

26 Ibid.

27 Bartel et al. 2015. Paid family leave, fathers' leave-taking, and leave-sharing in dual-earner households.

28 Appelbaum and Milkman. 2011. Leaves that pay.

29 Bartel et al. 2014. California's Paid Family Leave law.

30 Appelbaum and Milkman. 2011. Leaves that pay; Milkman and Appelbaum. 2013. *Unfinished business.*

31 O'Dea. 2018. Paid family-leave bill would mean more time, more money for workers.

32 Lerner and Appelbaum. 2014. Business as usual.

33 White, Houser, and Nisbet. 2013. Policy in action.

34 Ibid.

35 Silver, Mederer, and Djurdjevic. 2016. Launching the Rhode Island Temporary Caregiver Insurance Program.

36 New York State Paid Family Leave, https://www.ny.gov

37 Gale. 2018. The national fight for paid leave has moved to statehouses.

38 Sundell. 2018. Washington paid family leave premiums kick in January 1.

39 National Partnership for Women & Families. 2018. State paid family and medical leave insurance laws.

40 Johnston. 2018. Here's what we know about the state's paid leave program.

41 Gale, 2018.

42 Lemire. 2015. Paid parental leave programs starting to expand in US cities.

43 NYC Government. 2016. Mayor de Blasio signs paid parental leave personnel order for NYC workers.

44 Green. 2017. Historic SF parental leave law kicks in.
45 O'Connor. 2016. Washington, D.C. passes 8-week paid parental leave bill.
46 National Partnership for Women & Families. 2018. Leading on leave.
47 Desilver. 2017. Access to paid family leave varies widely across employers, industries.
48 Bureau of Labor Statistics. 2018. Employee tenure in 2018.
49 National Partnership for Women & Families. 2018. Leading on leave.
50 Ibid.
51 Ibid.
52 Margolin. 2016. Chobani offers moms, dads 6 weeks of parental leave at full pay.
53 National Partnership for Women & Families. 2018. Leading on leave.
54 Ibid.
55 Ibid.
56 Ibid.
57 Livingston. 2018. Most dads say they spend too little time with their children.
58 Ibid.
59 Ibid.
60 Cain. 2017. How a tech CEO's experience as a single dad convinced him to overhaul his $3 billion company's benefits.
61 Jackson. 2017. These photos of Mark Zuckerberg in Hawaii reveal a growing work trend for American dads.
62 National Partnership for Women & Families. 2018. Leading on leave.
63 Ibid.
64 Ibid.
65 Ibid.
66 Ibid.
67 Peck. 2016. Coca-Cola will offer more inclusive parental leave.
68 National Partnership for Women & Families. 2018. Leading on leave.
69 Ibid. Emphasis added.
70 Ibid.
71 Ibid.
72 Ibid.
73 Ibid.
74 Ibid.
75 Ibid.
76 Ibid.
77 Ibid.
78 All names are pseudonyms.
79 Gomby and Pei. 2009. Newborn family leave; Han, Ruhm, and Waldfogel. 2009. Parental leave policies and parents' employment and leave-taking; Zagorsky. 2017. Divergent trends in US maternity and paternity leave.
80 Nepomnyaschy and Waldfogel. 2007. Paternity leave and fathers' involvement with their young children.

81 Fass. 2009. Paid leave in the states; Milkman and Appelbaum. 2013. *Unfinished business*; Petts, Knoester, and Li. 2018. Paid paternity leave-taking in the United States.
82 Nepomnyaschy and Waldfogel, 2007; Zagorsky, 2017
83 Han, Ruhm, and Waldfogel, 2009; Zagorsky, 2017
84 Bowman et al. 2016. Making paid leave work for every family.
85 Bowman. 2017. How gay dads manage without paid paternity leave; Prescott. 2018. Queer families still struggle to access leave.
86 Horowitz et al. 2017. Americans widely support paid family and medical leave.
87 Ibid.
88 Ibid.
89 Ibid.
90 Peltz. 2016. Why paid parental leave won't go national.
91 Kaufman. 2013. *Superdads.*
92 Sweet. 2018. Tammy Duckworth is pregnant.
93 Leach. 2018. What maternity leave looks like when you're a sitting senator.
94 Hamedy and Diaz. 2018. Sen. Duckworth makes history, casts vote with baby on Senate floor.
95 Frothingham and West. 2017. Trump's paid parental leave plan won't work for women and families.

CHAPTER 2. PARENTAL LEAVE IS GOOD
1 Livingston. 2018. Most dads say they spend too little time with their children.
2 Parker and Livingston. 2017. 6 facts about American fathers.
3 Ibid.
4 Ibid.
5 Keck and Saraceno. 2013. The impact of different social-policy frameworks on social inequalities among women in the European Union; Stier, Lewin-Epstein, and Braun. 2001. Welfare regimes, family-supportive policies, and women's employment along the life-course.
6 Ejrnæs. 2011. The impact of family policy and career interruptions on women's perceptions of the negative occupational consequences of full-time home care; Rønsen and Sundström. 2002. Family policy and after-birth employment among new mothers.
7 Pettit and Hook. 2005. The structure of women's employment in comparative perspective.
8 Adema. 2013. Greater gender equality.
9 Ruhm. 1998. The economic consequences of parental leave mandates.
10 Akgunduz and Plantenga. 2013. Labour market effects of parental leave in Europe.
11 Thévenon and Solaz. 2013. Labour market effects of parental leave policies in OECD countries.
12 Kluve and Tamm. 2013. Parental leave regulations, mothers' labor force attachment and fathers' childcare involvement.

13 Pronzato. 2009. Return to work after childbirth.

14 Keck and Saraceno. 2013. The impact of different social-policy frameworks on social inequalities among women in the European Union.

15 Baker and Milligan. 2008. How does job-protected maternity leave affect mothers' employment?

16 Joesch. 1997. Paid leave and the timing of women's employment before and after birth.

17 Berger and Waldfogel. 2004. Maternity leave and the employment of new mothers in the United States.

18 Hofferth and Curtin. 2006. Parental leave statutes and maternal return to work after childbirth in the United States.

19 Baum and Ruhm. 2016. The effects of paid family leave in California on labor market outcomes.

20 Byker. 2016. Paid parental leave laws in the United States.

21 Ibid.

22 Han, Ruhm, and Waldfogel. 2009. Parental leave policies and parents' employment and leave-taking.

23 Keck and Saraceno. 2013. The impact of different social-policy frameworks on social inequalities among women in the European Union.

24 Rossin-Slater, Ruhm, and Waldfogel. 2013. The effects of California's paid family leave program on mothers' leave-taking and subsequent labor market outcomes.

25 Baum and Ruhm. 2016. The effects of paid family leave in California on labor market outcomes.

26 Edlund. 2017. The causal effect of paid parental leave on gender equality.

27 Jacobs. 1999. Trends in women's career patterns and in gender occupational mobility in Britain; McRae. 2008. Working full-time after motherhood.

28 Hennig, Gatermann, and Hägglund. 2012. Pros and cons of family policies for mothers' labour market participation.

29 Ibid.

30 Harrop and Moss. 1995. Trends in parental employment; Jacobs. 1999. Trends in women's career patterns and in gender occupational mobility in Britain.

31 Fagan and Norman. 2012. Trends and social divisions in maternal employment patterns following maternity leave in the UK.

32 Jonsson and Mills. 2001. The sooner the better? Parental leave duration and women's occupational career.

33 Waldfogel. 1998. Understanding the 'family gap' in pay for women with children.

34 Stier, Lewin-Epstein, and Braun. 2001. Welfare regimes, family-supportive policies, and women's employment along the life-course.

35 Albrecht, Edin, Sundström, and Vroman. 1999. Career interruptions and subsequent earnings.

36 Budig and England. 2001. The wage penalty for motherhood.

37 Baum. 2002. The effect of work interruptions on women's wages.

38 Stancyzk. 2016. Paid family leave may reduce poverty following a birth.

39 Johansson. 2010. The effect of own and spousal parental leave on earnings.

40 Fernández-Cornejo, Del Pozo-García, Escot, and Castellanos-Serrano. 2018. Can an egalitarian reform in the parental leave system reduce the motherhood labor penalty?

41 Burtle and Bezruchka. 2016. Population health and paid parental leave.

42 Aitken et al. 2015. The maternal health outcomes of paid maternity leave; Baker and Milligan. 2008. How does job-protected maternity leave affect mothers' employment?

43 Killien, Habermann, and Jarrett. 2001. Influence of employment characteristics on postpartum mothers' health; McGovern et al. 2011. A longitudinal analysis of total workload and women's health after childbirth.

44 Laughlin. 2011. Maternity leave and employment patterns of first-time mothers.

45 Goodman. 2018. Laboring until labor.

46 Guendelman et al. 2009. Maternity leave in the ninth month of pregnancy and birth outcomes among working women.

47 Dagher, McGovern, and Dowd. 2014. Maternity leave duration and postpartum mental and physical health; O'Hara and Swain. 1996. Rates and risk of postpartum depression.

48 Cooper and Murray. 1998. Fortnightly review; Goodman. 2004. Postpartum depression beyond the early postpartum period; Horowitz and Goodman. 2004. A longitudinal study of maternal postpartum depression symptoms.

49 Chatterji and Markowitz. 2012. Family leave after childbirth and the mental health of new mothers.

50 Gjerdingen and Chaloner. 1994. The relationship of women's postpartum mental health to employment, childbirth, and social support.

51 McGovern et al. 1997. Time off work and the postpartum health of employed women.

52 Chatterji and Markowitz. 2005. Does the length of maternity leave affect maternal health?

53 Chatterji and Markowitz. 2012. Family leave after childbirth and the mental health of new mothers.

54 Chatterji, Markowitz, and Brooks-Gunn. 2013. Effects of early maternal employment on maternal health and well-being.

55 Chatterji, Markowitz, and Brooks-Gunn. 2013. Effects of early maternal employment on maternal health and well-being; Gault et al. 2014. Paid parental leave in the United States.

56 Petts. 2018. Time off after childbirth and mothers' risk of depression, parenting stress, and parenting practices.

57 Avendano, Berkman, Brugiavini, and Pasini. 2015. The long-run effect of maternity leave benefits on mental health.

58 Bratberg and Naz. 2014. Does paternity leave affect mothers' sickness absence?

59 Haas and Rostgaard. 2011. Fathers' rights to paid parental leave in the Nordic countries.

60 Castro-Garcia and Pazos-Moran. 2016. Parental leave policy and gender equality in Europe.

61 Kotsadam and Finseraas. 2011. The state intervenes in the battle of the sexes.

62 Almqvist, Sandberg, and Dahlgren. 2011. Parental leave in Sweden.

63 Meil. 2013. European men's use of parental leave and their involvement in child care and housework.

64 Haas and Hwang. 1999. Parental leave in Sweden.

65 Johansson. 2011. Fatherhood in transition.

66 Greenstein. 1995. Gender ideology, marital disruption, and the employment of married women; Oláh. 2001. Gender and family stability; Sigle-Rushton. 2010. Men's unpaid work and divorce.

67 Unterhofer and Wrohlich. 2017. Fathers, parental leave and gender norms.

68 Fernández-Cornejo et al. 2018. Can an egalitarian reform in the parental leave system reduce the motherhood labor penalty?

69 Dex. 2010. Can state policies produce equality in housework?; Nepomnyaschy and Waldfogel. 2007. Paternity leave and fathers' involvement with their young children; Petts and Knoester. 2019. Paternity leave and parental relationships.

70 Drago. 2011. What would they do?

71 Haas and Hwang. 2008. The impact of taking parental leave on fathers' participation in childcare and relationships with children; Nepomnyaschy and Waldfogel. 2007. Paternity leave and fathers' involvement with their young children.

72 Tanaka and Waldfogel. 2007. Effects of parental leave and work hours on fathers' involvement with their babies.

73 Nepomnyaschy and Waldfogel. 2007. Paternity leave and fathers' involvement with their young children.

74 Schober. 2014. Parental leave and domestic work of mothers and fathers.

75 Boll, Leppin, and Reich. 2014. Paternal childcare and parental leave policies.

76 Petts and Knoester. 2018. Paternity leave-taking and father engagement; Pragg and Knoester. 2017. Paternity leave use among disadvantaged fathers.

77 Pleck. 1993. Are "family-supportive" employer policies relevant to men?

78 Seward et al. 2006. Fathers taking parental leave and their involvement with children.

79 Boll, Leppin, and Reich. 2014. Paternal childcare and parental leave policies; de Laat and Sevilla-Sanz. 2011. The fertility and women's labor force participation puzzle in the OECD countries; Chalasani. 2007. The changing relationship between parents' education and their time with children; Frenette. 2011. How does the stork delegate work?

80 Huttunen. 1996. Full-time fathers and their parental leave experiences.

81 Duvander and Jans. 2009. Consequences of fathers' parental leave use.

82 O'Brien. 2009. Fathers, parental leave policies, and infant quality of life, 207.

83 Brandth and Kvande. 1998. Masculinity and childcare.

84 Brandth and Kvande. 2001. Flexible work and flexible fathers.

85 Brandth and Kvande. 2003. Father presence in childcare.

86 Haas. 1992. *Equal parenthood and social policy*; Haas and Hwang. 1999. Parental leave in Sweden; Haas and Hwang. 2008. The impact of taking parental leave on fathers' participation in childcare and relationships with children.

87 Haas and Hwang. 2008. The impact of taking parental leave on fathers' participation in childcare and relationships with children.

88 Wisensale. 2001. *Family leave policy*.

89 Tanaka and Waldfogel. 2007. Effects of parental leave and work hours on fathers' involvement with their babies.

90 Rehel. 2014. When dad stays home too.

91 Boll, Leppin, and Reich. 2014. Paternal childcare and parental leave policies.

92 Coltrane. 1996. *Family man*; Lamb. 2000. The history of research on father involvement.

93 Huerta et al. 2014. Fathers' leave and fathers' involvement.

94 Meil. 2013. European men's use of parental leave and their involvement in child care and housework.

95 Almqvist and Duvander. 2014. Changes in gender equality?

96 Bonke and Greve. 2012. Children's health-related life-styles.

97 Lidbeck, Bernhardsson, and Tjus. 2018. Division of parental leave and perceived parenting stress among mothers and fathers.

98 Månsdotter and Lundin. 2010. How do masculinity, paternity leave, and mortality associate?

99 Ibid.

100 Feldman et al. 2010. Natural variations in maternal and paternal care are associated with systematic changes in oxytocin following parent-infant contact.

101 Abraham et al. 2014. Father's brain is sensitive to childcare experiences.

102 Staehelin, Bertea, and Stutz. 2007. Length of maternity leave and health of mother and child.

103 Heymann et al. 2017. Paid parental leave and family wellbeing in the sustainable development era.

104 Ruhm. 2000. Parental leave and child health.

105 Tanaka. 2005. Parental leave and child health across OECD countries.

106 Rossin. 2011. The effects of maternity leave on children's birth and infant health outcomes in the United States.

107 Galtry and Callister. 2005. Assessing the optimal length of parental leave for child and parental well-being.

108 Ueda, Kondo, Takada, and Hashimoto. 2014. Maternal work conditions, socioeconomic and educational status, and vaccination of children.

109 Berger, Hill, and Waldfogel. 2005. Maternity leave, early maternal employment and child health and development in the US.

110 Ibid.

111 Galtry and Callister. 2005. Assessing the optimal length of parental leave for child and parental well-being.

112 Skafida. 2012. Juggling work and motherhood.

113 Baker and Milligan. 2008. How does job-protected maternity leave affect mothers' employment?

114 Galtry. 2003. The impact on breastfeeding of labour market policy and practice in Ireland, Sweden, and the USA.

115 Ogbuanu et al. 2011. The effect of maternity leave length and time of return to work on breastfeeding.

116 Huang and Yang. 2015. Paid maternity leave and breastfeeding practice before and after California's implementation of the nation's first paid family leave program.

117 Lichtman-Sadot and Bell. 2017. Child health in elementary school following California's Paid Family Leave program.

118 Flacking, Dykes, and Ewald. 2010. The influence of fathers' socioeconomic status and paternity leave on breastfeeding duration.

119 Petts. 2018. Time off after childbirth and mothers' risk of depression, parenting stress, and parenting practices.

120 Hwang and Jung. 2016. Does paid maternity leave affect infant development and second-birth intentions?

121 McMunn, Martin, Kelly, and Sacker. 2017. Fathers' involvement.

122 Gredebäck et al. 2012. Individual differences in face processing.

123 Gaston, Edwards, and Tober. 2015. Parental leave and child care arrangements during the first 12 months of life are associated with children's development five years later.

124 Lichtman-Sadot and Bell. 2017. Child health in elementary school following California's Paid Family Leave program.

125 Berger, Hill, and Waldfogel. 2005. Maternity leave, early maternal employment and child health and development in the US.

126 Rasmussen. 2010. Increasing the length of parents' birth-related leave.

127 Danzer and Lavy. 2017. Paid parental leave and children's schooling outcomes.

128 Huerta et al. 2013. Fathers' leave, fathers' involvement and child development.

129 Cools, Fiva, and Kirkebøen. 2015. Causal effects of paternity leave on children and parents.

130 Carneiro, Løken, and Salvanes. 2015. A flying start.

131 National Partnership for Women & Families. 2017. New and expanded employer paid family leave policies.

132 Ibid.

133 Ibid.

134 Ibid.

135 Ibid.

136 Stroman et al. 2017. Why paid family leave is good business.

137 National Partnership for Women & Families. 2017. New and expanded employer paid family leave policies.

138 Ibid.

139 Ibid.

140 Stroman et al. 2017. Why paid family leave is good business.

141 Ibid.
142 National Partnership for Women & Families. 2017. New and expanded employer paid family leave policies.
143 Houser and Vartanian. 2012. Pay matters.
144 Appelbaum and Milkman. 2011. Leaves that pay.
145 Wojcicki. 2014. Paid maternity leave is good business; Vanderkam. 2016. Why offering paid maternity leave is good for business.
146 National Partnership for Women & Families. 2017. New and expanded employer paid family leave policies.
147 Lerner and Appelbaum. 2014. Business as usual; Stroman et. al. 2017. Why paid family leave is good business
148 National Partnership for Women & Families. 2017. New and expanded employer paid family leave policies.
149 Ibid.
150 Esping-Andersen, Gallie, Hemerijck, and Myles. 2002. *Why we need a new welfare state.*
151 Shambaugh, Nunn, and Portman. 2017. Lessons from the rise of women's labor force participation in Japan.
152 Weinstein. 2018. When more women join the workforce, wages rise.
153 Bassanini and Venn. 2008. The impact of labour market policies on productivity in OECD countries.
154 Houser and Vartanian. 2012. Pay matters; Ruhm. 1998. The economic consequences of parental leave mandates.
155 Lalive and Zweimüller. 2009. How does parental leave affect fertility and return to work?
156 Bassford and Fisher. 2016. Bonus babies?
157 Duvander, Lappegård, and Andersson. 2010. Family policy and fertility.

CHAPTER 3. TOO MUCH PARENTAL LEAVE IS NOT GOOD

1 Rønsen and Sundström. 2002. Family policy and after-birth employment among new mothers.
2 Mandel and Semyonov. 2005. Family policies, wage structures, and gender gaps; Mandel and Semyonov. 2006. A welfare state paradox.
3 Lister. 2002. The dilemmas of pendulum politics.
4 Lister. 1997. Citizenship.
5 Lister. 2002. The dilemmas of pendulum politics, 526.
6 Fraser. 1994. After the family wage.
7 Ibid., 609.
8 Edin and Gustavsson. 2008. Time out of work and skill depreciation.
9 Pettit and Hook. 2005. The structure of women's employment in comparative perspective.
10 Ondrich, Spiess, and Yang. 1996. Barefoot and in a German kitchen.
11 Hanratty and Trzcinski. 2009. Who benefits from paid family leave?

12 Ruhm. 1998. The economic consequences of parental leave mandates.

13 Jaumotte. 2003. Female labour force participation.

14 Akgunduz and Plantenga. 2013. Labour market effects of parental leave in Europe.

15 Fagan and Norman. 2012. Trends and social divisions in maternal employment patterns following maternity leave in the UK.

16 Ibid.

17 Hennig, Gatermann, and Hägglund. 2012. Pros and cons of family policies for mothers' labour market participation.

18 Aisenbrey, Evertsson, and Grunow. 2009. Is there a career penalty for mothers' time out?

19 De Henau, Meulders, and O'Dorchai. 2010. Maybe baby.

20 Klerman and Leibowitz. 1997. Labor supply effects of state maternity leave legislation.

21 Aisenbrey, Evertsson, and Grunow. 2009. Is there a career penalty for mothers' time out?

22 Ibid.

23 Ibid.

24 Mandel and Semyonov. 2006. A welfare state paradox, figures 6 and 7.

25 Mandel and Semyonov. 2006. A welfare state paradox, 1942.

26 Gupta, Smith, and Verner. 2008. The impact of Nordic countries' family friendly policies on employment, wages and children.

27 Ejrnaes. 2011. The impact of family policy and career interruptions on women's perceptions of the negative occupational consequences of full-time home care.

28 Evertsson and Grunow. 2012. Women's work interruptions and career prospects in Germany and Sweden.

29 Evertsson and Duvander. 2011. Parental leave—possibility or trap?

30 Aisenbrey, Evertsson, and Grunow. 2009. Is there a career penalty for mothers' time out?

31 Evertsson. 2016. Parental leave and careers.

32 Gupta, Smith, and Verner. 2008. The impact of Nordic countries' family friendly policies on employment, wages and children.

33 Albrecht et al. 1999. Career interruptions and subsequent earnings; Baum. 2002. The effect of work interruptions on women's wages; Budig and England. 2001. The wage penalty for motherhood; Gupta and Smith. 2002. Children and career interruptions; Gangl and Ziefle. 2009. Motherhood, labor force behavior, and women's careers; Gornick. 2004. Women's economic outcomes, gender inequality, and public policy; Waldfogel. 1997. The effect of children on women's wages.

34 Glauber. 2008. Race and gender in families and at work; Killewald. 2013. A reconsideration of the fatherhood premium.

35 Budig and England. 2001. The wage penalty for motherhood.

36 Glass. 2004. Blessing or curse?

37 Mandel and Semyonov. 2005. Family policies, wage structures, and gender gaps

38 Stier, Lewin-Epstein, and Braun. 2001. Welfare regimes, family-supportive policies, and women's employment along the life-course.
39 Gupta and Smith. 2002. Children and career interruptions
40 Pylkkanen and Smith. 2003. Career interruptions due to parental leave.
41 Glass and Fodor. 2007. From public to private maternalism?
42 Buligescu et al. 2008. Panel estimates of the wage penalty for maternal leave.
43 Albrecht et al. 1999. Career interruptions and subsequent earnings; Ruhm. 1998. The economic consequences of parental leave mandates.
44 Ziefle 2004 as cited in Hennig, Gatermann, and Hägglund. 2012. Pros and cons of family policies for mothers' labour market participation.
45 Ondrich, Spiess, and Yang. 2002. The effect of maternity leave on women's pay in Germany.
46 Ketsche and Branscomb. 2003. The long-term costs of career interruptions.
47 Budig, Misra, and Boeckmann. 2012. The motherhood penalty in cross-national perspective.
48 Angelov, Johansson, and Lindahl. 2013. Is the persistent gender gap in income and wages due to unequal family responsibilities?
49 Cooke. 2014. Gendered parenthood penalties and premiums across the earnings distribution in Australia, the United Kingdom, and the United States.
50 Bianchi et al. 2012. Housework; Hook. 2006. Care in context.
51 Hook. 2010. Gender inequality in the welfare state.
52 Fodor and Kispeter. 2014. Making the 'reserve army' invisible, 383.
53 Ibid., p. 384.
54 Glass and Fodor. 2011. Public maternalism goes to market.
55 Fodor and Kispeter. 2014. Making the 'reserve army' invisible; Glass and Fodor. 2011. Public maternalism goes to market; Misra, Moller, and Budig. 2007. Work–family policies and poverty for partnered and single women in Europe and North America.
56 Gábos. 2017. Hungary country note.
57 Fodor and Kispeter. 2014. Making the 'reserve army' invisible.
58 Ibid., p. 393.
59 Aisenbrey, Evertsson, and Grunow. 2009. Is there a career penalty for mothers' time out?
60 Mandel and Shalev. 2006. A class perspective on gender inequality.
61 Lundberg and Rose. 2000. Parenthood and the earnings of married men and women.
62 Orloff. 2009. Should feminists aim for gender symmetry?
63 Ibid., 145.
64 Charles and Grusky. 2004. *Occupational ghettoes*; Cobble. 2004. *The other women's movement*.
65 Orloff. 2009. Should feminists aim for gender symmetry?, 145.
66 Orloff. 2009. Gendering the comparative analysis of welfare states.
67 Budig and Hodges. 2010. Differences in disadvantage.

68 Aisenbrey and Fasang. 2017. The interplay of work and family trajectories over the life course, see Figure 3.
69 Dagher, McGovern, and Dowd. 2014. Maternity leave duration and postpartum mental and physical health.
70 Ibid., 394.
71 Hwang and Jung. 2016. Does paid maternity leave affect infant development and second-birth intentions?
72 Hochschild. 1997. *The time bind.*
73 Gaston, Edwards, and Tober. 2015. Parental leave and child care arrangements during the first 12 months of life are associated with children's development five years later.
74 Albrecht et al. 1999. Career interruptions and subsequent earnings.
75 Ibid., 310.
76 Ibid.
77 Coltrane et al. 2013. Fathers and the flexibility stigma; Rudman and Mescher. 2013. Penalizing men who request a family leave.
78 Davies and Frink. 2014. The origins of the ideal worker.
79 Stafford and Sundström. 1996. Time out for childcare.
80 Cools, Fiva, and Kirkebøen. 2015. Causal effects of paternity leave on children and parents; Johansson. 2010. The effect of own and spousal parental leave on earnings.
81 Rege and Solli. 2013. The impact of paternity leave on fathers' future earnings.
82 Ibid., 2275.
83 Horvath, Grether, and Wiese. 2018. Fathers' realizations of parental leave plans.
84 Brandth and Kvande. 2002. Reflexive fathers.
85 Valarino and Gauthier. 2016. Paternity leave implementation in Switzerland.
86 Evertsson and Grunow. 2012. Women's work interruptions and career prospects in Germany and Sweden.
87 Albrecht et al. 1999. Career interruptions and subsequent earnings
88 Johansson. 2010. The effect of own and spousal parental leave on earnings.
89 Evertsson. 2016. Parental leave and careers.

CHAPTER 4. FATHERS AS PARTNERS, NOT HELPERS

1 Heilman et al. 2016. State of America's fathers 2016.
2 Kaufman. 2016. Fathers also want to "have it all."
3 Gregory and Milner. 2011. What is "new" about fatherhood?
4 Henwood, Shirani, and Coltart. 2010. Fathers and financial risk-taking during the economic downturn.
5 Whitehouse, Diamond, and Baird. 2007. Fathers' use of leave in Australia.
6 Moss and Deven. 2015. Leave policies in challenging times.
7 Dermott. 2008. *Intimate fatherhood*; Kilkey. 2010. Men and domestic labor.
8 Allen and Hawkins. 1999. Maternal gatekeeping.
9 Lyonette, Kaufman, and Crompton. 2011. "We both need to work"; Miller. 2011. Falling back into gender?

10 McKay and Doucet. 2010. "Without taking away her leave."
11 Brady et al. 2017. "You can spend time . . . but not necessarily be bonding with them."
12 Duvander. 2014. How long should parental leave be?; Hyde, Essex, and Horton. 1993. Fathers and parental leave; McKay and Doucet. 2010. "Without taking away her leave."
13 Duvander. 2014. How long should parental leave be
14 Brady et al. 2017. "You can spend time . . . but not necessarily be bonding with them."
15 McKay and Doucet. 2010. "Without taking away her leave"; Miller. 2011. Falling back into gender?
16 Baird and O'Brien. 2015. Dynamics of parental leave in Anglophone countries.
17 Miller. 2011. Falling back into gender?
18 McKay and Doucet. 2010. "Without taking away her leave"
19 Baird and O'Brien. 2015. Dynamics of parental leave in Anglophone countries.
20 Risman. 1986. Can men "mother?"
21 Risman. 1987. Intimate relationships from a microstructural perspective.
22 Lamb. 2000. The history of research on father involvement.
23 Doucet. 2006. *Do men mother?*
24 see also Doucet. 2009. Dad and baby in the first year.
25 Rochlen et al. 2008. Predictors of relationship satisfaction, psychological well-being, and life satisfaction among stay-at-home fathers.
26 Hook and Chalasani. 2008. Gendered expectations?
27 Coles. 2009. *The best kept secret*; Kaufman. 2013. *Superdads.*
28 Rehel. 2014. When dad stays home, 122
29 Ibid., 126–127.
30 O'Brien and Wall. 2017. *Comparative perspectives on work-life balance and gender equality.*

CHAPTER 5. THE UK IS NOT A GOOD MODEL

1 Connolly and Gregory. 2008. Moving down.
2 Crompton. 2006. *Employment and the family.*
3 O'Brien and Shemilt. 2003. Working fathers.
4 Cousins and Tang. 2004. Working time and work and family conflict in the Netherlands, Sweden and UK; Lewis. 2002. The problems of fathers.
5 Featherstone. 2009. *Contemporary fathering*; Geisler and Kreyenfeld. 2011. Against all odds.
6 Dermott. 2008. *Intimate fatherhood.*
7 Tinson, Aldridge, and Whitham. 2016. Women, work and wages in the UK.
8 OECD. 2018. Part-time employment rate.
9 Gash. 2009. Sacrificing their careers for their families?
10 Atkinson. 2017. Shared parental leave in the UK.
11 Ejrnæs. 2011. The impact of family policy and career interruptions on women's perceptions of the negative occupational consequences of full-time home care, 248.

12 Sigle-Rushton and Waldfogel. 2007. The incomes of families with children.

13 Smith and Williams. 2007. Father-friendly legislation and paternal time across Western Europe.

14 Jarvis. 2010. The timeline.

15 Boll, Leppin, and Reich. 2014. Paternal childcare and parental leave policies.

16 Daly. 2010. Shifts in family policy in the UK under New Labour.

17 Baird and O'Brien. 2015. Dynamics of parental leave in Anglophone countries, 209.

18 Wall. 2007. Leave policy models and the articulation of work and family in Europe.

19 Adema, Clarke, and Frey. 2015. Paid parental leave.

20 Ibid.

21 Jarvis. 2010. The timeline.

22 Baird and O'Brien. 2015. Dynamics of parental leave in Anglophone countries.

23 Ibid., 201.

24 The following OECD countries have no paid paternity or parental leave *reserved* for fathers: Canada, Czech Republic, Ireland, Israel, New Zealand, Slovak Republic, Switzerland, Turkey, US.

25 Kilkey. 2006. New Labour and reconciling work and family life.

26 Kilkey, Perrons, and Plomien. 2013. *Gender, migration and domestic work.*

27 Kilkey. 2006. New Labour and reconciling work and family life.

28 Daly. 2010. Shifts in family policy in the UK under New Labour.

29 Lewis et al. 2008. Patterns of development in work/family reconciliation policies for parents in France, Germany, the Netherlands, and the UK.

30 Atkinson. 2017. Shared parental leave in the UK.

31 Deven and Moss. 2002. Leave arrangements for parents.

32 Ray, Gornick, and Schmitt. 2010. Who cares?

33 Atkinson. 2017. Shared parental leave in the UK, 358.

34 Kilkey. 2006. New Labour and reconciling work and family life.

35 Moss and Deven. 2015. Leave policies in challenging times, 139.

36 TUC. 2015. Two in five new fathers won't qualify for Shared Parental Leave.

37 Gordon and Szram. 2013. Paternity leave experiences of NHS doctors.

38 O'Brien and Koslowski. 2017. United Kingdom country note.

39 Baird and O'Brien. 2015. Dynamics of parental leave in Anglophone countries.

40 Atkinson. 2017. Shared parental leave in the UK.

41 Rush. 2015. *Between two worlds of father politics.*

42 TUC. 2015. Two in five new fathers won't qualify for Shared Parental Leave.

43 Miller. 2013. Shifting out of neutral on parental leave, 261.

44 Atkinson. 2017. Shared parental leave in the UK.

45 Ibid., 364.

46 Ibid., 360.

47 Ibid., 363.

48 The Telegraph. 2017. Did you know you can take unpaid leave to take care of your kids?

49 O'Brien and Koslowski. 2017. United Kingdom country note.

50 Kelly. 2016. Paternity leave.

51 O'Brien and Koslowski. 2017. United Kingdom country note.

52 Rush. 2015. *Between two worlds of father politics.*

53 Dermott. 2001. New fatherhood in practice?

54 Ibid.

55 Dermott. 2005. Time and labour, 102.

56 Williams. 2008. What is fatherhood?

57 Gregory and Milner. 2010. Fathers and work-life balance in France and the UK.

58 Kaufman. 2018. Barriers to equality.

59 Bygren and Duvander. 2006. Parents' workplace situation and fathers' parental leave use; McKay and Doucet. 2010. Without taking away her leave.

60 McKay and Doucet. 2010. Without taking away her leave.

61 Callan. 2007. Implications of family-friendly policies for organizational culture.

62 Burnett et al. 2013. Fathers at work.

63 Callan. 2007. Implications of family-friendly policies for organizational culture.

64 McKay and Doucet. 2010. Without taking away her leave.

65 Dahl, Løken, and Mogstad. 2014. Peer effects in program participation.

66 Burnett et al. 2013. Fathers at work.

67 Gatrell and Cooper. 2016. A sense of entitlement?

68 Fox, Pascall, and Warren. 2009. Work-family policies, participation, and practices.

69 Gatrell et al. 2014. Parents, perceptions and belonging, 482.

70 Kaufman, Lyonette, and Crompton. 2010. Post-birth employment leave among fathers in Britain and the United States.

71 Miller. 2011. Falling back into gender?

72 Gov.UK. Surrogacy: Legal rights of parents and surrogates.

73 Schober. 2014. Parental leave and domestic work of mothers and fathers.

74 Hobson, Lewis, and Siim. 2002. *Contested concepts in gender and social politics.*

75 Romero-Balsas, Muntanyola-Saura, and Rogero-Garcia. 2013. Decision-making factors within paternity and parental leaves.

76 My Family Care. 2016. Shared parental leave.

77 Fisher. 2018. Want men to share parental leave?

78 Ibid.

79 Ibid.

CHAPTER 6. THE SWEDISH MODEL IS GREAT—BUT NOT PERFECT

1 Weller. 2017. Sweden is the best country in the world for women.

2 Bennhold. 2010. In Sweden, men can have it all.

3 Wall Street Journal. 2018. Sweden is the world's finest home for families.

4   Drew. 2018. These are the 5 best countries to raise kids; Haines. 2017. Mapped; Martin. 2017. The 16 countries with the world's best healthcare systems; Mejia. 2018. These are the top 10 happiest countries in the world; Radu. 2018. These are the 5 best countries for women.

5   MacLellan. 2017. Sweden's gender-neutral preschools produce kids who are more likely to succed.

6   Kane. 2018. Sweden is apparently full of "latte dads" carrying toddlers.

7   CESifo. 2014. Parental leave entitlements.

8   Bergqvist, Bjarnegård, and Zetterberg. 2016. When class trumps sex, 175.

9   Eydal et al. 2015. Trends in parental leave in the Nordic countries.

10 Duvander, Haas, and Hwang. 2017. Sweden country note.

11 Ibid.

12 Ibid.

13 Crisp. 2017. Take five months parental leave, Swedish fathers told.

14 Lück. 2005. Cross-national comparison of gender role attitudes and their impact on women's life courses.

15 Korpi. 2000. Faces of inequality.

16 Earles. 2011. Swedish family policy; Oláh and Bernhardt. 2008. Sweden.

17 Ferrarini and Duvander. 2010. Earner-carer model at the crossroads.

18 Ibid.

19 Mandel and Semyonov. 2006. A welfare state paradox.

20 Thévenon and Luci. 2012. Reconciling work, family and child outcomes.

21 Knudsen and Waerness. 2001. National context, individual characteristics and attitudes on mothers' employment.

22 Bernhardt, Noack, and Lyngstad. 2008. Shared housework in Norway and Sweden.

23 Dribe and Stanfors. 2009. Does parenthood strengthen a traditional household division of labor?; Kaufman, Bernhardt, and Goldscheider. 2017. Enduring egalitarianism?

24 Haas. 1992. *Equal parenthood and social policy*, 12.

25 Johansson and Klinth. 2008. Caring fathers.

26 Valarino et al. 2018. Exploring leave policy preferences.

27 Wall. 2007. Leave policy models and the articulation of work and family in Europe.

28 Ferrarini. 2003. Parental leave institutions in eighteen post-war welfare states, 34.

29 Klinth 2002 as cited in Haas and Rostgaard. 2011. Fathers' rights to paid parental leave in the Nordic countries.

30 Haas and Rostgaard. 2011. Fathers' rights to paid parental leave in the Nordic countries, 193.

31 Dearing. 2016. Gender equality in the division of work.

32 Ray, Gornick, and Schmitt. 2010. Who cares?

33 Javornik and Kurowska. 2017. Work and care opportunities under different parental leave systems.

34 Johansson. 2011. Fatherhood in transition.
35 Duvander and Johansson. 2012. What are the effects of reforms promoting fathers' parental leave use?
36 Duvander. 2014. How long should parental leave be?
37 The Local. 2018. Dads in Sweden took more paternity leave than ever in 2017.
38 The Local Sweden. 2017. More dads taking paternity leave; The Local Sweden. 2017. Dads in Sweden took more parental leave than ever in 2017.
39 Mohdin. 2016. How Sweden's "daddy quota" parental leave helps with equal parenting.
40 Försäkringskassan 2009 as cited in Haas and Rostgaard. 2011. Fathers' rights to paid parental leave in the Nordic countries.
41 Duvander, Haas, and Hwang. 2017. Sweden country note.
42 Karu and Tremblay. 2018. Fathers on parental leave.
43 Ibid.
44 Swedish Social Insurance Agency. 2017. *Social Insurance in Figures 2017*.
45 Johansson. 2011. Fatherhood in transition, 169.
46 Bergman and Hobson. 2002. Compulsory fatherhood.
47 Johansson and Klinth. 2008. Caring fathers.
48 Rush. 2015. *Between two worlds of father politics*.
49 Johansson and Klinth. 2008. Caring fathers.
50 Klinth. 2008. The best of both worlds?
51 Bergqvist and Saxonberg. 2017. The state as a norm-builder?, 1481.
52 Kaufman and Almqvist. 2017. The role of partners and workplaces in British and Swedish men's parental leave decisions.
53 Sundström. 1999. Should mothers work?
54 Evertsson. 2013. The importance of work.
55 Almqvist, Sandberg, and Dahlgren. 2011. Parental leave in Sweden; Edlund and Öun. 2016. Who should work and who should care?
56 Geisler and Kreyenfeld. 2011. Against all odds.
57 Creighton, Brussoni, and Oliffe. 2015. Fathers on child's play.
58 Almqvist and Duvander. 2014. Changes in gender equality?
59 Haas and Hwang. 2008. The impact of taking parental leave on fathers' participation in childcare and relationships with children.
60 Kaufman and Grönlund. 2017. Doing the dual-earner family.
61 Haas and Hwang. 2013. Fatherhood and social policy in Scandinavia.
62 Crisp. 2017. Take five months parental leave, Swedish fathers told.

CONCLUSION
1 Fouché. 2008. Where tax goes up to 60 per cent, and everybody's happy paying it.
2 O'Brien. 2009. Fathers, parental leave policies, and infant quality of life.
3 McKay, Mathieu, and Doucet. 2016. Parental-leave rich and parental-leave poor.
4 Han, Ruhm, and Waldfogel. 2009. Parental leave policies and parents' employment and leave-taking.

5 Institute for Child, Youth and Family Policy. 2015. Working adults who are eligible for and can afford FMLA unpaid leave.

6 Employment Development Department, State of California. 2016. Disability Insurance (DI) and Paid Family Leave (PFL) weekly benefit amounts.

7 Appelbaum and Milkman. 2011. *Leaves that pay*; Milkman and Appelbaum. 2013. *Unfinished business.*

8 Keck and Saraceno. 2013. The impact of different social-policy frameworks on social inequalities among women in the European Union; Pronzato. 2009. Return to work after childbirth.

9 Stier, Lewin-Epstein, and Braun. 2001. Welfare regimes, family-supportive policies, and women's employment along the life-course.

10 Ogbuanu et al. 2011. The effect of maternity leave length and time of return to work on breastfeeding; Tanaka. 2005. Parental leave and child health across OECD countries.

11 Chatterji, Markowitz, and Brooks-Gunn. 2013. Effects of early maternal employment on maternal health and well-being.

12 Månsdotter and Lundin. 2010. How do masculinity, paternity leave, and mortality associate?

13 Boll, Leppin, and Reich. 2014. Paternal childcare and parental leave policies.

14 Castro-Garcia and Pazos-Moran. 2016. Parental leave policy and gender equality in Europe; Kotsadam and Finseraas. 2011. The state intervenes in the battle of the sexes.

15 National Partnership for Women & Families. 2018. State paid family and medical leave insurance laws.

16 Fraser. 1994. After the family wage.

17 Pettit and Hook. 2005. The structure of women's employment in comparative perspective.

18 De Henau, Meulders, and O'Dorchai. 2010. Maybe baby.

19 Gupta, Smith, and Verner. 2008. The impact of Nordic countries' family friendly policies on employment, wages and children.

20 Akgunduz and Plantenga. 2013. Labour market effects of parental leave in Europe; Jaumotte. 2003. Female labour force participation.

21 Dagher, McGovern, and Dowd. 2014. Maternity leave duration and postpartum mental and physical health.

22 Albrecht et al. 1999. Career interruptions and subsequent earnings.

23 Gaston, Edwards, and Tober. 2015. Parental leave and child care arrangements during the first 12 months of life are associated with children's development five years later.

24 McKay and Doucet. 2010. "Without taking away her leave."

25 O'Brien and Wall. 2017. *Comparative perspectives on work-life balance and gender equality.*

26 Ejrnæs. 2011. The impact of family policy and career interruptions on women's perceptions of the negative occupational consequences of full-time home care; McGuinness. 2018. Women and the economy.

27 TUC. 2015. Two in five new fathers won't qualify for Shared Parental Leave.

28 Fisher. 2018. Want men to share parental leave?

29 Karu and Tremblay. 2018. Fathers on parental leave; The Local. 2018. Dads in Sweden took more paternity leave than ever in 2017.

30 Bergqvist and Saxonberg. 2017. The state as a norm-builder?

31 Dearing. 2016. Gender equality in the division of work; Ray, Gornick, and Schmitt. 2010. Who cares?

32 Tervola, Duvander, and Mussino. 2017. Promoting parental leave for immigrant fathers.

33 Dinu. 2017. Parental leave directive.

34 EU legislation briefing. 2018. A new directive on work-life balance.

BIBLIOGRAPHY

Abraham, E., Hendler, T., Shapira-Lichter, I., Kanat-Maymon, Y., Zagoory-Sharon, O., & Feldman, R. (2014). Father's brain is sensitive to childcare experiences. *Proceedings of the National Academy of Sciences of the United States of America, 111,* 9792–9797.

Adema, W. (2013). Greater gender equality: What role for family policy? *Family Matters, 93,* 7–16.

Adema, W., C. Clarke, & Frey, V. (2015). Paid parental leave: Lessons from OECD countries and selected U.S. states. OECD Social, Employment and Migration Working Papers, No. 172, OECD Publishing, Paris.

Aisenbrey, S., Evertsson, M., & Grunow, D. (2009). Is there a career penalty for mothers' time out? A comparison of Germany, Sweden and the United States. *Social Forces, 88,* 573–606.

Aisenbrey, S., & Fasang, A. (2017). The interplay of work and family trajectories over the life course: Germany and the United States in comparison. *American Journal of Sociology, 122,* 1448–1484.

Aitken, Z., Garrett, C. C., Hewitt, B., Keogh, L., Hocking, J. S., & Kavanagh, A. M. (2015). The maternal health outcomes of paid maternity leave: A systematic review. *Social Science & Medicine, 182,* 97–105.

Akgunduz, Y. E., & Plantenga, P. (2013). Labour market effects of parental leave in Europe. *Cambridge Journal of Economics, 37,* 845–862.

Albrecht, James W., Per-Anders, E., Sundström, M. & Vroman, B. S., (1999). Career interruptions and subsequent earnings: A reexamination using Swedish data. *Journal of Human Resources, 34,* 294–311.

Allen, S. M., & Hawkins, A. J. (1999). Maternal gatekeeping: Mothers' beliefs and behaviors that inhibit greater father involvement in family work. *Journal of Marriage and Family, 61,* 199–212.

Almqvist, A.-L., & Duvander, A.-Z. (2014). Changes in gender equality? Swedish fathers' parental leave, division of housework and childcare. *Journal of Family Studies, 20,* 19–27.

Almqvist, A.-L., & Kaufman, G. (2016). What work-family conflicts do fathers experience in Sweden and in the US? In I. Crespi & E. Ruspini (Eds.), *Balancing work and family in a changing society: The father's perspective* (pp. 177–189). Basingstoke, UK: Palgrave Macmillan.

Almqvist, A.-L., Sandberg, A., & Dahlgren, L. (2011). Parental leave in Sweden: Motives, experiences, and gender equality amongst parents. *Fathering, 9,* 189–206.

Angelov, N., Johansson, P., & Lindahl, E. (2013). Is the persistent gender gap in income and wages due to unequal family responsibilities? Institute for Labour Market and Educational Policy Assessment, IFAU Working Paper 3.

Appelbaum, E., & Milkman, R. (2011). *Leaves that pay: Employer and worker experiences with Paid Family Leave in California*. Washington, D.C.: Center for Economic and Policy Research.

Atkinson, J. (2017). Shared parental leave in the UK: Can it advance gender equality by changing fathers into co-parents? *International Journal of Law, 13*, 356–368.

Avendano, M., Berkman, L. F., Brugiavini, A., & Pasini, G. (2015). The long-run effect of maternity leave benefits on mental health: Evidence from European countries. *Social Science & Medicine, 132*, 45–53.

Baird, M., & O'Brien, M. (2015). Dynamics of parental leave in Anglophone countries: The paradox of state expansion in the liberal welfare regime. *Community, Work & Family, 18*, 198–217.

Baker, M., & Milligan, K. (2008). How does job-protected maternity leave affect mothers' employment? *Journal of Labor Economics, 26*, 655–691.

Bartel, A., Baum, C., Rossin-Slater, M., Ruhm, C., & Waldfogel, J. (2014). *California's Paid Family Leave law: Lessons from the first decade*. Report prepared for the U.S. Department of Labor. Retrieved from: https://www.dol.gov/

Bartel, A., Rossin-Slater, M., Ruhm, C., Stearns, J., & Waldfogel, J. (2015). *Paid Family Leave, fathers' leave-taking, and leave-sharing in dual-earner households*. Report prepared for the U.S. Department of Labor. Retrieved from: https://www.dol.gov/

Bassanini, A., & Venn, D. (2008). The impact of labour market policies on productivity in OECD countries. *International Productivity Monitor, 17*, 3–15.

Bassford, M., & Fisher, H. (2016). Bonus babies? The impact of paid parental leave on fertility intentions. Working papers 2016–04, University of Sydney, School of Economics.

Baum, C. L. (2002). The effect of work interruptions on women's wages. *Labour, 16*, 1–37.

Baum, C. L., & Ruhm, C. J. (2016). The effects of paid family leave in California on labor market outcomes. *Journal of Policy Analysis and Management, 35*, 333–356.

Bennhold, K. (2010, June 9). In Sweden, men can have it all. *The New York Times*. Retrieved from: https://www.nytimes.com

Berger, L. M., Hill, J., & Waldfogel, J. (2005). Maternity leave, early maternal employment and child health and development in the US. *The Economic Journal, 115*, 29–47.

Berger, L. M., & Waldfogel, J. (2004). Maternity leave and the employment of new mothers in the United States. *Journal of Population Economics, 17*, 331–349.

Bergman, H., & Hobson, B. (2002). Compulsory fatherhood. In B. Hobson (Ed.), *Making men into fathers* (pp. 92–124). Cambridge: Cambridge University Press.

Bergqvist, C., Bjarnegård, E., & Zetterberg, P. (2016). When class trumps sex: The Social Democratic intra-party struggle over extending parental leave quotas in Sweden. *Social Politics, 23*, 169–191.

Bergqvist, C., & Saxonberg, S. (2017). The state as a norm-builder? The take-up of parental leave in Norway and Sweden. *Social Policy & Administration, 51*, 1470–1487.

Bernhardt, E., & Goldscheider, F. (2006). Gender equality, parenthood attitudes, and first births in Sweden. *Vienna Yearbook of Population Research, 4*, 19–39.

Bernhardt, E., Noack, T., & Lyngstad, T. (2008). Shared housework in Norway and Sweden: Advancing the gender revolution. *Journal of European Social Policy, 18*, 275–288.

Bianchi, S. M., Sayer, L. C., Milkie, M. A., & Robinson, J. P. (2012). Housework: Who did, does or will do it, and how much does it matter? *Social Forces, 91*, 55–63.

Boll, C., Leppin, J., & Reich, N. (2014). Paternal childcare and parental leave policies: Evidence from industrialized countries. *Review of Economics of the Household, 12*, 129–158.

Bonke, J., & Greve, J. (2012). Children's health-related life-styles: How parental child care affects them. *Review of the Economics of the Household, 10*, 557–572.

Borchorst, A., & Siim, B. (2008). Woman-friendly policies and state feminism. *Feminist Theory, 9*, 207–224.

Bowman, A. (2017, September 26). How gay dads manage without paid paternity leave. *Chicago Tribune.* Retrieved from: https://www.chicagotribune.com

Bowman, M., Durso, L. E., Gruberg, S., Kocolatos, M., Krishnamurthy, K., Make, J., McGovern, A., & Robbins, K. G. (2016). Making paid leave work for every family. Washington, DC: Center for American Progress.

Brady, M., Stevens, E., Coles, L., Zadoroznyj, M., & Martin, B. (2017). 'You can spend time . . . but not necessarily be bonding with them': Australian fathers' constructions and enactments of infant bonding. *Journal of Social Policy, 46*, 69–90.

Brandth, B., & Kvande, E. (1998). Masculinity and childcare. *The Sociological Review, 46*, 292–313.

Brandth, B., & Kvande, E. (2001). Flexible work and flexible fathers. *Work, Employment and Society, 15*, 251–267.

Brandth, B., & Kvande, E. (2002). Reflexive fathers: Negotiating parental leave and working life. *Gender, Work and Organization, 9*, 186–203.

Brandth, B., & Kvande, E. (2003). Father presence in childcare. In A. Jensen & L. McKee (Eds.), *Children and the changing family: Between transformation and negotiation* (pp. 61–75), Abingdon, UK: Routledge.

Bratberg, E., & Naz, G. (2014). Does paternity leave affect mothers' sickness absence? *European Sociological Review, 30*, 500–511.

Budig, M. J., & England, P. (2001). The wage penalty for motherhood. *American Sociological Review, 66*, 204–225.

Budig, M. J., & Hodges, M. J. (2010). Differences in disadvantage: Variation in the motherhood penalty across white women's earnings distribution. *American Sociological Review, 75*, 705–728.

Budig, M. J., Misra, J., & Boeckmann, I. (2012). The motherhood penalty in cross-national perspective: The importance of work-family policies and cultural attitudes. *Social Politics, 19*, 63–193.

Buligescu, B., De Crombrugghe, D., Mentesoglu, G. & Montizaan, R. (2008). Panel estimates of the wage penalty of leave. *Oxford Economic Papers, 61,* 35–55.

Bureau of Labor Statistics. (2013). Employee benefits survey. Retrieved from: https://www.bls.gov

Bureau of Labor Statistics. (2018). Employee benefits survey, access to paid personal leave. Retrieved from: https://www.bls.gov

Burnett, S. B., Gatrell, C. J., Cooper, C. L., & Sparrow, P. (2013). Fathers at work: A ghost in the organizational machine. *Gender, Work and Organization, 20,* 632–646.

Burtle, A., & Bezruchka, S. (2016). Population health and paid parental leave: What the United States can learn from two decades of research. *Healthcare, 4,* 30.

Bygren, M., & Duvander, A. (2006). Parents' workplace situation and fathers' parental leave use. *Journal of Marriage and Family, 68,* 363–372.

Byker, T. S. (2016). Paid parental leave laws in the United States: Does short-duration leave affect women's labor-force attachment? *American Economic Review, 106,* 242–246.

Cain, A. (2017, September 19). How a tech CEO's experience as a single dad convinced him to overhaul his $3 billion company's benefits. *Business Insider.* Retrieved from: http://www.businessinsider.com

Callan, S. (2007). Implications of family-friendly policies for organizational culture: Findings from two case studies. *Work, Employment and Society, 21,* 673–691.

Carneiro, P., Løken, K. V., & Salvanes, K. G. (2015). A flying start? Maternity leave benefits and long-run outcomes of children. *Journal of Political Economy, 123,* 365–412.

Castro-Garcia, C., & Pazos-Moran, M. (2016). Parental leave policy and gender equality in Europe. *Feminist Economics, 22,* 51–73.

Center for American Women and Politics. (2018). Women in Congress 2018. Retrieved from: www.cawp.rutgers.edu

CESifo. (2014). Parental leave entitlements: Historical perspective (around 1870–2014). Retrieved from: https://www.cesifo-group.de

Chalasani, S. (2007). The changing relationship between parents' education and their time with children. *International Journal of Time Use Research, 4,* 93–117.

Charles, M., & Grusky, D. (2004). *Occupational ghettoes: The worldwide segregation of women and men.* Stanford: Stanford University Press.

Chatterji, P., & Markowitz, S. (2005). Does the length of maternity leave affect maternal health? *Southern Economic Journal, 72,* 16–41.

Chatterji, P., & Markowitz, S. (2012). Family leave after childbirth and the mental health of new mothers. *The Journal of Mental Health Policy and Economics, 15,* 61–76.

Chatterji, P., Markowitz, S., & Brooks-Gunn, J. (2013). Effects of early maternal employment on maternal health and well-being. *Journal of Population Economics, 26,* 285–301.

Cobble, D.S. (2004). *The other women's movement: Workplace justice and social rights in modern America.* Princeton: Princeton University Press.

Coles, R. (2009). *The best kept secret: Single black fathers*. New York: Rowan & Littlefield.

Coltrane, S. (1996). *Family man: Fatherhood, housework, and gender equity*. New York: Oxford University.

Coltrane, S., Miller, E. C., DeHaan, T., & Stewart, L. (2013). Fathers and the flexibility stigma. *Journal of Social Issues, 69*, 279–302.

Connolly, S., & Gregory, M. (2008). Moving down: Women's part-time work and occupational change in Britain 1991–2001. *The Economic Journal, 118*, F52–76.

Cooke, L. P. (2014). Gendered parenthood penalties and premiums across the earnings distribution in Australia, the United Kingdom, and the United States. *European Sociological Review, 30*, 360–372.

Cools, S., Fiva, J. H., & Kirkebøen, L. J. (2015). Causal effects of paternity leave on children and parents. *Scandinavian Journal of Economics, 117*, 801–828.

Cooper, P. J., & Murray, L. (1998). Fortnightly review: Postnatal depression. *British Medical Journal, 316*, 1884–1886.

Cousins, C. R., & Tang, N. (2004). Working time and work and family conflict in the Netherlands, Sweden and UK. *Work, Employment and Society, 18*, 531–549.

Creighton, G., Brussoni, M., & Oliffe, J. (2015). Fathers on child's play: Urban and rural Canadian perspectives. *Men and Masculinities, 18*, 559–580.

Crisp, J. (2017, December 20). Take five months parental leave, Swedish fathers told. *The Telegraph*. Retrieved from: http://www.telegraph.co.uk

Crompton, R. (1999). *Restructuring gender relations and employment: The decline of the male breadwinner*. Oxford: Oxford University Press

Crompton, R. (2006). *Employment and the family: The reconfiguration of work and family life in contemporary societies*. Cambridge: Cambridge University Press.

Dagher, R. K., McGovern, P. M., & Dowd, B. E. (2014). Maternity leave duration and postpartum mental and physical health: Implications for leave policies. *Journal of Health Policy and Law, 39*, 369–416.

Dahl, G. B., Løken, K. V., & Mogstad, M. (2014). Peer effects in program participation. *American Economic Review, 104*, 2049–2074.

Daly, M. (2010). Shifts in family policy in the UK under New Labour. *Journal of European Social Policy, 20*, 433–443.

Danzer, N., & Lavy, V. (2017.) Paid parental leave and children's schooling outcomes. *The Economic Journal, 128*, 81–117.

Davies, A. R., & Frink, B. D. (2014). The origins of the ideal worker: The separation of work and home in the United States from the market revolution to 1950. *Work and Occupations, 41*, 18–39.

Dearing, H. (2016). Gender equality in the division of work: How to assess European leave policies regarding their compliance with an ideal leave model. *Journal of European Social Policy, 26*, 234–247.

De Henau, J., Meulders, D., & O'Dorchai, S. (2010). Maybe baby: Comparing partnered women's employment and child policies in the EU-15. *Feminist Economics, 16*, 43–77.

de Laat, J., & Sevilla-Sanz, A. (2011). The fertility and women's labor force participation puzzle in the OECD countries: The role of men's home production. *Feminist Economics, 17*, 87–119.

Dermott, E. (2001). New fatherhood in practice? Parental leave in the UK. *International Journal of Sociology and Social Policy, 21*, 145–164.

Dermott, E. (2005) Time and labour: Fathers' perceptions of employment and childcare. *The Sociological Review, 53*, 89–103.

Dermott, E. (2008). *Intimate fatherhood*. London: Routledge.

Desilver, D. (2017, March 23) Access to paid family leave varies widely across employers, industries. Washington, DC: Pew Research Center.

Deven, F., & Moss, P. (2002). Leave arrangements for parents: Overview and future outlook. *Community, Work & Family, 5*, 237–255.

Dex, S. (2010). Can state policies produce equality in housework? In J. Treas & S. Drobnic (Eds.), *Dividing the domestic: Men, women, and household work in cross-national perspective* (pp. 79–104). Stanford, CA: Stanford University Press.

Dinu, A. (2017). Parental leave directive. European Parliamentary Research Service. Retrieved from: http://www.europarl.europa.eu

Doucet, A. (2006). *Do men mother? Fathering, care, and domestic responsibility*. Toronto: University of Toronto Press.

Doucet, A. (2009). Dad and baby in the first year: Gendered responsibilities and embodiment. *The ANNALS of the American Academy of Political and Social Science, 624*, 78–98.

Drago, R. (2011). What would they do? Childcare under parental leave and reduced hours option. *Industrial Relations, 50*, 610–628.

Drew, K. (2018, January 23). These are the 5 best countries to raise kids. *US News and World Report*. Retrieved from: https://www.usnews.com

Dribe, M., & Stanfors, M. (2009). Does parenthood strengthen a traditional household division of labor? *Journal of Marriage and Family, 71*, 33–45.

Duvander, A. (2014). How long should parental leave be? Attitudes to gender equality, family, and work as determinants of women's and men's parental leave in Sweden. *Journal of Family Issues, 35*, 909–926.

Duvander, A, Haas, L., & Hwang, C. P. (2017). Sweden country note. In Blum, S., Koslowski, A., & Moss, P. (Eds.) *International Review of Leave Policies and Research 2017*. Retrieved from: https://www.leavenetwork.org

Duvander, A., & Jans, A. (2009). Consequences of fathers' parental leave use: Evidence from Sweden. *Finnish Yearbook of Population Research*, 51–62.

Duvander, A., & Johansson, M. (2012). What are the effects of reforms promoting fathers' parental leave use? *Journal of European Social Policy, 22*, 319–330.

Duvander, A., Lappegård, T., & Andersson, G. (2010). Family policy and fertility: Fathers' and mothers' use of parental leave and continued childbearing in Norway and Sweden. *Journal of European Social Policy, 20*, 45–57.

Earles, K. (2011). Swedish family policy: Continuity and change in the Nordic welfare state model. *Social Policy & Administration, 45*, 180–193.

Edin, P.-A. & Gustavsson, M. (2008). Time out of work and skill depreciation. *Industrial & Labor Relations Review, 61,* 163–180.

Edlund, J. (2017). The causal effect of paid parental leave on gender equality: A comparative analysis with a synthetic control method. Master's thesis for Lund University School of Economics and Management. Lund, Sweden.

Edlund, J., & Öun, I. (2016). Who should work and who should care? Attitudes towards the desirable division of labour between mothers and fathers in five European countries. *Acta Sociologica, 59,* 151–169.

Ejrnæs, A. (2011). The impact of family policy and career interruptions on women's perceptions of the negative occupational consequences of full-time home care. *European Societies, 13,* 239–256.

Elison, S. K. (1997). Policy innovation in a cold climate: The Family and Medical Leave Act of 1993. *Journal of Family Issues, 18,* 30–55.

Elving, R. D. (1995). *Conflict and compromise: How Congress makes the law.* New York: Simon and Schuster.

Employment Development Department, State of California. (2016). Disability Insurance (DI) and Paid Family Leave (PFL) weekly benefit amounts. Retrieved from: http://www.edd.ca.gov

Engeman, C. (2018). Time for care: A history of state leave legislation in the United States. Working Paper 9/2018, Swedish Institute for Social Research, Stockholm University.

Esping-Andersen, G. (1990). *The three worlds of welfare capitalism.* Princeton, NJ: Princeton University Press.

Esping-Andersen, G., Gallie, D., Hemerijck, A., & Myles, J. (2002). *Why we need a new welfare state.* Oxford: Oxford University Press.

EU legislation briefing. (2018). A new directive on work-life balance. Retrieved from: http://www.europarl.europa.eu

Evertsson, M. (2013). The importance of work: Changing work commitment following the transition to motherhood. *Acta Sociologica, 56,* 139–153.

Evertsson, M. (2016). Parental leave and careers: Women's and men's wages after parental leave in Sweden. *Advances in Life Course Research, 29,* 26–40.

Evertsson, M., & Duvander, A. (2011). Parental leave—possibility or trap? Does family leave length effect Swedish women's labour market opportunities? *European Sociological Review, 27,* 435–450.

Evertsson, M., & Grunow, D. (2012). Women's work interruptions and career prospects in Germany and Sweden. *International Journal of Sociology and Social Policy, 32,* 561–575.

Eydal, G. B., Gislason, I. V., Rostgaard, T., Brandth, B., Duvander, A., & Lammi-Taskula, J. (2015). Trends in parental leave in the Nordic countries: Has the forward march of gender equality halted? *Community, Work & Family, 18,* 167–181.

Fagan, C., & Norman, H. (2012). Trends and social divisions in maternal employment patterns following maternity leave in the UK. *International Journal of Sociology and Social Policy, 32,* 544–560.

Farrell, J., & Glynn, S. J. (2013). The FAMILY Act: Facts and frequently asked questions. Washington, DC: Center for American Progress.

Fass, S. (2009). *Paid leave in the states: A critical support for low-wage workers and their families.* National Center for Children in Poverty, Columbia University.

Featherstone, B. (2009). *Contemporary fathering.* Bristol: Policy Press.

Feldman, R., Gordon, I., Schneiderman, I., Weisman, O., & Zagoory-Sharon, O. (2010). Natural variations in maternal and paternal care are associated with systematic changes in oxytocin following parent-infant contact. *Psychoneuroendocrinology, 35,* 1133–1141.

Fernández-Cornejo, J. A., Del Pozo-García, E., Escot, L., & Castellanos-Serrano, C. (2018). Can an egalitarian reform in the parental leave system reduce the motherhood labor penalty? Some evidence from Spain. *Revista Española de Sociología, 27,* 45–64.

Ferrarini, T. (2003). *Parental leave institutions in eighteen post-war welfare states.* Stockholm: Institute for Social Research.

Ferrarini, T., & Duvander, A. (2010). Earner-carer model at the crossroads: Reforms and outcomes of Sweden's family policy in comparative perspective. *International Journal of Health Services, 40,* 373–398.

Fisher, D. (2018, February 15). Want men to share parental leave? Just give them equality. *The Guardian.* Retrieved from: https://www.theguardian.com

Flacking, R., Dykes, F., & Ewald, U. (2010). The influence of fathers' socioeconomic status and paternity leave on breastfeeding duration: A population-based cohort study. *Scandinavian Journal of Public Health, 38,* 337–343.

Fodor, E., & Kispeter, E. (2014). Making the 'reserve army' invisible: Lengthy parental leave and women's economic marginalization in Hungary. *European Journal of Women's Studies, 21,* 382–398.

Fouché, G. (2008, November 15). Where tax goes up to 60 per cent, and everybody's happy paying it. *The Guardian.* Retrieved from: https://www.theguardian.com

Fox, E., Pascall, G., and Warren, T. (2009). Work-family policies, participation, and practices: Fathers and childcare in Europe. *Community, Work & Family, 12,* 313–326.

Fraser, N. (1994). After the family wage: Gender equity and the welfare state. *Political Theory, 22,* 591–618.

Frenette, M. (2011). How does the stork delegate work? Childbearing and the gender division of paid and unpaid labour. *Journal of Population Economics, 24,* 895–910.

Frothingham, S., & West, R. (2017). *Trump's paid parental leave plan won't work for women and families.* Washington, DC: Center for American Progress.

Gábos, A. (2017). Hungary country note. In: Blum S., Koslowski A., and Moss P. (eds.) *International Review of Leave Policies and Research 2017.* http://www.leavenetwork. org

Gale, R. (2018, May 2). The national fight for paid leave has moved to statehouses. *Slate.* Retrieved from: https://slate.com

Galtry, J. (2003). The impact on breastfeeding of labour market policy and practice in Ireland, Sweden, and the USA. *Social Science and Medicine, 57,* 167–77.

Galtry, J., & Callister, P. (2005). Assessing the optimal length of parental leave for child and parental well-being: How can research inform policy? *Journal of Family Issues, 26*, 219–246.

Gangl, M., & Ziefle, A. (2009). Motherhood, labor force behavior, and women's careers: An empirical assessment of the wage penalty for motherhood in Britain, Germany, and the United States. *Demography, 46*, 341–369.

Gash, V. (2009). Sacrificing their careers for their families? An analysis of the penalty to motherhood in Europe. *Social Indicators Research, 93*, 569–586.

Gaston, A., Edwards, S. A., & Tober, J. (2015). Parental leave and child care arrangements during the first 12 months of life are associated with children's development five years later. *International Journal of Child, Youth and Family Studies, 6*, 230–251.

Gatrell, C., Burnett, S. B., Cooper, C. L., & Sparrow, P. (2014). Parents, perceptions and belonging: Exploring flexible working among UK fathers and mothers. *British Journal of Management, 25*, 473–487.

Gatrell, C., & Cooper, C. L. (2016). A sense of entitlement? Fathers, mothers and organizational support for family and career. *Community, Work & Family, 19*, 134–147.

Gault, B., Hartmann, H., Hegewisch, A., Milli, J., & Reichlin, L. (2014). *Paid parental leave in the United States: What the data tells us about access, usage, and economic and health benefits.* Washington, DC: Institute for Women's Policy Research.

Geisler, E., & Kreyenfeld, M. (2011). Against all odds: Fathers' use of parental leave in Germany. *Journal of European Social Policy, 21*, 88–99.

Gjerdingen, D. K., & Chaloner, K. M. (1994). The relationship of women's postpartum mental health to employment, childbirth, and social support. *Journal of Family Practice, 38*, 465–472.

Glass C., & Fodor E. (2007). From public to private maternalism? Gender and welfare in Poland and Hungary after 1989. *Social Politics, 14*, 323–350.

Glass, C., & Fodor, E. (2011). Public maternalism goes to market: Recruitment, hiring, and promotion in postsocialist Hungary. *Gender & Society, 25*, 5–26.

Glass, J. (2004). Blessing or curse? Work-family policies and mother's wage growth over time. *Work and Occupations, 31*, 367–394.

Glauber, R. (2008). Race and gender in families and at work: The fatherhood wage premium. *Gender & Society, 22*, 8–30.

Goldscheider, F., Bernhardt, E., & Lappegård, T. (2015). The gender revolution: A framework for understanding changing family and demographic behavior. *Population and Development Review, 41*, 207–239.

Gomby, D. S., & Pei, D. (2009). *Newborn family leave: Effects on children, parents, and business.* The David and Lucile Packard Foundation.

Goodman, J. (2004). Postpartum depression beyond the early postpartum period. *Journal of Obstetric, Gynecologic, and Neonatal Nursing, 33*, 410–420.

Goodman, J. M. (2018). Laboring until labor: The prevalence and correlates of antenatal maternity leave in the United States. *Maternal and Child Health Journal, 22*, 184–194.

Gordon, H., & Szram, J. (2013). Paternity leave experiences of NHS doctors. *Journal of the Royal College of Physicians, 13,* 426–430.

Gornick, J. C. (2004). Women's economic outcomes, gender inequality, and public policy: Lessons from the Luxembourg income study. *Socio-Economic Review, 2,* 213–238.

Gornick, J. & Meyers, M. (2003). *Families that work: Policies for reconciling parenthood and employment.* New York, Russell Sage Foundation.

Gov.UK. Surrogacy: Legal rights of parents and surrogates. Retrieved from: https://www.gov.uk

Gredebäck, G., Eriksson, M., Schmitow, C., Laeng, B., & Stenberg, G. (2012). Individual differences in face processing: Infants' scanning patterns and pupil dilations are influenced by the distribution of parental leave. *Infancy, 17,* 79–101.

Green, E. (2017, January 3). Historic SF parental leave law kicks in. *SF Gate.* Retrieved from: http://www.sfgate.com

Greenstein, T. N. (1995). Gender ideology, marital disruption, and the employment of married women. *Journal of Marriage and Family, 57,* 31–42.

Gregory, A., & Milner, S. (2010). Fathers and work-life balance in France and the UK: Policy and practice. *International Journal of Sociology and Social Policy, 31,* 34–52.

Gregory, A. & Milner, S. (2011). What is 'new' about fatherhood? The social construction of fatherhood in France and the UK. *Men and Masculinities, 14,* 588–606.

Guendelman, S., Pearl, M., Graham, S., Hubbard, A., Hosang, N., & Kharrazi, M. (2009). Maternity leave in the ninth month of pregnancy and birth outcomes among working women. *Women's Health Issues, 19,* 30–37.

Gupta, N. D., & Smith, N. (2002). Children and career interruptions: The family gap in Denmark. *Economica, 69,* 609–629.

Gupta, N. D., Smith, N. & Verner, M. (2008). The impact of Nordic countries' family friendly policies on employment, wages and children. *Review of the Economics of the Household, 6,* 65–89.

Haas, L. (1992). *Equal parenthood and social policy: A study of parental leave in Sweden.* Albany: State University of New York Press.

Haas, L., & Hwang, C. P. (1999). Parental leave in Sweden. In P. Moss and F. Deven (Eds.), *Parental leave: Progress or pitfall?* Groningen, Netherlands: NIDI/CGBS Publications.

Haas, L., & Hwang, C. P. (2008). The impact of taking parental leave on fathers' participation in childcare and relationships with children: Lessons from Sweden. *Community, Work & Family, 11,* 85–104.

Haas, L., & Hwang, C. P. (2013). Fatherhood and social policy in Scandinavia. In D. Schwalb, B. Schwalb, & M. Lamb (Eds.), *Fathers in cultural context* (pp. 303–330). New York: Routledge.

Haas, L., & Rostgaard, T. (2011). Fathers' rights to paid parental leave in the Nordic countries: Consequences for the gendered division of leave. *Community, Work & Family, 14*(2), 177–195.

Haines, G. (2017, November 4). Mapped: The best (and worst) countries for gender equality. *The Telegraph*. Retrieved from: https://www.telegraph.co.uk

Hamedy, S., & Diaz, D. (2018, April 20). Sen. Duckworth makes history, casts vote with baby on Senate floor. *CNN*. Retrieved from: https://www.cnn.com

Han, W., Ruhm, C., & Waldfogel, J. (2009). Parental leave policies and parents' employment and leave-taking. *Journal of Policy Analysis and Management, 28*, 29–54.

Hanratty, M., & Trzcinski, E. (2009). Who benefits from paid family leave? Impact of expansions in Canadian paid family leave on maternal employment and transfer income. *Journal of Population Economics, 22*, 693–711.

Harrop, A. & Moss, P. (1995). Trends in parental employment. *Work, Employment & Society, 9*, 421–444.

Heilman, B., Cole, G., Matos, K., Hassink, A., Mincy, R., & Barker, G. (2016). *State of America's fathers 2016*. Washington, DC: Promundo-US.

Hennig, M., Gatermann, D., & Hägglund, A. E. (2012). Pros and cons of family policies for mothers' labour market participation. *International Journal of Sociology and Social Policy, 32*, 502–512.

Henwood, K., Shirani, F., & Coltart, C. (2010). Fathers and financial risk-taking during the economic downturn: Insights from a QLL study of men's identities-in-the-making. *Twenty-First Century Society, 5*, 137–147.

Hernes, H. (1987). *Welfare state and woman power: Essays in state feminism*. London: Norwegian University Press.

Heymann, J., Sprague, A. R., Nandi, A., Earle, A., Batra, P., Schickedanz, A., Chung, P. J., & Raub, A. (2017). Paid parental leave and family wellbeing in the sustainable development era. *Public Health Reviews, 38*, 21.

Hobson, B., Lewis, J., & Siim, B. (Eds.). (2002). *Contested concepts in gender and social politics*. Cheltenham: Edward Elgar.

Hochschild, A. R. (1997). *The time bind: When work becomes home and home becomes work*. New York: Holt Paperbacks.

Hofferth, S. L., & Curtin, S. C. (2006). Parental leave statutes and maternal return to work after childbirth in the United States. *Work and Occupations, 33*, 73–105.

Hook, J. L. (2006). Care in context: Men unpaid work in 20 countries, 1965–2003. *American Sociological Review, 71*, 639–660.

Hook, J. L. (2010). Gender inequality in the welfare state: Sex segregation in housework, 1965–2003. *American Journal of Sociology, 115*, 1480–1523.

Hook, J., & Chalasani, S. (2008). Gendered expectations? Reconsidering single fathers' child-care time. *Journal of Marriage and Family, 70*, 978–990.

Horowitz, J. A., & Goodman, H.J. (2004). A longitudinal study of maternal postpartum depression symptoms. *Research and Theory for Nursing Practice, 18*, 149–163.

Horowitz, J. M., Parker, K., Graf, N., and Livingston, G. (2017, March 23). Americans widely support paid family and medical leave, but differ over specific policies. Washington, DC: Pew Research Center.

Horvath, L. K., Grether, T., & Wiese, B. S. (2018). Fathers' realization of parental leave plans: Leadership responsibility as help or hindrance? *Sex Roles, 79*, 163–175.

Houser, L., & Vartanian, T. (2012). *Pay matters: The positive economic impacts of paid family leave for families, businesses and the public.* Rutgers, NJ: Rutgers Center for Women and Work.

Huang, R., & Yang, M. Z. (2015). Paid maternity leave and breastfeeding practice before and after California's implementation of the nation's first paid family leave program. *Economics and Human Biology, 16,* 45–59.

Huerta, M. C., Adema, W., Baxter, J., Han, W., Lausten, M., Lee, R., & Waldfogel, J. (2013). Fathers' leave, fathers' involvement and child development: Are they related? Evidence from four OECD countries. OECD Social, Employment and Migration Working Papers, No. 140, OECD Publishing, Paris.

Huerta, M. C., Adema, W., Baxter, J., Han, W., Lausten, M., Lee, R., & Waldfogel, J. (2014). Fathers' leave and fathers' involvement: Evidence from four OECD countries. *European Journal of Social Security, 16,* 308–346.

Huttunen, J. (1996). Full-time fathers and their parental leave experiences. In U. Björnberg & A. Kollind (Eds.), *Men's family relations* (pp. 79-90). Göteborg, Sweden: Göteborg University.

Hwang, W., & Jung, E. (2016). Does paid maternity leave affect infant development and second-birth intentions? *Family Relations, 65,* 562–575.

Hyde, J. S., Essex, M. J., & Horton, F. (1993). Fathers and parental leave: Attitudes and experiences. *Journal of Family Issues, 14,* 616–638.

Institute for Child, Youth and Family Policy. 2015. Working adults who are eligible for and can afford FMLA unpaid leave. Retrieved from: http://www.diversitydatakids.org

International Labour Organization. (2014). Maternity and paternity at work: Law and practice across the world. Retrieved from: http://www.ilo.org

Jackson, A. (2017, December 15). These photos of Mark Zuckerberg in Hawaii reveal a growing work trend for American dads. *Business Insider.* Retrieved from: http://www.businessinsider.com

Jacobs, S. (1999). Trends in women's career patterns and in gender occupational mobility in Britain. *Gender, Work and Organization, 6,* 32–46.

Jarvis, A. (2010, October 22). The timeline: Maternity leave. *Independent.* Retrieved from: https://www.independent.co.uk

Jaumotte, F. (2003). Female labour force participation: Past trends and main determinants in OECD Countries. OECD Economics Department Working Papers no. 376.

Javornik, J., & Kurowska, A. (2017). Work and care opportunities under different parental leave systems: Gender and class inequalities in northern Europe. *Social Policy & Administration, 51,* 617–637.

Joesch, J. M. (1997). Paid leave and the timing of women's employment before and after birth. *Journal of Marriage and Family, 59,* 1008–1021.

Johansson, E. (2010). The effect of own and spousal parental leave on earnings. Institute for Labour Market Policy Evaluation Working Paper. Uppsala, Sweden.

Johansson, T. (2011). Fatherhood in transition: Paternity leave and changing masculinities. *Journal of Family Communication, 11,* 165–180.

Johansson, T., & Klinth, R. (2008). Caring fathers: The ideology of gender equality and masculine positions. *Men and Masculinities, 11,* 42–62.

Johnston, K. (2018, June 22). Here's what we know about the state's paid leave program. Retrieved from: https://www.bostonglobe.com

Jonsson, J. O., & Mills, C. (2001). The sooner the better? Parental leave duration and women's occupational career. In J.O. Jonsson & C. Mills (Eds), *Cradle to grave: Life-course change in modern Sweden* (pp. 97–114). Mill Valley, CA: Sociology Press.

June, L. (2016, March 8). Why is maternity leave so terrible in this country? *New York Magazine.* Retrieved from: https://www.thecut.com

Kane, L. (2018, April 4). Sweden is apparently full of 'latte dads' carrying toddlers—and it's a sign of critical social change. *Business Insider.* Retrieved from: https://www .businessinsider.com

Karr, J. E. (2017). Where's my dad? A feminist approach to incentivized paternity leave. *Hastings Women's Law Journal, 28,* 225–263.

Karu, M., & Tremblay, D. (2018). Fathers on parental leave: An analysis of rights and take-up in 29 countries. *Community, Work & Family, 21,* 344–362.

Kaufman, G. (2013) *Superdads: How fathers balance work and family in the 21ˢᵗ century.* New York: New York University Press.

Kaufman, G. (2016, June 15). Fathers also want to 'have it all,' study says. *The Conversation.* Retrieved from: https://theconversation.com

Kaufman, G., & Almqvist, A. (2017). The role of partners and workplaces in British and Swedish men's parental leave decisions. *Men and Masculinities, 20,* 533–551.

Kaufman, G. (2018). Barriers to equality: Why British men do not use parental leave. *Community, Work & Family, 21,* 310–325.

Kaufman, G., & Bernhardt, E. (2012). His and her job: What matters most for fertility plans and actual childbearing. *Family Relations, 61,* 686–697.

Kaufman, G., & Bernhardt, E. (2015). Gender, work and parenthood: Couple analysis of work adjustments after the transition to parenthood. *Community, Work, and Family, 18,* 1–18.

Kaufman, G., Bernhardt, E., and Goldscheider, F. (2017). Enduring egalitarianism? Family transitions and gender role attitude change in Sweden. *Journal of Family Issues, 38,* 1878–1898.

Kaufman, G., & Grönlund, A. (2017). Doing the dual-earner family: Mothers and fathers balancing work and care in Sweden, the UK and the US. Paper presented at the Southern Sociological Society, Greenville, March.

Kaufman, G., Lyonette, C., & Crompton, R. (2010). Post-birth employment leave among fathers in Britain and the United States. *Fathering, 8,* 321–340.

Keck, W., & Saraceno, C. (2013). The impact of different social-policy frameworks on social inequalities among women in the European Union: The labour-market participation of mothers. *Social Politics, 20,* 297–328.

Kelly, G. (2016, January 6). Paternity leave: How Britain compares with the rest of the world. *The Telegraph.* Retrieved from https://www.telegraph.co.uk

Ketsche, P.G. & Branscomb, L. (2003). The long-term costs of career interruptions. *Journal of Health Care Management, 48*, 30–44.

Kilkey, M. (2006). New Labour and reconciling work and family life: Making it fathers' business? *Social Policy & Society, 5*, 167–175.

Kilkey, M. (2010). Men and domestic labor: A missing link in the global care chain. *Men and Masculinities, 13*, 126–149.

Kilkey, M., Perrons, D., & Plomien, A. (2013). *Gender, migration and domestic work: Masculinities, male labour and fathering in the UK and USA*. Basinstoke: Palgrave Macmillan.

Killewald, A. (2013). A reconsideration of the fatherhood premium: Marriage, coresidence, biology, and fathers' wages. *American Sociological Review, 78*, 96–116.

Killien, M. G., Habermann, B., & Jarrett, M. (2001). Influence of employment characteristics on postpartum mothers' health. *Women and Health, 33*, 63–81.

Klerman, J. A., Daly, K., & Pozniak, A. (2014). Family and Medical Leave in 2012: Technical report. Cambridge, MA: Abt Associates Inc. Retrieved from: https://www.dol.gov

Klerman, J. A., & Leibowitz, A. (1997). Labor supply effects of state maternity leave legislation. In F. D. Blau & R. G. Ehrenberg (Eds.), *Gender and family issues in the workplace* (pp. 65–91). New York: Russell Sage Foundation.

Klinth, R. (2008). The best of both worlds? Fatherhood and gender equality in Swedish paternity leave campaigns, 1976–2006. *Fathering, 6*, 20–38.

Kluve, J., & Tamm, M. (2013). Parental leave regulations, mothers' labor force attachment and fathers' childcare involvement: Evidence from a natural experiment. *Journal of Population Economics, 26*, 983–1005.

Knudsen, K., & Waerness, K. (2001). National context, individual characteristics and attitudes on mothers' employment: A comparative analysis of Great Britain, Sweden and Norway. *Acta Sociologica, 44*, 67–79.

Korpi, W. (2000). Faces of inequality: Gender, class, and patterns of inequalities in different types of welfare states. *Social Politics, 7*, 127–191.

Kotsadam, A., & Finseraas, H. (2011). The state intervenes in the battle of the sexes: Causal effects of paternity leave. *Social Science Research, 40*, 1611–1622.

Lalive, R., & Zweimüller, J. (2009). How does parental leave affect fertility and return to work? Evidence from two natural experiments. *The Quarterly Journal of Economics, 124*, 1363–1402.

Lamb, M. (2000). The history of research on father involvement: An overview. *Marriage and Family Review, 29*, 23–42.

Laughlin, L. (2011). Maternity leave and employment patterns of first-time mothers: 1961–2008. Current Population Report, 70–128. Washington, DC: US Census Bureau.

Leach, S. (2018, January 25). What maternity leave looks like when you're a sitting senator. *Glamour*. Retrieved from: https://www.glamour.com

Lemire. J. (2015, December 25). Paid parental leave programs starting to expand in US cities. *CNS news*. Retrieved from: http://www.cnsnews.com

Lerner, S., & Appelbaum, E. (2014). *Business as usual: New Jersey employers' experiences with Family Leave Insurance.* Washington, DC: Center for Economic and Policy Research.

Lewis, J. (2002). The problem of fathers: Policy and behavior in Britain. In B. Hobson (Ed.), *Making men into fathers: Men, masculinities and the social politics of fatherhood* (pp. 125–149). Cambridge: Cambridge University Press.

Lewis, J., Knijn, T., Martin, C., & Ostner, I. (2008). Patterns of development in work/family reconciliation policies for parents in France, Germany, the Netherlands, and the UK in the 2000s. *Social Politics, 15,* 261–286.

Lichtman-Sadot, S., & Bell, N. P. (2017). Child health in elementary school following California's Paid Family Leave program. *Journal of Policy Analysis and Management, 36,* 790–827.

Lidbeck, M., Bernhardsson, S., & Tjus, T. (2018). Division of parental leave and perceived parenting stress among mothers and fathers. *Journal of Reproductive and Infant Psychology, 36,* 406–420.

Lipset, S. M. (1997). *American exceptionalism: A double-edged sword.* W. W. Norton & Company.

Lister, R. (1997). Citizenship: Towards a feminist synthesis. *Feminist Review, 57,* 28–48.

Lister, R. (2002). The dilemmas of pendulum politics: Balancing paid work, care and citizenship. *Economy and Society, 31,* 520–532.

Livingston, G. (2018, January 8). Most dads say they spend too little time with their children; about a quarter live apart from them. Washington, DC: Pew Research Center.

The Local Sweden. (2017, February 17). More dads taking paternity leave. *The Local Sweden.* Retrieved from: https://www.thelocal.se

The Local Sweden. (2018, January 17). Dads in Sweden took more paternity leave than ever in 2017. *The Local Sweden.* Retrieved from: https://www.thelocal.se

The Local Sweden. (2018, September 18). In stats: How gender equal is Sweden's new parliament? *The Local Sweden.* Retrieved from: https://www.thelocal.se

Lück, D. (2005). Cross-national comparison of gender role attitudes and their impact on women's life courses. Globalife Working Paper No. 67.

Lundberg, S., & Rose, E. (2000). Parenthood and the earnings of married men and women. *Labour Economics, 7,* 689–710.

Lyonette, C., Kaufman, G., & Crompton, R. (2011). "We both need to work": Maternal employment, childcare and health care in Britain and the U.S. *Work, Employment and Society, 25,* 34–50.

MacLellan, L. (2017, June 18). Sweden's gender-neutral preschools produce kids who are more likely to succeed. *Quartz.* Retrieved from: https://qz.com

Mandel, H., & Semyonov, M. (2005). Family policies, wage structures, and gender gaps: Sources of earnings inequality in 20 countries. *American Sociological Review, 70,* 949–967.

Mandel, H., & Semyonov, M. (2006). A welfare state paradox: State interventions and women's employment opportunities in 22 countries. *American Journal of Sociology, 111,* 1910–1949.

Mandel, H., & Shalev, M. (2009). How welfare states shape the gender pay gap: A theoretical and comparative analysis. *Social Forces*, 87, 1873–1911.

Månsdotter, A., & Lundin, A. (2010). How do masculinity, paternity leave, and mortality associate? A study of fathers in the Swedish parental and child cohort of 1988/89. *Social Science & Medicine*, 71, 576–583.

Margolin, E. (2016, October 6). Chobani offers moms, dads 6 weeks of parental leave at full pay. *NBC News*. Retrieved from: https://www.nbcnews.com

Martin, W. (2017 January 13). The 16 countries with the world's best healthcare systems. *Business Insider*. Retrieved from: https://nordic.businessinsider.com

McGovern, P. M., Dagher, R.K., Rice, H.R., Gjerdingen, D. Dowd, B., Ukestad,L.K., & Lundberg, U. (2011). A longitudinal analysis of total workload and women's health after childbirth. *Journal of Occupational and Environmental Medicine*, 53, 497–505.

McGovern, P. M., Dowd, B., Gjerdingen, D., Moscovice, I., Kochevar, L., & Lohman, W. (1997). Time off work and the postpartum health of employed women. *Medical Care*, 35, 507–521.

McGuinness, F. (2018). Women and the economy. House of Commons Briefing Paper Number CBP06838.

McKay, L., & Doucet, A. (2010). Without taking away her leave: A Canadian case study of couples' decisions on fathers' use of paid parental leave. *Fathering*, 8, 300–320.

McKay, L., Mathieu, S., & Doucet, A. (2016). Parental-leave rich and parental-leave poor: Inequality in Canadian labour market-based leave policies. *Journal of Industrial Relations*, 58, 543–562.

McMunn, A., Martin, P., Kelly, Y., and Sacker, A. (2017). Fathers' involvement: Correlates and consequences for child socioemotional behavior in the United Kingdom. *Journal of Family Issues*, 38, 1109–1131.

McRae, S. (2008). Working full-time after motherhood. In Scott, J., Dex, S., & Joshi, H. (Eds.), *Women and employment: Changing lives and new challenges* (pp. 179–198). Cheltenham: Edward Elgar.

Meil, G. (2013). European men's use of parental leave and their involvement in child care and housework. *Journal of Comparative Family Studies*, 44, 557–570.

Mejia, Z. (2018, March 16). These are the top 10 happiest countries in the world. *CNBC.com*. Retrieved from: https://www.cnbc.com

Milkman, R., & Appelbaum, E. (2013). *Unfinished business: Paid family leave in California and the future of US work-family policy*. Ithaca, NY: Cornell University Press.

Miller, T. (2011). Falling back into gender? Men's narratives and practices around first-time fatherhood. *Sociology*, 45, 1094–1109.

Miller, T. (2013). Shifting out of neutral on parental leave: Making fathers' involvement explicit. *Public Policy Research*, 19, 258–262.

Misra J., Moller S., & Budig M.J. (2007). Work–family policies and poverty for partnered and single women in Europe and North America. *Gender and Society*, 21, 804–827.

Mohdin, A. (2016, January 6). How Sweden's "daddy quota" parental leave helps with equal parenting. *Quartz*. Retrieved from: https://qz.com

Moss, P. (2012). Caring and learning together: Exploring the relationship between parental leave and early childhood education and care. *European Journal of Education, 47,* 482–493.

Moss, P. (2013). *International review of leave policies and related research 2013.* Institute of Education. University of London.

Moss, P., & Deven, F. (2015). Leave policies in challenging times: Reviewing the decade 2004–2014. *Community, Work & Family, 18,* 137–144.

My Family Care. (2016, April 5). Shared parental leave: Where are we now? London. Retrieved from: https://www.myfamilycare.co.uk

National Partnership for Women & Families. (2017). New and expanded employer paid family leave policies (2015–2017). Washington, DC: NPWR.

National Partnership for Women & Families. (2018). State paid family and medical leave insurance laws. Washington, DC: NPWR.

National Partnership for Women & Families. (2018). Leading on leave: Companies with new or expanded paid leave policies (2015–2018). Washington, DC: NPWR.

Nepomnyaschy, L., & Waldfogel, J. (2007). Paternity leave and fathers' involvement with their young children: Evidence from the American Ecls-B. *Community, Work and Family, 10,* 427–453.

Newport, F. (2018, August 13). Democrats more positive about socialism than capitalism. Retrieved from: https://news.gallup.com

NYC Government. (2016, January 7). Mayor de Blasio signs paid parental leave personnel order for NYC workers. Retrieved from: http://www1.nyc.gov

O'Brien, M. (2009). Fathers, parental leave policies, and infant quality of life: International perspectives and policy impact. *The Annals of the American Academy of Political and Social Science, 624,* 190–213.

O'Brien, M., & Koslowski, A. (2017). United Kingdom country note. In Blum, S., Koslowski, A., and Moss, P. (Eds.), *International review of leave policies and research 2017* (pp. 414-426). International Network on Leave Policies & Research.

O'Brien, M., & Shemilt, I. (2003). *Working fathers: Earning and caring.* Manchester: Equal Opportunities Commission.

O'Brien, M., & Wall, K. (2017). *Comparative perspectives on work-life balance and gender equality: Fathers on leave alone.* New York: Springer.

O'Connell, M. (2015, January 15). Obama authorizes up to six weeks of paid parental leave. *Federal News Radio.* Retrieved from: https://federalnewsradio.com

O'Connor, C. (2016, December 20). Washington, D.C. passes 8 week paid parental leave bill. *Forbes.* Retrieved from: https://www.forbes.com

O'Dea, C. (2018, May 11). Paid family-leave bill would mean more time, more money for workers. *NJ Spotlight.* Retrieved from: http://www.njspotlight.com

Ogbuanu, C., Glover, S., Probst, J., Liu, J., & Hussey, J. (2011). The effect of maternity leave length and time of return to work on breastfeeding. *Pediatrics, 127,* 1414–1427.

O'Hara, M. W., & Swain, A. M. (1996). Rates and risk of postpartum depression— A meta-analysis. *International Review of Psychiatry, 8,* 37–54.

Oláh, L. S. (2001). Gender and family stability: Dissolution of the first parental union in Sweden and Hungary. *Demographic Research, 4*, 29–96.

Oláh, L. S., & Bernhardt, E. (2008). Sweden: Combining childbearing and gender equality. *Demographic Research, 19*, 1105–1143.

Ondrich, J., Spiess, K. C. & Yang, Q. (1996). Barefoot and in a German kitchen: federal parental leave and benefit policy and return to work after childbirth in Germany, *Journal of Population Economics, 9*, 247–266.

Ondrich, J., Spiess, K. C. and Yang, Q. (2002). The effect of maternity leave on women's pay in Germany 1984–1994. DIW Discussion Paper no. 289.

Organisation for Economic Co-operation and Development. (nd). OECD family database. Retrieved from: https://www.oecd.org

Organisation for Economic Co-operation and Development. (2011). *Doing better for families.* OECD Publishing. Retrieved from: http://www.oecd.org

Organisation for Economic Co-operation and Development. (2016). Trends in parental leave policies since 1970. Retrieved from: http://www.oecd.org

Organisation for Economic Co-operation and Development. (2017). Key characteristics of parental leave systems. Retrieved from: https://www.oecd.org

Organisation for Economic Co-operation and Development. (2018). Part-time employment rate (indicator). Retrieved from: https://data.oecd.org

Orloff, A. S. (2009). Should feminists aim for gender symmetry? Why the dual-earner/dual-carer model may not be every feminist's utopia. In J. Gornick & M. Meyers (Eds.), *Gender equality: Transforming family divisions of labor* (pp.129–160). New York: Verso.

Orloff, A. S. (2009). Gendering the comparative analysis of welfare states: An unfinished agenda. *Sociological Theory, 27*, 317–343.

Parker, K., & Livingston, G. (2017, June 15). 6 facts about American fathers. Washington, DC: Pew Research. Retrieved from: www.pewresearch.org

Peck, E. (2016, April 11). Coca-Cola will offer more inclusive parental leave, because millenials. *Huffington Post.* Retrieved from: https://www.huffingtonpost.com

Peltz, J. P. (2016, April 28.). Why paid parental leave won't go national. *Los Angeles Times.* Retrieved from: http://www.latimes.com

Pettit, B. & Hook, J. (2005). The structure of women's employment in comparative perspective. *Social Forces, 84*, 779–801.

Petts, R. J. (2018). Time off after childbirth and mothers' risk of depression, parenting stress, and parenting practices. *Journal of Family Issues, 39*, 1827–1854.

Petts, R. J., & Knoester, C. (2018). Paternity leave-taking and father engagement. *Journal of Marriage and Family, 80*, 1144–1162.

Petts, R. J., & Knoester, C. (2019). Paternity leave and parental relationships: Variations by gender and mothers' work statuses. *Journal of Marriage and Family, 81*, 468-486.

Petts, R. J., Knoester, C., & Li, Q. (2018). Paid paternity leave-taking in the United States. *Community, Work & Family.* doi:10.1080/13668803.2018.1471589.

Pleck, J. H. (1993). Are "family-supportive" employer policies relevant to men? In J. C. Hood (Ed.), *Research on men and masculinities series* (pp. 217–237). Thousand Oaks, CA: Sage.

Pragg, B., & Knoester, C. (2017). Paternity leave use among disadvantaged fathers. *Journal of Family Issues, 38*, 1157–1185.

Prescott, S. (2018, February 7). Queer families still struggle to access leave. *Slate.* Retrieved from: https://slate.com

Pronzato, C. D. (2009). Return to work after childbirth: does parental leave matter in Europe? *Review of the Economics of the Household, 7*, 341–360.

Pylkkanen, E. & Smith, N. (2003). Career interruptions due to parental leave: A comparative study of Denmark and Sweden. OECD Social, Employment and Immigration working paper No 1. Directorate for Employment, Labour and Social Affairs.

Radu, S. (2018, January 23). These are the 5 best countries for women. *US News and World Report.* Retrieved from: https://www.usnews.com

Rasmussen, A. W. (2010). Increasing the length of parents' birth-related leave: The effect on children's long-term educational outcomes. *Labour Economics, 17*, 91–100.

Ray, R., Gornick, J. C., & Schmitt, J. (2010). Who cares? Assessing generosity and gender equality in parental leave policy designs in 21 countries. *Journal of European Social Policy, 20*, 196–216.

Rege, M., & Solli, I. (2013). The impact of paternity leave on fathers' future earnings. *Demography, 50*, 2255–2277.

Rehel, E. (2014). When dad stays home: Paternity leave, gender, and parenting. *Gender & Society, 28*, 110–132.

Risman, B. J. (1986). Can men "mother"? Life as a single father. *Family Relations, 35*, 95–102.

Risman, B. J. (1987). Intimate relationships from a microstructural perspective: Men who mother. *Gender & Society, 1*, 6–32.

Rochlen, A., McKelley, R. A., Suizzo M., & Scaringi, V. (2008). Predictors of relationship satisfaction, psychological well-being, and life satisfaction among stay-at-home fathers. *Psychology of Men and Masculinity, 9*, 17–28.

Romero-Balsas, P., Muntanyola-Saura, D., & Rogero-Garcia, J. (2013). Decision-making factors within paternity and parental leaves: Why Spanish fathers take time off from work. *Gender, Work and Organization, 20*, 678–691.

Rønsen, M. & Sundström, M. (2002). Family policy and after-birth employment among new mothers: A comparison of Finland, Norway and Sweden. *European Journal of Population, 18*, 121–152.

Rossin, M. (2011). The effects of maternity leave on children's birth and infant health outcomes in the United States. *Journal of Health Economics, 30*, 221–239.

Rossin-Slater, M., Ruhm, C. J., & Waldfogel, J. (2013). The effects of California's paid family leave program on mothers' leave-taking and subsequent labor market outcomes. *Journal of Policy Analysis and Management, 32*, 224–245.

Rubery, J. (2015). Regulating for gender equality: A policy framework to support the universal caregiver vision. *Social Politics, 22*, 513–538.

Rubin, R. (2016, April 6). U.S. dead last among developed countries when it comes to paid maternity leave. *Forbes.* https://www.forbes.com

Rudman, L. A., & Mescher, K. (2013). Penalizing men who request a family leave: Is flexibility stigma a femininity stigma? *Journal of Social Issues, 69,* 322–340.

Ruhm, C. J. (1998). The economic consequences of parental leave mandates: Lessons from Europe. *Quarterly Journal of Economics, 113,* 285–317.

Ruhm, C. J. (2000). Parental leave and child health. *Journal of Health Economics, 19,* 931–960.

Rush, M. (2015). *Between two worlds of father politics. USA or Sweden?* Manchester, UK: Manchester University Press.

Sainsbury, D. (1999). Gender, policy regimes, and politics. In D. Sainsbury (Ed.), *Gender and welfare state regimes* (pp. 245–276). Oxford: Oxford University Press.

Schober, P. S. (2014). Parental leave and domestic work of mothers and fathers: A longitudinal study of two reforms in West Germany. *Journal of Social Policy, 43,* 351–372.

Seward, R. R., Yeatts, D. E., Zottarelli, L. K., & Fletcher, R. G. (2006). Fathers taking parental leave and their involvement with children. *Community, Work & Family, 9,* 1–9.

Shambaugh, J., Nunn, R., & Portman, B. (2017). Lessons from the rise of women's labor force participation in Japan. Brookings Institute.

Shepherd-Banigan, M., & Bell, J. F. (2014). Paid leave benefits among a national sample of working mothers with infants in the United States. *Maternal and Child Health Journal, 18,* 286–295.

Sigle-Rushton, W. (2010). Men's unpaid work and divorce: Reassessing specialization and trade in British families. *Feminist Economics, 16,* 1–26.

Sigle-Rushton, W., & Waldfogel, J. (2007). The incomes of families with children: A cross-national comparison. *Journal of European Social Policy, 17,* 299–318.

Silver, B. E., Mederer, H., & Djurdjevic, E. (2016). Launching the Rhode Island Temporary Caregiver Insurance Program (TCI): Employee experiences one year later. Submitted to the U.S Department of Labor, Women's Bureau. RI Department of Training and Labor. Retrieved from: http://www.dlt.ri.gov

Skafida, V. (2012). Juggling work and motherhood: The impact of employment and maternity leave on breastfeeding duration; A survival analysis on growing up in Scotland data. *Maternal and Child Health Journal, 16,* 519–527.

Smith, A. J., & Williams, D. R. (2007). Father-friendly legislation and paternal time across Western Europe. *Journal of Comparative Policy Analysis, 9,* 175–192.

Staehelin, K., Bertea, P. C., & Stutz, E. Z. (2007). Length of maternity leave and health of mother and child—a review. *International Journal of Public Health, 52,* 202–209.

Stafford, F. P., & Sundström, M. (1996). Time out for childcare: Signalling and earnings rebound effects for men and women. *Labour, 10,* 609–629.

Stancyzk, A. B. (2016). Paid family leave may reduce poverty following a birth: Evidence from California. Chicago: University of Chicago, The Employment Instability, Family Well-Being, and Social Policy Network.

Stier, H., Lewin-Epstein, N., & Braun, M. (2001). Welfare regimes, family-supportive policies, and women's employment along the life-course. *American Journal of Sociology, 106,* 1731–1760.

Strauss, E. (2018, February 5). Paid parental leave elusive 25 years after Family and Medical Leave Act. *CNN*. Retrieved from: https://www.cnn.com

Stroman, T., Woods, W., Fitzgerald, G., Unnikrishnan, S., & Bird, L. (2017). *Why paid family leave is good business*. Boston: The Boston Consulting Group.

Sundbye, A., & Hegewisch, A. (2011). Maternity, paternity, and adoption leave in the United States. Washington, DC: Institute for Women's Policy Research.

Sundell, A. (2018, November 30). Washington paid family leave premiums kick in January 1. *King 5 News*. https://www.king5.com

Sundström, E. (1999). Should mothers work? Age and attitudes in Germany, Italy and Sweden. *International Journal of Social Welfare, 8*, 193–205.

The Swedish Institute. (nd). Gender equality in Sweden. Retrieved from: www .sweden.se

Swedish Social Insurance Agency. (2017). *Social insurance in figures 2017*. Stockholm, Sweden.

Sweet, L. (2018, January 23). Tammy Duckworth is pregnant; will be 1st senator to give birth. *Chicago Sun-Times*. Retrieved from: https://chicago.suntimes.com

Tanaka, S. (2005). Parental leave and child health across OECD countries. *The Economic Journal, 115*, F7–F28.

Tanaka, S., & Waldfogel, J. (2007). Effects of parental leave and work hours on fathers' involvement with their babies: Evidence from the Millenium Cohort Study. *Community, Work and Family, 10*, 409–426.

The Telegraph (2017, July 4). Did you know you can take unpaid leave to take care of your kids? The hidden rules that could save you £1800 a year. *The Telegraph*. Retrieved from: https://www.telegraph.co.uk

Tervola, J., Duvander, A., & Mussino, E. (2017). Promoting parental leave for immigrant fathers: What role does policy play? *Social Politics, 24*, 269–297.

Thévenon, O. (2011). Family policies in OECD countries: A comparative analysis. *Population and Development Review, 37*, 57–87.

Thévenon, O., & Luci, A. (2012). Reconciling work, family and child outcomes: What implications for family support policies? *Population Research and Policy Review, 31*, 855–882.

Thévenon, O., & Solaz, A. (2013). Labour market effects of parental leave policies in OECD countries. OECD Social, Employment and Migration Working Papers, No. 141. Paris: OECD Publishing.

Tinson, A., Aldridge, H., & Whitham, G. (2016). Women, work and wages in the UK: Understanding the position of women in the UK labour market and the need for an effective policy response. London: New Policy Institute. Retrieved from: https:// www.npi.org.uk

TUC. (2015). Two in five new fathers won't qualify for Shared Parental Leave, says TUC. London: Trades Union Congress. Retrieved from: https://www.tuc.org.uk

Ueda M., Kondo N., Takada M., & Hashimoto H. (2014). Maternal work conditions, socioeconomic and educational status, and vaccination of children: A community-based household survey in Japan. *Preventive Medicine, 66*, 17–21.

U.S. Department of Labor. (2000). The 2000 survey report. Retrieved from: https://www.dol.gov

Unterhofer, U., & Wrohlich, K. (2017). Fathers, parental leave and gender norms. DIW Discussion Papers, DIW, Berlin.

Valarino, I., Duvander, A., Haas, L., & Neyer, G. (2018). Exploring leave policy preferences: A comparison of Austria, Sweden, Switzerland, and the United States. *Social Politics, 25,* 118–147.

Valarino, I., & Gauthier, J. (2016). Paternity leave implementation in Switzerland: A challenge to gendered representations and practices of fatherhood? *Community, Work & Family, 19,* 1–20.

Vanderkam, L. (2016, September 27). Why offering paid maternity leave is good for business. *Fast Company.* Retrieved from: https://www.fastcompany.com

Waldfogel, J. (1997). The effect of children on women's wages. *American Sociological Review, 62,* 209–217.

Waldfogel, J. (1998). Understanding the 'family gap' in pay for women with children. *Journal of Economic Perspectives, 12,* 137–156.

Wall, K. (2007). Leave policy models and the articulation of work and family in Europe: A comparative perspective. *International Review of Leave Policies and Related Research 2007.* Employment Relations Research Series No. 80.

Wall Street Journal. (2018, July 15). Sweden is the world's finest home for families. *Wall Street Journal.* Retrieved from: https://www.wsj.com

Weinstein, A. (2018, January 31). When more women join the workforce, wages rise—including for men. *Harvard Business Review.* Retrieved from: https://hbr.org

Weller, C. (2017, March 18). Sweden is the best country in the world for women. *Business Insider.* Retrieved from: https://www.businessinsider.com

White, K., Houser, L., and Nisbet, E. (2013) *Policy in action: New Jersey's Family Leave Insurance program at age three.* New Brunswick, NJ: Center for Women and Work, January.

Whitehouse, G., Diamond, C., & Baird, M. (2007). Fathers' use of leave in Australia. *Community, Work & Family, 10,* 387–407.

Williams, S. (2008). What is fatherhood? Searching for the reflexive father. *Sociology, 42,* 487–502.

Wisensale, S. K. (2001). *Family leave policy: The political economy of work and family in America.* New York: M.E. Sharpe, Inc.

Wojcicki, S. (2014, December 16.). Paid maternity leave is good business. *Wall Street Journal.*

World Bank. (2018). *Women, business and the law 2018.* Washington, DC: World Bank.

World Bank. (2018). Proportion of seats held by women in national parliaments. Retrieved from: www.data.worldbank.org

World Economic Forum. (2018). The global gender gap report 2018. Retrieved from: http://www3.weforum.org/

Zagorsky, J. L. (2017). Divergent trends in US maternity and paternity leave, 1994–2015, *American Journal of Public Health, 107,* 460–465.

Zigler, E., Muenchow, S., & Ruhm, C.J. (2012). *Time off with baby: The case for paid care leave.* Washington, D.C.: Zero To Three.

Zillman, C. (2017, February 7). Kirsten Gillibrand is giving her paid family leave proposal its first Trump-era test. *Fortune.* Retrieved from: http://fortune .com/2017/02/07/trump-paid-family-leave-gillibrand/

INDEX

obstacles to taking parental leave, in US: class, race, and family status and, 59; LGBTQ individuals and, 59; Mateo and, 58–59; work environment and, 56; work pressure and, 57

OECD. *See* Organisation for Economic Co-operation and Development

Oliver (father, UK), 143–44, 167

Omar (father, UK): on breastfeeding, 119; workplace context and, 139, 140

one-and-a-half earner model, 128

OPL. *See* Ordinary Paternity Leave

OppenheimerFunds, 41, *48*

Ordinary Paternity Leave (OPL), 131–32, 133

Organisation for Economic Co-operation and Development (OECD), 12, 65, 66, 160; too much leave and, 93

Orloff, Ann Shola, 15, 103–4

Paid Family Leave (PFL), 30–31, 67, 80, 107–8; ADHD and, 81; retention and, 86

paid parental leave benefits, 4; American consensus and, 64; children and, 65, 78–81, 89, 171–72; company, 82–88, 89–90; fathers and, 65, 73–78, 89, 191n100; gender equality and, 71–72; mothers and, 65–71, 89; societal, 65, 88–89, 90

Paige (mother, UK): career advancement and, 96; gatekeeping of, 116–17; mother-centered parental leave and, 114; workplace context and, 138

Papua New Guinea, 23, 170, 177

parental leave, 20; defining, 6; EU and, 7–8, *160*, 160–61; family policies and, 17–18; funding for, 7; well-paid leave and, 9, 11, 12. *See also specific topics*

parental leave, Sweden, 8, *8*, 11, 12–13, 166; citizenship and, 155; current policy of, 154–55, *155*; daddy month and, 152–53, 158, 176; development of, 153–54, *154*; fathers and, 4, 6, 9, *10*, 12–13, 109, 151, 153–54, 157, 158–59, 161–62, *162*; Fer-

rarini on, 157; flexibility of, 154; gender equality bonus and, 153; mommy quota and, 153; non-parents and, 155; non-transferrable leave and, 152–53, 178; policy development of, 153–54, *154*; sickness and, 155; stories on, 163–66; too much leave and, 176; users of, 158–61, *159*, *160*. *See also* daddy quota

parental-leave-rich households, 170

paternity leave: defining, 6; flexibility stigma and, 107; gendered company policies and, 50–52; high-income countries and, 9, *10*; human capital depreciation and, 108; too much, 106–10; in UK, 9, *10*, 12, 131–33, 146–47; in US, 9, *10*, 12, 24, 50–52. *See also* daddy quota; parental leave, Sweden

PayPal, *39*, *48*, 88

pendulum politics, 92

Petts, Richard, 71

PFL. *See* Paid Family Leave

Plantenga, Janneke, 93–94, 96

policy design, 177

policy recommendations: alternative caregivers and, 179; equal parental leave and, 178; FAMILY Act and, 180; gender-neutral policies as, 178; ideal leave length and, 174, 178; non-transferrable leave as, 179–80; policy design and, 177; Sweden and, 180; for UK, 180

postpartum depression, 70–71, *105*, 172; Edinburgh Postnatal Depression Scale and, 104; ideal leave length and, 178; too much leave and, 173

poverty rates: Anglo-Saxon countries and, 17–18; in California, 68

Pregnancy Discrimination Act, 27

presidential campaign (2016): Clinton, H., and, 62–63; Trump and, 63

primary and secondary caregiver policies, US: adoption and, 52, 53, 54–55; gender-neutral framing of, 53; same sex couples and, 54

ABOUT THE AUTHOR

Gayle Kaufman is Nancy and Erwin Maddrey Professor of Sociology and Gender & Sexuality Studies at Davidson College.